The Global Dimensions
of Irish Identity

The Global Dimensions of Irish Identity

Race, Nation, and the
Popular Press,
1840–1880

Cian T. McMahon

The University of North Carolina Press
Chapel Hill

Published with the assistance of the Authors Fund of the University of North Carolina Press

Set in ITC Charter by Westchester Publishing Services
Manufactured in the United States of America

The paper in this book meets the guidelines for permanence and
durability of the Committee on Production Guidelines for Book
Longevity of the Council on Library Resources.

The University of North Carolina Press has been a member of the
Green Press Initiative since 2003.

Cover illustrations: "The British Empire in Allegory," illustration from the New York
Irish World (newspaper), October 19, 1878; courtesy of New-York Historical Society,
http://www.nyhistory.org. Vintage aged old paper (background of title);
© depositphotos.com/cranach2.

Library of Congress Cataloging-in-Publication Data

McMahon, Cian T.
    The global dimensions of Irish identity : race, nation, and the popular press, 1840–1880 /
Cian T. McMahon.—1 Edition.
        pages cm
    Includes bibliographical references and index.
    ISBN 978-1-4696-2010-7 (pbk : alk. paper)—ISBN 978-1-4696-2011-4 (ebook)
    1. Ireland—Civilization—19th century.   2. Ireland—History—19th century.
3. Group identity—Ireland.   4. National characteristics, Irish.   5. Ireland—
Emigration and immigration.   I. Title.
    DA950.1.M35 2015
    941.5081—dc23
                                                                          2014034898

To all those storytellers,
in seminars and saloons,
who taught me the tricks of the trade

CONTENTS

ILLUSTRATIONS

ACKNOWLEDGMENTS

When we were preparing for our doctoral qualifying exams several years ago, my wife and I used to enjoy recounting to each other the poignant notes of acknowledgment we had discovered that day in the books we read. We mostly did so to break the monotony of heavy-duty exam prep. Yet in retrospect, there was something deeper at work. If the chapters of a book illuminate the lives lived by historical actors, the acknowledgments reveal the lives lived by the authors and their supporters during the course of research and writing. For a couple of frazzled grad students, reading and recounting these hidden lives served as cheerful reminders that history writing is, in the end, a team sport.

There were many members on the team that contributed to this book, although all errors of fact and interpretation are entirely my own. At Carnegie Mellon University, I had the pleasure of working closely for several years with David W. Miller, Scott Sandage, Richard Maddox, and Steven Schlossman. Their influences are all over this project. Other department members who helped me at Carnegie Mellon include Caroline Acker, Jay Aronson, Alex Bennett, Kevin Brown, Kate Chilton, Allyson Creasman, Paul Eiss, Peter Gilmore, Wendy Goldman, Carrie Hagan, Donna Harsch, Naum Kats, Mary Lindemann, Katherine Lynch, Jason Morgan, Roger Rouse, John Soluri, Jim Soto, David Struthers, Joel Tarr, Joe Trotter, Lee Vinsel, and Pat Zimmerman.

Many other scholars graciously took time to share their thoughts on my work. I am especially grateful to Kevin Kenny, whose thought-provoking article in the *Journal of American History* encouraged me to follow the global Irish wherever they led me. More importantly, his friendly encouragement and honest criticism along the way helped me to make sense of what I found. David Gleeson, Patrick Griffin, Kerby Miller, Marcus Rediker, and David Wilson posed critical questions at important junctures. Malcolm Campbell, Donna Gabaccia, and Joe Lee kindly read the entire manuscript in its latter stages and offered indispensable comments. I am also indebted to Colin Barr, Michael de Nie, Seymour Drescher, Sean Farrell, Mark Gabbert, Luke Gibbons, Ely Janis, Michael Laffan, Elizabeth Malcolm, Timothy McMahon, Matt O'Brien, Paul Townend, and Nicholas Wolf for all of their help along the way. At the University of Nevada, Las Vegas, where I was generously granted the time and space to finish revising the manuscript, I received help and encouragement from Willy Bauer, Raquel Casas, Kevin Dawson, Andy Fry, David Holland, Andy Kirk, Gene Moehring, David Tanenhaus, Michelle Tusan, Paul Werth, and David Wrobel. It was a pleasure to publish this book with the University of North Carolina Press. I am particularly indebted to my editor, Chuck Grench, his assistants Alison Shay and Lucas Church, and the two anonymous readers whose criticisms did much to improve the final product.

I traveled several thousands of miles in search of manuscripts and rare newspapers for this project and found great help wherever I went. I must thank the library and archival staffs at the American Antiquarian Society (especially Vincent Golden and Jaclyn Penny), Boston Public Library, Carnegie Mellon Hunt Library (especially Sue Collins, Joan Stein, and Barry Schles), Columbia University Butler Library, Boston College John J. Burns Library, Massachusetts Historical Society, National Library of Ireland (especially Tom Desmond and Gerry Lyne), New-York Historical Society (especially Edward O'Reilly), New York Public Library, Royal Irish Academy, Trinity College Dublin, University of Pittsburgh Hillman Library, and University of Nevada, Las Vegas Lied Library (especially Priscilla Finley and Dan Werra). I received fellowships from the Center for the Study of American Catholicism and the New-York Historical Society. I also received grants from the Department of History, Division of University Advancement, and the Graduate Student Association at Carnegie Mellon University. All historians need help from family, especially those living in close proximity to far-flung archives, and I am deeply indebted to my mother (Sheena), father (Dermot), evil stepmother (Áine), brothers (Tadhg, Daithí, Milo), sister (Finn), and many kind in-laws (especially Aisling O'Connor and Frank and Claudia Clemente).

When I first met Deirdre, I asked her what she wanted to do with her life. "To raise kids and write books," she replied. I am deeply grateful to her for sharing that adventure with me. My greatest thanks go to her and to our children, Fionnuala, Dymphna, Clodagh, and Lorcan. Together they continually remind me that life, like history writing, is a team sport.

NOTE ON TEXT

On October 25, 1856, the editor of the New York weekly *Irish News* issued a public apology for the many errors marring that week's columns. "While lowering the second form [of hand-set type] from the composing-room," he explained, "the machinery used for that purpose gave way, precipitating types, chase, leads, rules, &c., down four stories, and reducing all to a lugubrious mass of mince 'pi.'" Ironically, an advertisement further down the same page announced that the *Irish News* office "neatly and expeditiously executed" job printing for customers at reasonable rates.

For a project heavily reliant on weekly journals as primary sources, the apology reminds us of the difficulties facing those tasked with setting newspaper type by hand in the mid-nineteenth century. Mistakes abounded among even the most meticulous professionals. Handwritten letters were similarly prone to error. Rather than distract the reader by inserting "[sic]" countless times throughout my text, I have quietly corrected most spelling and grammatical errors while carefully maintaining the message of the original words. The footnotes contain all the information necessary for those interested in tracking down the exact spelling or phrasing of any quotation cited. Unless otherwise noted, all emphases appear in the original quotes.

The Global Dimensions
of Irish Identity

Introduction

As global capitalism hit full stride in the mid-nineteenth century, its inherent paradoxes came to fruition. While connecting people around the world in new ways, capitalism also disrupted preexisting networks of power and community. Notions of nationhood shifted accordingly. Some drew inward, seeking solidarity in heritage and race. Others looked outward, building unity on ideals and values. The four and a half million Irish people who migrated around the world between 1840 and 1880 were caught in this modern dilemma. Loyal to both their old and new homes, they found themselves at the heart of a dialectical tug-of-war between migration and identity. This book explores their struggle to construct a flexible sense of belonging suited for the modern world.

In January 1871, Patrick Ford defined the Irish race in his New York weekly *Irish World*. "All Irishmen, and all Irishmen's sons, the world over, are parts of one mighty whole," he wrote. "Perhaps there is no other people on the face of the earth whose identity is more clearly marked and defined. There are forces of attraction, ever at work, which draw the members of our race instinctively together, and knit them into an integral body." This supranational ethnic solidarity did not, however, preclude loyalty to the host community. Later in the year, another editorial reflected on the nature of the American population. "This people are not one," Ford declared. "In blood, in religion, in traditions, in social and domestic habits, they are many. Leaving out the aborigines, the veritable Americans (but who are now falsely called Indians), there are the Anglo-Americans, the Franco-Americans, the Irish-Americans, the Spanish-Americans, the German-Americans, and the African-Americans." The United States was not an assimilative melting pot but a pluralist mosaic, composed of various peoples united by the Constitution. The steady movement of vast numbers of people across national borders had created transnational communities capable of pledging dual loyalty to both their new and old homes. "Though American by nationality," Ford editorialized, "we are yet Irish by race."[1]

Using a wealth of manuscript and printed primary sources from Ireland, the United States, and Australia, I argue that their "whiteness" was not the most pressing issue facing mid-nineteenth-century Irish migrants. They mainly felt threatened by the notion, prevalent in the Western mainstream media at the time, that New World countries such as the United States and Australia were Anglo-Saxon nations with no room for Catholic Celts. Unwilling to renounce their Celtic self-image and "become Saxon," however, the Irish developed a diasporic identity that I call global nationalism. Constantly adapting to the practical exigencies of given times and places—by vacillating between ethnic solidarity and civic pluralism—global nationalism portrayed the Irish as an international community capable of simultaneous loyalty to their old and new worlds. This was a complicated discourse often marked by paradox and contradiction. Yet by laying claim to this multivalent identity, the Irish joined other migrant groups in expanding the modern parameters of citizenship and mobility. Moreover, this transnational identity was constructed in the columns of a globally integrated, yet uniquely Irish, popular press. By reading, writing, and physically transmitting individual copies of the weekly rag to friends and family overseas, the Irish created what one editor called an "empire of the press" where, though physically apart, they could virtually assemble once a week to debate and define information and identity.[2]

Three conceptual tools help to corral such a complicated project. First, the notion of race as an element of nineteenth-century nationalism, in the United States and elsewhere, is often inadequately problematized. Following previous scholars, especially Thomas Guglielmo, I divide "race" into color and nation. Yet unlike Guglielmo, who zooms in on the Italians in Chicago in the early twentieth century, I zoom out, to view the Irish on an international stage. From this perspective, immigrant racial discourse is about both nation and color. The second conceptual tool relates to theoretical framework. Kevin Kenny has argued that it is only by combining both transnational and comparative approaches that "the history of American immigration and ethnicity [can] be integrated into its wider global context." This book strives to unearth the multilayered nature of a global Irish identity by acknowledging that it was shaped by both the particularities of individual nation-states and by transnational networks. These people saw themselves as both emigrants and immigrants living in communities that were both global and local, on the borders between ethnic and civic solidarity. The third conceptual tool builds on the works of Jürgen Habermas and Benedict Anderson. Previous scholars have understated how print culture connected mid-nineteenth-century migrant communities. In fact, weekly newspapers constituted a transnational public sphere where fluctuating notions of race and nation were formulated and exchanged. This book uses these conceptual tools to compare, contrast, and connect the world-scattered Irish.[3]

Three key themes dominate each chapter. The first relates to the idioms and features of Irish racial discourse. This was, for the most part, a language of "Celts and Saxons" rather than "blacks and whites," because, from the perspective of Irish migrants, the differences between the white races were just as important as those separating whites from people of color. As such, Irish racial discourse reflected contemporary trends in Western race thinking. The Scottish ethnologist Robert Knox's *The Races of Men: A Fragment* (1850), for example, sought to prove that "the European races, so called, differ from each other as widely as the Negro does from the Bushman; the Caffre from the Hottentot; the Red Indian of America from the Esquimaux; the Esquimaux from the Basque." Irish nationalists may have disagreed with Knox's negative characterization of the Celtic race, but they accepted his fundamental premise: that physiological differences resulted in dissimilar cultural attributes, which rendered Celts and Saxons eternally at odds. This rhetoric served the Irish wherever they went. In Ireland in the 1840s, the image of themselves as valiant Celts struggling against Saxon oppression buttressed the political struggle for independence from Britain. As newcomers in the immigrant-friendly Australian colonies in the 1850s, the language became less combative by depicting Irish Celts as hardy settlers capable of blending with other races to form new communities at the ends of the earth. In the antebellum United States, by contrast, where antiforeign nativism was rife, Irish racial discourse bellicosely challenged the mainstream media's portrayal of American society as an Anglo-Saxon inheritance. During the Civil War, Irish immigrants on both sides of the Mason-Dixon Line freely shed their blood, in part to prove the Celts' fealty to their old and new worlds.[4]

Yet it is impossible to discuss mid-nineteenth-century Irish racial discourse without addressing people of color. The second theme running through each chapter relates to Irish nationalist attitudes toward slavery and imperialism. In some ways, the pages that follow confirm the conclusions of earlier scholars. Fearing that antislavery would undermine American support for Irish political independence from Britain, many Irish nationalists in the 1840s were loath to vocally support American abolitionism. In the Antipodes, Irish settlers were willing participants in the systematic dispossession of Aboriginal Australians and often opposed the importation of Chinese and Indian "coolie" laborers. Similarly, in the United States, they were some of the most voluble opponents of slave emancipation. At the same time, Irish attitudes toward people of color were more complicated than previous historians have suggested. As this book demonstrates, many in Ireland saw parallels between Afghani and Irish struggles against British oppression, while their unwillingness to support American antislavery was often predicated on constitutional, as opposed to racial, grounds. The Irish diaspora clearly included thuggish racists. Yet there were also noisy elements in Australia and the United States who were willing to defend the rights of people of color. The Irish Australian Sydney *Freeman's Journal,* for example, decried imperialists who trampled on "the common rights of humanity" by dispossessing Aboriginal Australians, while in the antebellum United States the political exile Michael Doheny publicly professed to "detest and abhor the slavery of an African negro, a Hill coolie or any coolie." There was more to the story than white supremacy.[5]

By publishing and reprinting letters, editorials, articles, and speeches, Irish people created their own transnational public sphere. The international Irish popular press, where racial discourse was formulated and exchanged, is the third theme in every chapter. The mid-nineteenth century was a golden age for political scribblers and hack editors. Repeals of press taxation combined with increased advertising revenue to dilute government interference and increase editorial independence. There were also seismic changes in technology, such as mechanized papermaking, steam-powered presses, and multiple-cylinder stereotype printing, as well as better roads, expanding railroads, and steam transportation. Clearer type and the ability to print woodcut cartoons broadened their appeal. Rising literacy rates also helped, but illiteracy did not prohibit consumption of the printed word. Reading the newspaper was often a public event in the nineteenth century. Building upon older traditions of storytelling and oral history, the weekly rag was regularly read aloud in pubs, coffeehouses, and reading rooms. An English laborer's evidence before a British parliamentary select committee on newspaper stamps in 1851 demonstrated the dangers inherent in the practice. "I tell you, Sir, I never go to the public-house for beer, I go for the news," he insisted. "I have no other way of getting it; I cannot afford to pay five-pence, but unfortunately I go on drinking till I have spent a shilling, and I might as well have bought the paper in the first instance; still, that is my reason, my only reason for going to the public house; I hear people read the paper, and say what is going on in London, and it is the only place where I get the news." Reanimating aspects of Benedict Anderson's work, this book shows that the press did more than merely articulate Irish opinion. By connecting the worldwide Irish, newspapers provided the intellectual basis for an international imagined community. Close examination of each chapter's endnotes reveals the global transmission of these ideas.[6]

As a transnational study of Irish identity, this book builds on the existing scholarship in two fields. First and foremost, it owes much to recent advances in Irish migration studies. In the mid-twentieth century, historians such as Oscar Handlin and Thomas N. Brown offered brilliant analyses of the immigrant Irish mind-set that moved beyond traditional hagiographies of leading men. Yet these studies also tended to overemphasize the host community's role in shaping Irish American identity. In the mid-1980s, Kerby Miller broke that mold by arguing that Irish American nationalism reflected a worldview that was more an artifact of Ireland than of the United States. In the past twenty years, subsequent studies have sought to blend analyses of both the old and new worlds, while others, such as Timothy Meagher's *Inventing Irish America* (2001), have offered multigenerational studies of the subject. Some have transcended the Atlantic connection. Donald Harman Akenson's works on the Irish in Canada and the Caribbean have overturned many of the field's comfortable assumptions. Others have built on the scholarship of Patrick O'Farrell to bring the Irish in Australia and New Zealand into the discussion. In his excellent monograph *Ireland's New Worlds* (2008), Malcolm Campbell offered a uniquely comparative analysis of the Irish in Australia and the United States. While these and other works have made great strides, my work aims to push the limits of this literature even further by offering a more fully international portrait of mid-nineteenth-century Irish identity.[7]

My work also draws on the historiography of American immigration. Reading books by authors such as David Roediger, Noel Ignatiev, and Matthew Frye Jacobson convinced me that there was still much work to be done on Irish America and race. While impressed by their commitment to rethink a complicated question, I felt that these "whiteness" historians had overemphasized the host community's role in immigrant identity formation, gone some distance toward blaming the immigrants for the American racial structure, and largely missed Irish America's connections to the outside world. Most troubling, the early whiteness scholars seemed overly interested in what others thought of the immigrants, to the detriment of the voices of

INTRODUCTION : 5

the newcomers themselves. In recent years, scholars such as Thomas Gu-glielmo, Russell Kazal, and Eric Goldstein have successfully blunted the sharpest edges of these earlier books. Nevertheless, my work seeks to go beyond whiteness by reintroducing older, European concepts of race as "nation" (as well as "color") into the Civil War era debate over American citizenship. This book is also part of a recent trend in American immigration studies that seeks to unearth the transnational dimensions of migrant communities. Works by Donna Gabaccia, Eiichiro Azuma, and Mark Choate inspired me to connect the dots between the international Irish. Delving into the often-overlooked mid-nineteenth century, my approach seeks to acknowl-edge the power of the nation-state while giving voice to the global dimensions of an imagined community.[8]

The gripping, globe-trotting adventures of a group of romantic national-ists known as Young Ireland drive the book's narrative and provide its main source-base. Between 1840 and 1880, this coterie of radical journalists and editors were key players in the global Irish secular intelligentsia. Through-out the mid-1840s, they practically invented Irish racial discourse by popu-larizing it in the columns of their wildly successful weekly newspaper, the Dublin *Nation*. Following the failure of their 1848 rebellion, seven of the Young Irelanders were arrested and transported to the British penal colony of Van Diemen's Land in present-day southern Australia. By the mid-1850s, most had escaped to the United States, where they joined the middle class of a wider exodus of Irish escaping the Great Famine. Between 1845 and 1855, over one and a half million Irish people migrated to the United States and British North America. With Young Ireland's stature as a cadre of lead-ers already consolidated at home, these massive numbers of Irish American voters instantly made the exiles a serious factor in antebellum American politics. This book uses a broad sample of their newspapers, printed speeches, cartoons, poems, personal correspondence, and diaries to track the Young Irelanders through their adventures. Owning, editing, and contributing to newspapers throughout their careers, the Young Irelanders publicized not only their own opinions, but also those of their allies, followers, and ene-mies, whose opinions they often printed in order to more soundly refute them. Similarly, while the letters they wrote form an important source for material, the letters they received from others are useful too. As a result, although this book relies heavily on materials produced by Young Ireland, it also includes the opinions of a wide range of other people, placing the Young Irelanders squarely within the context of public discourse at home and abroad.[9]

Yet no book can speak for all Irish-born people in a given time period. Limits on the scope of this project, therefore, mean that in this book, the term "Irish" refers to a mostly Catholic, nationalist, male community. While the Young Ireland émigrés came from various Christian denominations (Catholic, Anglican, and Presbyterian), their audience was largely Catholic. The diasporic identity of Irish Protestants, who dominated the ranks of the previous century's emigration from Ireland, is an important question and one finally enjoying, in recent years, the historiographical attention it deserves. Historians have begun to offer transnational examinations of how the identities of Irish Anglicans, Presbyterians, and others changed upon transplantation across the ocean. Other have shown how, as Kerby Miller has written, "by the mid-1800s Irish American Protestant political culture was dominated by what later critics would call a 'Scotch-Irish myth' that encompassed nearly all non-Catholic Irish immigrants and their descendants in a shared sense of social and cultural superiority [over Irish Catholics]." This anti-Catholicism encouraged many mid-nineteenth-century Irish Protestants, both Anglican and Presbyterian, to establish common cause both with each other and with American nativists. While that process is an important piece of the broader Irish American puzzle, a full investigation of it would exceed the limits of this project. This is also a story primarily utilizing primary sources produced by men. How women's experiences differed and the role gender played in the construction of this diasporic identity must be left to another historian.[10]

One of this book's main arguments is that the worldwide secular press was critical to the creation of Irish global nationalism in the nineteenth century. Yet it must be admitted that the press was not the only transnational dynamic at work. By following the British Empire wherever it went, the Roman Catholic Church also fostered a strong sense of connectedness among the worldwide Irish during this time period. In recent years, Colin Barr has discerned "a pattern of what might be called Irish Episcopal Imperialism" that first took shape in the United States in the 1830s before extending to British North America, southern Africa, the Antipodes, and Scotland. Under the guiding hand of the Irish prelate Paul Cullen, whose unique connections in Rome endowed him with disproportionate influence over episcopal appointments, Irish bishops were systematically assigned to key positions throughout the English-speaking world. During the nineteenth century, Barr concludes, "Paul Cullen and his allies 'borrowed' the British empire and more besides to build a transnational Irish spiritual empire of their own." The discourse of Celts and Saxons was popular among these

Irish clergymen; yet, while the hierarchy's views on identity enjoy some attention in the pages that follow, secular republicans produced the bulk of evidence presented. To compare and contrast both groups was too much for one monograph. In sum, this book does not pretend to paint all mid-nineteenth-century Irish with the same brush. To do so would rob them of their countless shades and perspectives.[11]

This is a study of the intelligentsia rather than of Irish migrants in general. For a historian deeply influenced by works of "history from the bottom up," focusing on the words and experiences of a coterie of editors and journalists required some hard decisions, but it also imbued the study with several important advantages. It is true, for example, that this book analyzes the dimensions of Irish racial discourse without delving deeply into its social origins. To clearly and consistently maintain the distinctions within the worldwide Irish community based on language, class, gender, age, and local origin would simply be too much for one monograph. At the same time, concentrating on the Young Irelanders strengthened the book in important ways. Its focus on their international misadventures gives real narrative drive and a human face to the story I am telling. Focusing on specific members of the Irish intelligentsia, and closely analyzing the actual processes of newspaper publication and distribution, also allows me to develop one of the most important contributions of this work: a deeper understanding of the myriad ways in which the worldwide popular press knit the Irish together. Finally, while other historians have written about Irish American racial attitudes during the nineteenth century, my book's focus on a handful of people over a specific period of time allows me to complicate our periodization of the subject. For example, I extend Angela Murphy's transnational analysis of Irish attitudes toward American slavery in the 1840s into the following decades. I also complement Bruce Nelson's recent longue durée approach to the making of the Irish race by carefully tightening the focus on a few decades.[12]

The following pages illustrate that the inherent flexibility of Irish global nationalism allowed it to constantly adapt to the unique political, social, and religious particularities of various host communities. Between 1845 and 1855, about 300,000 Irish settled permanently in Great Britain, while approximately 9,000 moved to South Africa. Over 50,000 headed to the Antipodes, where they formed part of a broader stream of rapid immigration, which led to a 450 percent increase in the size of the general settler population in the colony of Victoria between 1851 and 1861. Global nationalism allowed Irish immigrants to adapt to different host communities. In eastern Austra-

Thesis [handwritten annotation in left margin]

lia in the early 1850s, where Catholic immigrants generally received a friendly welcome, the Irish portrayed themselves as hearty Celtic pioneers, entirely suitable for the settler colonialism of the Antipodean colonies. Australian Anglo-Saxonism was widespread but not triumphalist, allowing Irish Celts to settle in as charter members of a self-governing collection of colonies powered by a rapidly expanding pastoral economy.[13]

Those Irish who landed in the United States, by contrast, found themselves in a much more hostile social climate. Their sheer numbers partly shaped the reception they received. The 781,000 Irish who came to the United States in the 1840s represented a staggering 45.6 percent of total immigration to the country for that period. In the 1850s, another 914,000 arrived, constituting 35.2 percent of that period's total influx. Faced with nativist hostility, Irish Catholics responded with a unique brand of global nationalism, which depicted the Celt as a universal proponent of the civic republican ideals that America was allegedly built on. Abandoned by the Whig/Republican Party, who considered their religion, work habits, and alcoholism as incompatible with free labor, Irish Catholic immigrants flocked to the Democratic Party. Being welcomed with open arms, however, required acquiescing to the Democrats' other main constituency: the slave-owning South. Vociferously rejected by the Whig/Republicans, whose evangelical Protestantism brought back bad memories from home, many Catholic immigrants found this a simple step to take. The Democrats' emphasis on states' rights (which echoed the Irish nationalist campaign for self-government) and the Catholic Church's ambivalence over slavery also made the Democrats the easy choice. When linked to claims of a Celtic republican heritage reaching back to the American War of Independence, this voting power rendered Irish Catholics, and their middle-class leaders, a force in American politics.[14]

The Young Irelanders' international adventures dictate the book's outline. The first chapter roots the story in the soil, people, idioms, and history of Ireland. Buoyed by a rising tide of popular support for political independence from Britain, yet wracked by an unprecedented natural disaster in the form of the Great Famine, weekly periodicals such as the Young Irelanders' Dublin *Nation* constructed and disseminated a highly elastic historical image of Irish Catholics as "the original Celtic owners of the soil." Once it was dislocated from the Irish natural environment, this dexterous discourse subsequently provided the template for global nationalism. Following their abortive rebellion in 1848, many of the Young Ireland leaders were arrested and sentenced to exile in Britain's Australian penal colonies. Chapter 2 shows how almost constant access to newspapers from home aided the Irish in *identity w/o being in Ireland*

In Australia in developing a new sense of themselves as Celts that was no longer rooted in the soil and climate of the island of Ireland. Though sentenced to between ten years and life in Tasmanian exile, most of the Young Irelanders escaped to the United States in the early 1850s, where anti-Irish nativism was at a fever pitch. Chapter 3 analyzes how Irish Americans depicted Know-Nothingism as merely the latest avatar of Saxon oppression. Against the background of the Civil War, chapter 4 examines how Irish on both sides of the Mason-Dixon Line employed the racial discourse of Celts and Saxons to contextualize their military service and their claim on American citizenship. Finally, chapter 5 demonstrates that, with social relations in a state of flux after the war, many Irish editors pressed an agenda that sought to break down, rather than build up, walls around the American polity. By demanding the right, bought with their blood, to pledge simultaneous loyalty to their new and old homes, the Irish successfully broadened how postbellum Americans thought about citizenship and mobility.[15]

It is hard for many historians to picture the nineteenth-century Irish as advocates of civic pluralism. Most are content to retain their monochromatic group portrait of an embittered community of blue-collar racists. Indeed, the Irish themselves have done much to perpetuate that image, whether rioting against the draft in the 1860s or against busing a century later. As the following pages make clear, white supremacy was undoubtedly a part of mid-nineteenth-century Irish identity. Yet when we situate the words of the Irish themselves in the transnational context in which they were written, published, reprinted, and read, we see a much more complicated community, one that included decent folks committed to human equality. The goal of this project is, in part, to recover and remember those lost voices.

CHAPTER ONE

L'Esprit et les Lois

Celts and Saxons in Ireland, 1840–1848

One afternoon in the summer of 1842, three young journalists went for a walk through Dublin. Thomas Davis, John Blake Dillon, and Charles Gavan Duffy rendezvoused at Trinity College before ambling down to the Liffey and west along the quays, all the way to Phoenix Park. As they walked, they bemoaned the state of Irish nationalism. The eighteenth-century Patriotism of Grattan, Charlemont, and Flood was gone. The United Irishmen of 1798 were dead or in exile. Their successor, Daniel O'Connell's Loyal National Repeal Association (LNRA), was popular, but its argument that Irish prosperity had declined since Ireland joined the United Kingdom in 1801 was too materialistic. "Passions and imagination have won victories which reason and self-interest have attempted in vain," figured Duffy. It was these "lessons of profounder influence over the human breast" that he and his friends believed in. What Irish nationalism needed was a vibrant new voice that would, regardless of religion or class, unite the people behind repeal of the union with Britain by emphasizing the historical, philological, and cultural differences between Ireland and England. Sitting on a bench beneath an elm tree overlooking an entrance to Phoenix Park, the three agreed that this new voice should be manifested in a weekly newspaper named after their ultimate objective: the *Nation*. Its motto was "To create and to foster public opinion in Ireland—to make it racy of the soil." In time, an English newspaper would nickname Duffy and the *Nation*'s staff "Young Ireland."[1]

This chapter investigates the form and function of Irish racial discourse during the 1840s. Embedded in an international network of weekly periodicals sympathetic to Ireland's cause, the Dublin *Nation* played a critical role in developing the language of Celts and Saxons. While portrayed as a coherent philosophy, the Celt/Saxon dichotomy was in fact a flexible, practical instrument riddled with ambivalence and contradiction. On the one hand, Irish nationalists used it to buttress their claim for legislative independence from Britain by situating the Celts in a timeless struggle for freedom from their oppressive Saxon neighbors. England's laws, they argued, could never suit the Irish temperament. On the other hand, this racial rhetoric simultaneously undermined the Young Ireland national project by deepening the sense of difference within Ireland between Catholics (Celts) and Protestants (Saxons). In the short run, their Celtic discourse, which effectively portrayed the English as the eternal enemy, was equally fatal to the Young Irelanders' dream of unifying Irish Catholics and Protestants. In the long run, however, this flexible language of race and nation proved useful to the Irish when famine and exile scattered them overseas.

Race and Nation in Pre-Famine Ireland

The steady expansion of capitalism throughout the nineteenth century shaped how Europeans thought about race and nation. As tens of millions of laborers and managers circulated around the earth, national identities morphed and shifted. Pre-Famine Irish society was deeply affected by these changes. The Irish population exploded from about 2.3 million in the middle of the eighteenth century to 7.2 million in 1821 and 8.4 million in 1841. In 1834, 80 percent of the population (6,428,000) were Catholic, just over 10 percent (852,000) were Church of Ireland (Anglican), about 8 percent (642,000) were Presbyterian, and a tiny fraction (22,000) were other dissenters, including Methodists and Quakers. The rapid increase in population had been stoked, in part, by the success of Irish commerce. Stimulated by Britain's sprawling urbanization and aggressive militarism, the value of Irish annual exports trebled between 1750 and 1810, and continued to increase even with the collapse of wartime inflation after Waterloo. At the same time, the main means of production in Ireland—land—remained in the hands of a tiny (mostly Protestant) minority, and since the Act of Union had incorporated Ireland into the United Kingdom in 1801, legislative power remained in London. This strengthening of the state and commerce brought with it the increased use of English as the language of law, business, and politics during the 1830s and 1840s. This process eroded remaining vestiges of Gaelic society, but it also handed Irish nationalists a tool for uniting their constituents. In touch with the intellectual currents then circulating throughout Europe, the Young Irelanders used racial discourse to make sense of this fluctuating world.[2]

European racialism in the 1840s was a hodgepodge of various concepts and methodologies rather than a hard science in the modern sense of the term. Its three basic building blocks were German linguistic philology, French physiology, and English pro-Saxonism, but as Robert J. C. Young has shown, it borrowed indiscriminately from a wide variety of disciplines, "providing a common source of cultural capital that writers of all kinds were able to draw on." This popular science held that there were, fundamentally, two races in Europe: the Celts and the Saxons, distinguished by cultural differences ingrained in physiological incongruence. Primarily produced by English and Lowland Scottish ethnologists like Thomas Arnold, John Mitchell Kemble, Thomas Carlyle, and Robert Knox, this reading of the races of humankind described Anglo-Saxons as rational, freedom-loving, self-reliant people—nineteenth-century avatars of the stout, sylvan Germans described by Tacitus. By contrast, the Celts were imaginative, slavish boors dependent on leaders for direction. The two races were irreconcilable. Writing in 1820, the influential French historian Augustin Thierry believed that recent studies in physiology had shown that "the physical and moral constitution of nations depends far more on their descent from certain primitive ancestors than on the influence of climate." Almost three decades later, the London *Times* agreed. "For three hundred years there has been a continued succession of attempts to infuse the Anglo-Saxon spirit into these miserable [Celtic] imbeciles," it editorialized. "So far it is all in vain." Many agreed with Thierry that the main dynamic of human history was "the conflict of different races."[3]

The Celtic Revival of the late eighteenth and early nineteenth centuries also shaped European racialism. Beginning around 1750, a burst of popular interest in all things Celtic encouraged men of letters to deepen contemporary literature with the myths, histories, and legends of their forebears. The most famous works to emerge from this genre included James MacPherson's fraudulent *Fragments of Ancient Poetry* (1760), which, despite his vehement claims to the contrary, actually consisted of modern compositions by MacPherson himself. What was most remarkable about MacPherson's work was not its alleged antiquity but rather the public interest it sparked in rediscovering Celtic languages and traditions. In response, men like William Stukeley, Thomas Gray, and Lewis Morris produced extensive tracts on the superstitions, laws, and literatures of northwestern Europe's earliest inhabitants. At root, the Celtic Revival was an auxiliary of the broader romantic movement, which sought to replace classical mythology with a renewed emphasis on the mysteries of nature. By the 1840s, it had built a massive body of scholarly literature, some of which was dedicated to outlining the perceived racial differences between Celts and Saxons. In an era of what Eric Hobsbawm has termed "invented traditions," racialism offered the basis for national histories that could legitimate or challenge the contemporary political map. If the goal of the modern nation-state was to find the perfect balance between what Montesquieu had called *l'esprit et les lois* of any given country, racialism could define both.[4]

Ironically, while many Europeans were busy drawing national borders around races, international migration lay at the heart of their origin myths. Since the sixteenth century, English nationalism had rested on the Teutonic or Anglo-Saxon myth, which held that the English people's ancestral roots were brought north from Germany when Hengist and Horsa landed in Kent in 449 CE. Similarly, the Celts' roots were believed to lie in central Europe, where, by 600 BCE, the Greeks were referring to them as Keltoi (although many Irish Celts traced their ancestors to the Milesian migration from Spain several centuries BCE). In the ever-changing context of the industrial revolution, it is no surprise that Europeans described themselves in terms of people moving over a border-free earth. Folks like Carlyle and Knox took the Hengist and Horsa legend as historical evidence that God had put them in that time and place to cement Saxon hegemony. Those who identified as the descendants of Celts, by contrast, believed that the Milesian story confirmed native sovereignty over the island of Ireland. In later years, these stories of their migratory ancestors provided the Famine-era Irish with evidence that their exodus was only the latest in a grand tradition of great tribes roaming the earth.[5]

In the decades after the French Revolution, Irish nationalists sought to balance *l'esprit et les lois* of Ireland. During the 1790s, the United Irishmen tried to smash the Anglican monopoly and bring Catholics and Presbyterian dissenters into the polity. In their minds, a handful of privileged, corrupt Anglicans, propped up by the British government, misruled Ireland. Breaking the connection with England would topple this oligarchy and open the way for a new parliament representative of all segments and sects of the Irish population. Yet their original hopes for political reform devolved into violence. After their bloody rebellion was put down in 1798, the Act of Union (1801) drew Ireland into the United Kingdom by abolishing the parliament in Dublin and giving the Irish seats in Westminster. Popular interest in Irish independence, which waned in the early 1800s, was reinvigorated by Daniel O'Connell's brand of constitutional nationalism. The scion of a wealthy landowning Catholic family in County Kerry, O'Connell grew to become one of early nineteenth-century Britain's leading legal minds. Convinced that Ireland's political woes were attributable to Catholic exclusion from the polity, he successfully mobilized the masses behind a campaign for Catholic Emancipation, which he achieved in 1829. A decade later, he regathered the people into a new political instrument called the Loyal National Repeal Association, which was designed to repeal the Act of Union and replace it with a form of—purposefully ill-defined—self-government. For O'Connell, as for the United Irishmen, political health demanded that the spirit of the people be reflected in the laws of the nation-state.[6]

If a healthy body politic depended on harmony between the laws of the land and the soul of the people, it was critical to define that community's *esprit*. Early Irish nationalists found themselves caught between antithetical definitions based on ethnic solidarity and civic pluralism. The universalist roots of the United Irishmen were reflected in their desire for "a cordial union among ALL PEOPLE OF IRELAND, to maintain that balance which is essential to the preservation of our liberties." Catholics, Presbyterians, and Anglicans alike must unite in a representative parliament. At the same time, sectarian violence in the countryside encouraged armed bands of Catholics to join the United Irishmen in the hope that revolution would undo the seventeenth-century conquest, which had transferred the land into Protestant hands. Years later, under O'Connell, this tension between ethnic and civic nationalism remained. Steeped in the rationalist liberalism of the Enlightenment, he shared a commitment to diversity. Yet O'Connellism was also characterized by what Kevin Whelan has described as "an embryonic cultural nationalism," which equated confessional allegiance and national identity. In 1843, for example, O'Connell published an account of Irish history entitled *A Memoir on Ireland, Native and Saxon*, whose title page quoted a couplet from Thomas Moore: "On *our* side is Virtue and Erin, On *theirs* is Saxon and Guilt." Irish nationalists seeking to define the Irish *esprit* in the early nineteenth century were, therefore, locked in a dialectical struggle between ethnic solidarity and civic pluralism. The Young Irelanders would wrestle with the same quandary.[7]

Though they often spoke wistfully of pikes and swords, the most effective weapon in the armory of nineteenth-century Irish nationalists was the printed word. Through a fluid but reliable network of communication and exchange, national identity and political unity were exported from urban centers to the countryside through newspapers, pamphlets, song-sheets, posters, and handbills. Theobald Wolfe Tone's widely circulated pamphlet *An Argument on Behalf of the Catholics of Ireland* (1791) galvanized the Society of United Irishmen, which subsequently founded a semiweekly newspaper in Belfast entitled the *Northern Star*. Though its readership was largely limited to the island's eastern littoral, it soon became one of the country's most widely diffused periodicals. Through a potent mixture of domestic satire, news from France, and radical opinion from England, the *Northern Star* successfully contributed to the democratization of Irish political culture by expanding the limits of its imagined community. Daniel O'Connell also employed print culture in his campaigns for Catholic Emancipation and Repeal by using sympathetic Dublin weeklies such as the *Freeman's Journal* and *Pilot* as semi-official mouthpieces. Through these newspapers, O'Connell advertised meetings, raised cash, and disseminated ideas. For early nineteenth-century Irish nationalists, the printed word was the most effective medium for spreading their message. It was in this context that Duffy and his associates founded the Dublin *Nation*.[8]

The Dublin *Nation*

The Young Irelanders came from a variety of backgrounds. Duffy was a Catholic from the northern province of Ulster who had grown up experiencing Protestant bigotry. Largely self-educated until the age of eighteen, Duffy met Dillon (and through him, Davis) when he took terms at the King's Inns law school in Dublin. His financial capital and editorial experience with a previous newspaper, the Belfast *Vindicator*, provided the new organ with stability. John Blake Dillon was a Catholic farmer's son from Ballaghaderreen in the poor western province of Connaught. His background kept the newspaper in touch with the country folk whose numbers it was trying to harness. Thomas Osborne Davis, by contrast, was an Anglican from Munster, in the south, where he had enjoyed a more affluent upbringing than his colleagues. Protected from the hardscrabble experiences of Duffy and Dillon, Davis, with his unabashed idealism and wide reading in history and literature, imbued the *Nation* with intellectual authenticity. Selling itself as physically "the LARGEST WEEKLY PAPER IN IRELAND," the *Nation* boasted an impressive list of contributors, including members of the LNRA's top leadership. Yet it was a handpicked coterie of close colleagues who contributed the most to the *Nation*. John Cornelius O'Callaghan was a historian whose *The Green Book* had recently enjoyed widespread popularity. James Clarence Mangan was an eccentric, highly talented, starving poet. Fellow students from Trinity College made important contributions as well. Over the next few years, its staff hardened into a dedicated band of intellectuals that rival Dublin editor Dicky Barrett cynically referred to as the "Clique." In time, the Young Irelanders went from followers to critics to enemies of O'Connell and the LNRA.[9]

The *Nation*'s first number met with instant success when it appeared on the morning of Saturday, October 15, 1842. The first edition sold out by noon "and could have sold twice as many more if they had been printed, as they ought to have been," Davis wrote to a friend. He was delighted and boasted that one of the windows in the *Nation*'s office at 12 Trinity Street "was actually broken by the newsmen in their impatience to get more [copies]." The success continued through the following week: "4,000 copies to-day," gushed Davis excitedly, "equal to the Freeman and double any other weekly paper." Neither of the other pro-Repeal weeklies, Wilson Gray's *Freeman's Journal* and Dicky Barrett's *Pilot*, could compete for readership with the *Nation*, which owed much of its success to its rural popularity. The "country people are delighted with us if their letters speak true," Davis told a friend. Dillon found the same thing when he returned to his remote hometown a couple of months later. "I was quite astonished to find how successful the Nation has been [here]," he wrote to Duffy. "You would not guess how many Nations came in to it on Sunday last—no less than 23. There are scarcely so many houses in the town . . . !" The paper's popularity was confirmed in correspondence sent to the editorial office by the readers themselves. "My calendar for the week dates from the time the 'Nation' arrives," wrote one rural reader, "till the day I may hope for another 'Nation.' I often walk three miles to the post-office to bring it home a few hours earlier than it could otherwise reach us." An anonymous Dublin tradesman agreed. "I work hard all the week," he wrote, "and on Sunday I am repaid by lying in bed an additional hour or two to read the 'Nation.'"[10]

It is hard to establish concrete figures on how many people the *Nation* reached each week. Literacy rates in Ireland, subject to dramatic regional and class differences, sat at about 50 percent during the mid-nineteenth century and were increasing slowly. Yet illiteracy did not prohibit consumption of the newspaper. Pre-Famine Ireland had strong traditions of oral history and group storytelling that easily translated into collective readings of the weekly rag. The *Nation*'s historical tales, poems, and ballads (often arranged to contemporary tunes), made for exciting group readings, and Duffy would later recall "the young tradesmen in the towns and the young peasants who listened to the 'Nation' read aloud around the forge fire of an evening, or in the chapel yard on a Sunday morning." Individuals also shared newspapers. James Fintan Lalor had to wait until midweek to receive his copy because his subscription was "in partnership with another person." In later years, Duffy explained that the *Nation*'s unique distribution increased its readership exponentially. "Three hundred copies went to newsrooms and Teetotal Societies, and were read by at least fifty persons each," he estimated. "Eleven hundred copies went to Repeal Wardens to be read aloud at weekly meetings, and each copy served from fifty to a hundred persons. Nine thousand copies were sold by agents or went directly to subscribers; and as the 'Nation' was handed about like a magazine, and preserved for binding, it is certain that each of these copies reached more than a dozen readers, probably more than a score." Moreover, articles and poems "were copied extensively in the Colonies and wholesale in the United States." Given all of this, Duffy estimated the *Nation*'s weekly readership at over "a quarter of a million." While that figure needs to be treated with some skepticism, it is not outrageous. Given the traditions of group reading, the excitement of the new newspaper, the huge list of agents published in the paper, and, as seen later, the popular willingness to become active participants in the Repeal movement in 1843, Duffy's estimate is probably a fair number, especially during the first phase of the Young Ireland movement between 1842 and 1845.[11]

Nor was the *Nation*'s circulation limited to Ireland. In the United States, entrepreneur Patrick Donahoe was striving to transcend the regionalism of the Irish American press by fashioning a national circulation for his struggling *Boston Pilot* (which he had renamed in honor of Dicky Barrett's Dublin *Pilot*). Donahoe's plan for national circulation hinged on innovatively pitching the paper as "Irish American" rather than "American Catholic." He published more Irish news, vehemently supported the Repeal movement, and established contacts and reciprocal exchange agreements with Irish newspapers in Ireland and around the United States. The strategy paid off. The circulation of his newspaper increased from 680 in December 1838 to 7,000 in 1844. The establishment of closer contacts with Repeal newspapers back home was an important part of Donahoe's plan to become more "Irish" in America, and the Dublin *Nation* was a perfect candidate. By December 1842, the *Boston Pilot* told its readers that it had received "the three first numbers issued" of the *Nation*, "and unhesitatingly award to it the highest merit." Committed to nurturing the fledgling transatlantic network of Irish news and opinion, the *Pilot* added the *Nation* to its list of exchange agreements "and should be pleased to do the same with every liberal Repeal paper in Ireland." Donahoe was annoyed that the Dublin *Freeman's Journal* was the only Irish paper his publication "received regularly as an exchange," and he

A group reading of the Dublin *Nation*, ca. 1843. Collective readings of weekly newspapers were an important element of the Irish public sphere in the mid-nineteenth century as evidenced in this engraving, which accompanied Charles Gavan Duffy's history of the Young Ireland movement. Charles Gavan Duffy, *Young Ireland: A Fragment of Irish History, 1840–1845* (Dublin: M. H. Gills and Son, 1884), ii.

hoped that "a more liberal and *Irish* spirit will in future govern the Irish Press in their intercourse with the Repeal Press of America." The "mutual advantages" of exchange and intercourse should never be lost sight of "in any selfish desire for pay."[12]

Back in Ireland, the Dublin *Nation* sought to encourage a national ardor that transcended sectarian and class divisions. "Protestant, Catholic, and Dissenter—Milesian and Cromwellian—the Irishman of a hundred generations, and the stranger who is within our gates," were welcome in this new nation. National identity, having instilled in the people "a lofty and heroic love of country," would pave the way for political independence. To support their cause, they often cited Edmund Burke's definition of nationality as "a moral essence, not a geographical arrangement, or a denomination of the nomenclator." Popular education was the key to national identity. "Speeches are wind, petitions are waste paper," editorialized Duffy, "if, day by day, the People are not training themselves in the knowledge that is power, and the union that is strength, and which, in their combination, make this public opinion that nothing can withstand." *Nation* contributor Thomas MacNevin called for a national education "uncontaminated by bigotry and . . . influencing the spirit of a People." The national system of education created by the Whig ministry in the 1830s had begun to increase Irish literacy rates, but these schools were not national. Parents ought to procure books on Irish history and customs for their children. Similarly, the *Nation* allowed the Irish to formulate their own foreign policy. No nationality could coexist, Duffy argued, "with the mean and mendicant spirit . . . which looks at all the rest of the world through the spectacles of Anglican prejudice." Thomas Davis agreed. England "shuts us up in a dark dungeon," he argued, "and tells us what she likes of herself and of the rest of the world." There was freedom in the printed word.[13]

If popular education was the engine of national independence, historical knowledge was its fuel. O'Callaghan considered "a nation without a history to be like a religion without a Scriptures." The writings of leading scholars were valuable arrows in the *Nation*'s historical quiver, and Thomas Davis maintained regular correspondence with leading antiquarians such as John O'Donovan, John Windele, and Eugene O'Curry. The *Nation* also cited Cicero and Plato in an attempt to marry, as David Dwan has written, "the principles of ancient citizenship and the institutional realities of modern politics." To render historical material accessible to even the humblest classes, the newspaper published a "National Gallery" series, which offered biographical sketches of historical heroes, and an ancillary series entitled "The Library of Ireland" that featured essays on great moments in Irish history. At the same time, letters to the editor allowed readers to contribute snippets of input, correction, and opinion and thus invest something of themselves in these history lessons. When the Dublin Corporation considered passing a resolution lauding recent British victories in Afghanistan and China, an angry letter from "Patricius" hoped that "by looking into the pages of Irish history," the members of the corporation "would find, in the treatment of their martyred ancestors by the Saxon invader, cases parallel to the preceding ones [in Asia]." Archaeology, literature, biography, and hagiography were all important topics in these history lessons, but the theme with the most currency for Irish political independence from Britain was the racial discourse of Celts and Saxons.[14]

Thomas Davis's unexpected demise, which corresponded with the outbreak of the Famine in the autumn of 1845, ended the first phase of the Young Ireland movement. The second phase, between 1845 and 1848, was as intensely energetic, if far more fractious, as the first. The previous year or two had seen several young men join the group. Thomas Francis Meagher was the son of a wealthy Catholic merchant from County Waterford. In 1844, after returning from a Jesuit education at Stonyhurst in England with a lisping, upper-class accent and a taste for fine clothes, Meagher joined the Repeal Association and immediately fell in with the Young Irelanders, who were attracted to his powerful, florid oratory. Another gifted speaker who joined around this time was Richard O'Gorman. Also the son of a Catholic merchant, O'Gorman was a practicing barrister in Dublin. Although these men brought new energy and rhetorical ability to the Nation, they could not replace Davis as chief contributor.[15]

Duffy achieved this by hiring two other men. The first was John Mitchel, who became lead writer of the Nation. The son of a County Down nonsubscribing Presbyterian minister, Mitchel had been working as a solicitor in Banbridge, where he was happily married to Jenny Verner, with whom he had eloped in 1837. Mitchel was no stranger to Repeal, having been both a member of the LNRA and an occasional contributor to the Nation since the spring of 1843. He and fellow County Down Repealer John Martin had sent the Nation to each other since its early days. "I send you by this post the second number of the Nation," wrote Mitchel in October 1842, feeling assured that the new newspaper "will do very well." Mitchel was therefore no stranger to either the Nation or its wide circulation. He also had firsthand experience with anti-Catholic bigotry in the north of Ireland. In Banbridge, where he had practiced law, he witnessed the bullying tactics of the Orangemen during their annual marching season, and as a Presbyterian solicitor he had worked on behalf of many maltreated Catholics. In explaining why he joined Repeal, Mitchel described "the butchery and assassination, which appear to be the means of opposing Repeal, contemplated by the Northern Orangemen, and recommended by certain Thug newspapers." As the *Nation*'s lead writer, Mitchel soon found himself on the radical edge of Young Ireland. Two months after taking up the position, he published an editorial entitled "Threats of Coercion" in which he explicitly endorsed the sabotaging of Irish railways in the event of an uprising. Duffy was prosecuted for having published the article and, though subsequently acquitted, got the point: Mitchel was going to be a handful.[16]

The second person Duffy hired to help with the writing in the *Nation* was a Catholic from County Louth named Thomas D'Arcy McGee. Having already served as editor of the *Boston Pilot* from 1844 to 1845 and as a correspondent for the Dublin *Freeman's Journal*, McGee brought a wealth of international newspaper experience to the *Nation*. This background, figured Duffy, combined with his "sweet and flexible voice" and "fertile brains and great originality" to make him a "serviceable recruit." But McGee's experience abroad also made him a bit of an outsider in the political and social circles that Duffy introduced him to in Dublin. Thomas Davis liked McGee but feared that his "Irish nature" had been "spoiled by the Yankees." His personal appearance was also noteworthy. McGee, according to Duffy, "looked illdressed and underbred" among the "self-confident and somewhat dandified young men" of Young Ireland. Even more noticeable were his facial features. "His face was odd, and might even be considered ugly," remarked Duffy. "An unaccountable Negro cast of features was a constant source of jesting allusions, and induced his enemies, of whom he came to have a plentiful supply, to distort his name from Darcy McGee into Darky McGee."[17]

The Dublin *Nation* embodied a wildly popular network of communication for the transmission of Irish nationalist rhetoric. Its affordability, wide circulation, and reciprocal exchange with other Irish newspapers garnered it extensive circulation at home and abroad. The paper's founders were well-educated, middle-class professionals, but they possessed strong connections with their rural readership and were as eager to write as their readers were to read. At a time when literacy rates were rising, they contributed to the development of a vernacular print culture designed to welcome, rather than exclude, the majority of the population. The *Nation*'s popularity also lay in its ability to incorporate the opinions of its readers. The weekly Answers to Correspondents column, a prominent part of the editorial page, featured unsolicited letters, poems, and historical notes from readers along with editorial comment on these letters. In this way, readers were engaged members, rather than passive observers, of the construction and dissemination of racial discourse. This partly explains why Duffy later referred to Answers to Correspondents as "the first column read in the 'Nation.'" The newspaper was more than mere paper and ink. It was a national network for communicating ideas about race and nation.[18]

Celts and Saxons

Daniel O'Connell dominated early nineteenth-century Irish politics. After mobilizing the Catholic masses to secure emancipation in 1829, "the Liberator" led a sizable number of Irish MPs through the 1830s in a series of alliances with Whig administrations. The results were disappointing, and when Sir Robert Peel and the Tories came to power early in the following decade, O'Connell decided that the time had come to remobilize the population, this time in pursuit of Irish legislative independence through repeal of the Act of Union. Between the founding of the LNRA in 1840 and his death in 1847, O'Connell was the figurehead of Europe's first political mass movement. Through a penny-a-month program called the Repeal Rent, tiny droplets of financial contributions from all over the country united to form a torrent of cash for the organization. While peasants and tradesmen made up the bulk of the LNRA's membership, its leadership was drawn from Ireland's growing stratum of underemployed, middle-class professionals. Headquartered in Dublin's Conciliation Hall, the LNRA spread throughout the country in a complicated network of local chapters, each run by a "Repeal warden." These branches were often superimposed on existing local structures, especially Catholic Church parish halls and the Teetotal Societies that had sprung up under Father Theobald Mathew's wildly successful Temperance movement in the late 1830s and early 1840s. These local outfits collected the Repeal Rent, organized meetings, and disseminated newspapers and pamphlets.[19]

O'Connell opened 1843 by declaring it the Repeal Year and embarking on a countrywide series of mass assemblies nicknamed "monster meetings." His intention was, as it had been in 1829, to garner concessions from the government through the brute physics of mass mobilization. Meetings were carefully scheduled at historically electrified sites intended to remind the audience of ancient Irish glory, English perfidy, or both. Unprecedented numbers of people attended these peaceful meetings. Although the contemporary estimates of crowd numbers must be handled with great care, assemblies in Limerick and Kells in April may have attracted up to 120,000 and 150,000 participants, respectively. In Cork in mid-May, according the nationalist press, as many as 500,000 showed up. Support from Catholic bishops and local priests gave lift and impetus to O'Connell's movement. The Repeal Rent climbed to £2,000 a week. Meanwhile, the monster meetings continued to grow throughout the summer. Three hundred thousand assembled at Cashel, probably more at Mallow, and as many as 750,000 at Tara, the ancient seat of the high kings of Ireland. Young Ireland newcomer Thomas MacNevin was impressed. "O'Connell is still going on, and not likely to stop," he editorialized in the *Nation* in late September 1843; "he is still at work, agitating the Celtic masses, awakening the power of the people, passing like a spirit over the deep, and evoking the wild things there."[20]

The Young Irelanders' paramount concern for promoting a national identity among the people was reflected in the *Nation*'s motto ("To create and to foster public opinion in Ireland—to make it racy of the soil"). In an anonymous letter published in the *Nation* under the pseudonym "A Protestant," Thomas Davis built an intellectual framework for nationalism around this quote, which survived over the coming decades among the Irish at home and abroad. To make public opinion racy of the soil, he explained, "is to lay the foundations of nationality . . . in the hearts and intelligence of the people." The physiology of the Celts was set, but it was up to their leaders to develop and encourage "the tendencies of their race and organization." Acknowledging the checkered history of sectarian relations in Ireland, Davis concluded, "A public opinion, 'racy of the soil,' should be full of these things as a healthy tree is full of sap. The fibres make the skeleton of the tree, but the sap is its life. Lands and population make the frame of a nation; a thoughtful, proud, valorous, pious mind, deriving its nature from the peculiar nature and history of the country, is its life." His letter also made a subtle point about the relationship between race and the natural environment, which reflected the thread of migration running through European racial discourse at the time. A nationality rooted in the hearts and minds of the people would prove resilient, "and though time should destroy it, still time would produce it again—in our island, if it existed; in other lands, if Ireland—the pile of rock and clay—should have perished; for, as Edmund Burke said, 'a nation is a spiritual essence.' While a people feels and understands its national existence, it is imperishable." National identity need not be bounded by the sovereign state. Races still roamed the earth.[21]

At this point, however, mass migration was largely buried in a broader discourse, which tied Irish nationality to the natural environment of Ireland. "All the climate and soil suggest to us, we should do," exhorted Davis, "and so doing, should grow to be different from men of other climes and soils." O'Connell's speeches, faithfully reprinted in every issue of the *Nation*, were laden with similar references. Ireland was the most beautiful land on earth, he declared, with fertile valleys, magnificent hills, "and streams pouring down with a voice, as it were, from eternity, calling on the people to make their country a nation again (tremendous cheers)." Duffy dreamed of seeing "a race of men full of a more intensely Irish character and knowledge" living on the soil and seas of Ireland, while W. J. O'Neill Daunt echoed the United Irishmen when he rued that English policy had ransacked the Irish countryside. God had endowed Ireland with treasures and advantages, he told an LNRA audience, that "the vile, the hideous policy" of England had squandered. The soils, rivers, and seas of Ireland belonged to the Celtic race.[22]

The landscape played an important role in Young Ireland racial discourse. Every Saturday evening, after that week's number had been issued, the closest confidantes gathered to discuss editorial policy, share new ideas, and enjoy a "frugal supper." On Sunday afternoons they often visited the historical ruins that dot the hills of Dublin and Wicklow. "The rudest peasant has *some* history," editorialized Davis in April 1843, "and much would it afflict and degrade him to take from him . . . those names and stories which people the hills and tombs and ruins of his neighbourhood with heroes, victims, fairies, kings, and ghosts." Every aspect of the Irish landscape had a local name, the knowledge of which "was a topography, and a history, and romance, walking by your side, and helping your discourse." Museums and historical walking tours were far preferable to books and historical novels. While on one such walking tour, Young Irelander John Martin wrote of having marveled at the "ruins dear to Irish hearts—seats of ancient learning, dwellings of Irish power and pride." In a letter to the editor, "A Delcassian" urged all Repealers to discontinue employing "modern Saxon designations of places." Some even blamed affection for the Union with Britain on the dislocation of Irish (Saxon) Protestants from the soil of Ireland. "For them the battle-field is unpeopled and inexplicable—the temple and the castle recall nor saint nor chieftain," complained Davis, a fellow Anglican, "and the cairn is a grey heap, and no more." To find true harmony, the Irish people needed to understand their collective soul. It was rooted in the natural environment they shared.[23]

Although the Dublin *Nation* was published almost exclusively in English, and few of the Young Irelanders had more than a smattering of Irish (Gaelic), Thomas Davis still referred to the use of foreign language as "the worst badge of conquest, the chain on the soul." "A nation should guard its language more than its territories," he declared; "'tis a surer barrier and more important frontier than fortress or river." A native language was, after all, conformed to the physiology, climate, history, and soil of its people. To force a foreign language on a race was "to send their history adrift among the accidents of translation—'tis to tear their identity from all places." The Irish Celt's historical distinctiveness from Saxon England was important as well. "Among the whole civilized race," wrote Michael Doheny in 1843, the Irish had "no foes but the Saxon—no opponent but the clumsy and decrepit thing that calls itself our master." National strength depended on uniqueness and peculiarity. Thomas MacNevin echoed Augustin Thierry when he described "the original Celtic owners of the soil—those who have survived the bloody struggles of the conquest and legal oppression of confiscation, standing aloof from the descendants of the oppressor." Excerpts from historical books that supported these arguments were eagerly reviewed and reprinted. Samuel Smiles's *History of Ireland and the Irish People under the Government of England* (1844) argued that while the conquerors and conquered of other countries such as Scotland had largely integrated into one people, the opposite was true of Ireland. The Young Irelanders agreed. For centuries, the British government's policy had been to "divide and conquer—to set the children of one sky and soil at loggerheads," they editorialized. To undo the damage, the Irish must rediscover themselves. "Ireland must be unSaxonised," read an 1843 editorial, "before it can be pure and strong."[24]

At the monster meetings themselves, O'Connell and his lieutenants consistently invoked the timeless struggle between Celts and Saxons. One meeting place, the Curragh of Kildare, was the mythological meeting ground of the legendary Fianna of yore and, more recently, the site of the massacre of 350 surrendering rebels by yeomen under Sir James Duff during the 1798 rebellion. At a meeting there in May 1843, O'Connellite lieutenant Thomas Steele reminded his listeners of the time when unarmed prisoners were slaughtered "under the sanction of the Saxon alien government, in cold blood (renewed shouts of execration and horror)!!!" At Castlebar, County Mayo, local MP Robert Dillon Browne urged his audience to "submit no further to the sad mockery of Saxon despotism and dastardism," while the Very Reverend Mr. Hughes, a parish priest from nearby Claremorris, decried the fact that the quiet and peaceable political agitation of the Irish for Repeal had been threatened by "Saxon yeomanry, Saxon soldiery, and Saxon artillery." At Cashel in May 1843, O'Connell told the crowd that he had been heartened to see, as he was traveling through the nearby town of Cahir, a homemade banner that read "Tipperary acknowledges no superiority in the Saxon." O'Connell urged his audience to acknowledge "no superiority in the Saxon or the stranger" nor "in the inhabitants of any other country on the face of the earth (cheers)." In using this language, O'Connell and the *Nation's* editors both sought to authenticate Repeal by situating Irish Celts in a timeless struggle against Saxon oppression.[25]

When it came to spreading the national message, printed materials were as critical as the monster meetings themselves. Through subscription and exchange agreements with friendly periodicals around the Atlantic Ocean, Dublin newspapers such as the *Nation, Freeman's Journal*, and *Pilot* were embedded in a lively international network. Individual editors often simply subscribed to foreign newspapers to get the news, but the preferred method was an "exchange agreement" by which editors would send each other weekly issues for free. In March 1843, an article from the New York Catholic *Truth Teller*, which was reprinted in the Dublin *Nation*, offered insights into the uniquely international role of the popular press. Pro-Repeal papers "should be put in the reading rooms of England and Scotland" and "distributed along the shores of the Mediterranean and the Nile—along the Rhine and the Danube." Sympathy for Ireland's cause, the *Truth Teller* concluded, "should be courted on every side and in every quarter" of the globe. In June 1843, a "Letter from America," probably by émigré Thomas Mooney, described how an important address by Daniel O'Connell to Robert Tyler, the president's son, "was copied entire in the *Washington Madisonian*, the leading paper of the capital, and on the wings of that journal has it passed to all parts of the Union. It was in part copied or commented on," wrote Mooney enthusiastically, "by all the American press." The dissemination of Irish ideas throughout the United States was having a tangible effect. "America has previously derived her impressions of Ireland through the calumniating medium of the Saxon press," complained Mooney. Imported Irish papers provided the antidote.[26]

The transmission of news, opinion, and racial discourse between Ireland and its emigrant communities, therefore, went both ways. Editors were cognizant of the legal stipulations prohibiting the publication of seditious material in Ireland and often worked around it. When the British government hinted at using force to deflate O'Connell's monster meetings, for example, there were big meetings in the United States in support of Repeal. The speeches and resolutions from these meetings were sent to Ireland, but Thomas Davis admitted that the Dublin *Nation* "dare not print one of the speeches, nor one of the Repeal articles of the American press" for fear of imprisonment. "But with wise foresight of our cramped and crippled position," he editorialized, friends in the United States "have sent TWO THOUSAND COPIES of the New York journals containing the proceedings." The international web of Irish nationalist periodicals found ways to dodge the law.[27]

While the historical language of Celts and Saxons was of great service to O'Connell's monster meetings, a simultaneous thread of implicitly threatened violence proved their undoing. Clontarf was chosen as the site of the penultimate meeting of the year. As the battlefield where the high king Brian Boru had defeated the Danes on Good Friday, 1014, Clontarf was a shining symbol of one of Gaelic Ireland's greatest victories. When the poster for the October meeting referred to the mustering of "Repeal cavalry," however, the Conservative government seized the opportunity to prohibit the assembly and send out troops. Fearing bloodshed, O'Connell canceled the meeting. The Repeal Year had ended early—and without Repeal. The government subsequently convicted several leaders of sedition, and in May 1844, O'Connell, Duffy, and others were sentenced to a year in jail. This brought other leaders to the fore. The most important new recruit was a stately Anglican landlord named William Smith O'Brien. An MP for County Limerick who claimed familial descent from the legendary Brian Boru, Smith O'Brien was a well-known public figure in Irish politics and a landowner, which made him an invaluable recruit. In the months after joining the LNRA in October 1843, Smith O'Brien rose so quickly through the ranks of leadership that by the time the "traversers" were committed to prison in 1844, he was O'Connell's second in command and de facto leader on the outside. The sentences were overturned after four months and all were released, but the affair had further complicated the leadership of the Repeal movement. O'Connell's grip on Irish nationalism was no longer beyond question.[28]

The racial discourse of Celts and Saxons was thrust into the spotlight again in August 1845 when the London *Times*' "Special Commissioner" arrived in Ireland. Edited since 1842 by John Thadeus Delane, an anti-Catholic young man of Protestant Irish descent, the *Times* was by far the most popular newspaper in Britain, with a daily circulation of 40,000. In the summer of 1845, Delane sent Thomas Campbell Foster, who had no experience of the country, to write regular reports for the *Times* that appeared under the title

"On the Condition of Ireland." Foster's thirty-six reports between August 1845 and January 1846 painted an unflattering portrait of an island inhabited by indolent Celts and industrious Saxons. Until it was proven, wrote Foster, "that Orangeism and Protestantism will add six inches to the average height and proportionate bulk to the men," he would continue to hold that Irish Catholic poverty and physical weakness "must chiefly be attributed to the characteristics of *race*." Celtic laziness was to blame for the underdevelopment of the predominantly Catholic south and west of Ireland. "It is because the poor Celt is content to put up with bad fare, and worse clothing and shelter, that he is *made* to put up with them," concluded Foster. "It is because the man of Saxon descent *will* live comfortably and well, or, if his exertions cannot accomplish this, make his grumblings heard and *felt*, that he *does* live comfortably and well."[29]

The tone of Foster's reports was in keeping with the racial language circulating in Europe and Britain at the time, including many of the pro-Saxonist ideas Thomas Carlyle had floated in *Chartism* (1839) six years before. Carlyle was willing to acknowledge that British misgovernment had affected Ireland's "very heart and soul," but he also blamed the island's endemic poverty on the "headlong, violent, mendacious" nature "of the wretched Irishman." Fellow Scot and leading ethnologist Robert Knox probably influenced Foster and the *Times* as well. Although his most famous work, *The Races of Men*, was not published until 1850, Knox was an esteemed professor of Edinburgh's Royal College of Surgeons who spent much of the 1840s testing racial theories in periodicals like the *Medical Times*. In these and other journals he forcefully argued that the Celts were genetically inferior to their Saxon neighbors and imbued with "furious fanaticism; a love of war and disorder; a hatred for order and patient industry; no accumulative habits; restless, treacherous, uncertain." As intellectual prime movers of the 1840s, Carlyle and Knox undoubtedly influenced Foster. Their theories, combined with the *Times'* own editorial positions, shaped his racialized reports.[30]

In their vehement denunciations of the *Times'* commissioner, whom Daniel O'Connell called the "gutter commissioner," Irish Repealers inadvertently echoed the contradiction lying at the heart of Irish nationalist racial discourse. Despite his many and varied articles on the subject, Thomas Davis now derided what he called the "imaginary classification" and "pestilent and lying distinction" between Celts and Saxons. "He is a fool, or worse," wrote Davis, "who seeks to find a cause for our poverty or our crimes in the inferiority of our race." It was the rapacity of Irish landlords and the lack of tenant-right that was to blame for Irish woes, not racial inferiority. Racial distinctions were legitimate subjects for antiquarians but wholly unsuitable in politics. Others, such as Repeal lieutenant Captain Broderick, continued to reaffirm them. Having attributed the better material condition of Fermanagh Protestants over Leitrim Catholics not to "difference of race, or difference of religion, but because one was the favoured of government," Broderick pointed out that, contrary to what the commissioner had claimed, "the Celt was not content with his bad condition, and exhibited no signs of contentment." At an LNRA meeting in September 1845, John O'Connell wished they could settle the dispute by allowing a Saxon and a Celt to kick the *Times'* commissioner and then asking him to decide "which kicked harder."[31]

Having forcefully employed the racial language of Celts and Saxons to legitimate Irish independence from England, Thomas Davis now saw the dichotomy fragmenting the nation along sectarian divisions between Catholics and Protestants. The quandary spurred him to pen what is perhaps his most famous editorial. In it, Davis sought, once and for all, to provide the intellectual underpinning for a nonsectarian Irish national identity. While Saxons and Celts would always be essentially different, Davis's independent Ireland would see them living in harmony. After giving up the hopeless dream of a "Celtic kingdom with the old names and the old language, without the old quarrels," Davis described what he saw as a durable, inclusive Irish nationality. "It must contain and represent the races of Ireland," he explained. "It must not be Celtic, it must not be Saxon—it must be Irish. The Brehon law, and the maxims of Westminster, the cloudy and lightning genius of the Gael, the placid strength of the Sassenach, the marshalling insight of the Norman . . . these are components of *such* a nationality." The article signaled a desire to return to the civic pluralism that the United Irishmen had hoped would unite Catholic and Protestant under a single national flag. Davis's colleagues were impressed. "I am delighted with the article in yesterday's nation respecting the prospect of a union between Orange and Green," Smith O'Brien excitedly told him. "It makes me for a moment believe that the dream of my life is about to be realized." Smith O'Brien suggested they reprint the article on individual handbills and mail them to their Protestant compatriots in the north of Ireland.[32]

In mid-August 1845, Duffy temporarily turned the reins of the *Nation* over to Davis while he went on a walking holiday in County Wicklow, equipped with detailed instructions from Davis of what to do and how to do it. Follow "the new roads of Bray Head—'tis the best cliff in Leinster & the vale between it & *Little* Sugar Loaf very beautiful," Davis told him. "Rise early and after abundant cold water, walk half-an-hour before your seven or

eight o'clock breakfast. . . . There's good advice, which you won't follow!"
Soon after Duffy's return to Dublin in September, Davis caught scarlatina,
which Thomas MacNevin made fun of as "English cholera." "Why the d——l
did he not get an Irish cholera?" he asked Duffy jocularly, adding that the
victim's "stomach is too Saxon." MacNevin even joked with Davis himself
about it, regretting that "your ailment took so unpatriotic a turn as 'English'
cholera." He was sure Davis would rally, assuring him that the "unfortunate
disease won't remain long in your Celtic constitution." But MacNevin and
his friends had underestimated the gravity of the illness, and on September
16, 1845, Davis died at his family home on Baggot Street in Dublin. Tributes
from across the political spectrum of Ireland and Britain streamed in, and a
huge procession followed his corpse to its final resting place in Mount Jerome Cemetery, Dublin. Duffy's loss was compounded even further when
his wife died eight days later. Finally, in mid-September, a London newspaper announced that a black blight had been found in parts of Ireland on that
year's potato harvest. The Great Famine had begun.[33]

At first, the discovery of *Phytophthora infestans* did not provoke universal alarm. Many thought the blight's appearance merely heralded the return of one of the periodic regional food shortages that had pockmarked
eighteenth-century Ireland. The following autumn, however, excess mortality began to mount. The rural population of the island had grown exponentially during the previous hundred years on the back of the "lumper," a
reliable and flexible strain of potato capable of producing high yields on
marginal land. The lumper was also particularly susceptible to the blight,
however, and when it disappeared, so did the main source of caloric intake
and financial security for the majority of the population. Evictions, deaths,
and emigration followed. By 1851, about a million people had died who
would not otherwise have, while approximately another million had emigrated. The British government's response to the catastrophe was mud-
dled, trapped between knowledge of the indisputable suffering around
the country and, as Peter Gray has argued, the "belief that the blight was
a providential visitation, sent to bring Ireland into a higher state of social
and moral organization through a necessary measure of pain." The London *Times* fanned the flames by blaming the famine on the Irish themselves and disapproving of charity relief by publishing letters attacking
"an attempt so ill-advised as again to fatten the lazy Celt on the daily
bread of the industrious Saxon." As impoverished Catholics fled the island, they carried with them the notion of themselves as Celts fleeing
Saxon oppression.[34]

In the early 1840s, Irish nationalists sought to legitimate their campaign for Irish political independence with the language of Celts and Saxons. The discourse was, however, riddled with contradictions and ambiguities because "Celt" and "Saxon" each had two meanings in Irish popular culture. The former could mean Irish or Catholic, the latter English or Protestant. O'Connell and the Young Irelanders failed to effectively tease these meanings apart. On the one hand, they justified, somewhat successfully, the repeal of the Act of Union on the grounds that history, language, and physiology all stood opposed to the unnatural union of Celtic Ireland and Saxon England. The United Kingdom was an instrument for attaching the "mask of a slavish uniformity" to Ireland and her people. On the other hand, the success of this racial discourse simultaneously undermined their attempt to unite the Catholics and Protestants of Ireland into one nation. If only Irish Protestants could relate to the battlefields, cairns, and ruins of the landscape, Davis reasoned, they would surely share in the "valorous, pious mind" of nationality. The immutable facts of history, which justified the disunion of the Irish and English, could, according to this reading, simultaneously unify Catholics and Protestants within Ireland. Unfortunately for Irish nationalists, they could not have it both ways. Their hopes for a new nation foundered on the rock of race. Yet, as we shall see, while the rhetoric's paradoxical nature plagued Irish nationalism in the 1840s, its flexibility rendered it invaluable to later migrants.[35]

Imperialism and Slavery

Pre-Famine Irish nationalist racial discourse was not limited to the ageless struggle between Celts and Saxons. The *Nation*'s staff was aware that imperialism and slavery were oppressing people of color around the world, but Irish realpolitik dictated how they handled each issue. Attacking British imperialism lent authenticity to the Irish national movement, while deriding American slavery weakened Irish America's support for the campaign. As a result, the *Nation* portrayed these questions in fundamentally different terms. The Young Irelanders' handling of the oppression of people of color was as contradictory and given to practical considerations as was their Celtic racial discourse. As with the latter, it also situated Irish nationalism in a global context. Seeing in it a sort of auxiliary movement in support of Repeal, the Young Irelanders portrayed imperialism as a transnational, universal problem. "Justice and pity know no distinction of clime, or race, or time," declared Thomas Davis in only the second month of the *Nation*'s existence. He envisioned the *Nation* in global communion with other lovers of freedom. "We are battling for Ireland," he exhorted; "if we conquer, 'twill be for mankind." England was "a sort of world-hydra" of imperialism. "From Canada to the Cape, from Ireland to Australia, from India and China to Western Africa, and the distant realms of South America," wrote Davis, "no nation but has felt the teeth, and claws, and venom of this incongruous and pitiless monster." Through slavery, hypocrisy, and brute violence Britain had built an international enterprise that "spared no infliction, and despised no gain."[36]

With Western European civilization marching in step against aboriginal peoples, the language of "savages" was popular at the time, and contemporary travel literature often described the Irish peasantry in uncomplimentary terms. In *Travels in Ireland* (1844), the Austrian traveler J. G. Kohl wrote that in comparison to the average Irish hovel, "even the condition of savages will appear endurable, and to be preferred. . . . A log hut carefully stuffed with moss—what a luxury!" Gustave De Beaumont was even less flattering. "I have seen the Indian in his forests, and the negro in his chains, and thought, as I contemplated their pitiable condition, that I saw the very extreme of human wretchedness," he wrote in *Ireland: Social, Political, and Religious* (1839), "but I did not then know the condition of unfortunate Ireland." The *Nation* had an ambivalent relationship with the language of savages. On the one hand, it sometimes used common tropes to attack enemies. With an eye on the upcoming Protestant marching season in 1843, Duffy derided the sight of an Orangeman with "a tawdry ribbon on his breast, in the fashion of a penny-show-man." "A savage of New Holland might treat such a creature as this with contempt, as a lower grade in the species," assured Duffy, "and rather farther removed from sense or civilization." Repealers should merely feel sorry for "these poor fellows . . . who think they can alter the resolution of a great people, by crying 'No Popery,' and beating their big drums, as some Indian tribes sound their gongs to frighten away an eclipse."[37]

In general, however, editorials in the *Nation* more often than not declared support for aboriginal people facing white encroachment. The subject was brought to the attention of Dubliners in the summer of 1843 when the famed American naturalist George Catlin brought his traveling show of American Indian life to the city for four evening and two matinee shows. The show's advertisement, printed in the *Nation*, promised to feature a "splendid Indian Wardrobe, on 20 living figures, with numerous changes, giving their Dances, Games, Songs, War-Whoops, &c., &c." The following week, Davis reviewed the show in the columns of the *Nation*. Overall, he was "greatly pleased," although he did complain that Catlin apologized too much for the natives. "Uncorrupted by the European race, they are gallant, good, and graceful men, an honor to our common humanity," wrote Davis, who wanted to see them stick up for themselves. "Why does not some bold spirit rally and combine them in language and war," he asked, "and drive back corruption and pale faces ere it be too late? The Red Americans (they are not Indians) must not be allowed to perish." A few years later, another lead article scoffed at the debate between England and the United States over Oregon. "Both parties are robbers of the Red-men," editorialized the *Nation*, "and the priority of claim is the priority of crime."[38]

While the Young Irelanders' anti-imperialism espoused support for colored victims of oppression, their position on the slavery question was another matter. A proponent of abolition since at least the mid-1820s, O'Connell gave his first major address on the subject in January 1842 when he, Father Mathew, and 60,000 members of the Irish public signed a petition urging Irish American support for the movement in the United States. Throughout the early 1840s, O'Connell continued to labor the point. Slavery was nothing more and nothing less than "huckstering in human flesh." He refused to accept money from slave owners in America and derided "the filthy aristocracy of the skin." All the races of man had "the same origin, and were partakers of the same common humanity." O'Connell sought to intertwine Repeal and antislavery, but Irish Americans rejected this message on the grounds that support for immediate abolition threatened their status as loyal American citizens. Unwanted by the Whigs, Irish Catholics had streamed into the Democratic Party, which offered them a voice in American politics. Supporting the Democrats meant supporting states' rights, especially on the subject of slavery. The crisis crested in March 1845 with O'Connell's infamous "Eagle Speech," in which he implicitly threatened Irish support for English designs against the United States in North America. Caught between contending loyalties to O'Connell and their new home, the Irish American Repeal movement sided with the latter and, for all intents and purposes, collapsed.[39]

Nevertheless, it is remarkable how rarely Irish Americans used racist language to undermine O'Connell's abolitionism. Leading Catholic bishop J. J. Hughes opposed O'Connell's 1842 address "not precisely because of the doctrines it contains, but because of their having emanated from a foreign source, and of their tendency to operate on questions of domestic and foreign policy." The editor of the *Boston Pilot*, Thomas D'Arcy McGee, who later joined the Dublin *Nation* staff, admitted that though the United States had many faults, including "the evils of Negro slavery," the Irish in Ireland should "respect your brethren [in America] more than to vilify the homes of which they are justly proud." When white supremacy did emanate from Irish American Repeal organizations, it often did so from the pen of American surrogate leaders. A July 1843 letter to O'Connell on behalf of the Cincinnati Repeal Association by its corresponding secretary, D. T. Disney (an American-born Cincinnati Democrat), expressed such racism. "Really inferior as a race," Disney wrote, "slavery has stamped its debasing influence upon the Africans, and between him and the white almost a century would be required to elevate the character of the one and destroy the antipathies of the other." An open letter from the Irish Repealers in the mining town of Pottsville, Pennsylvania, greeted the 1842 O'Connell antislavery address with similar language, decrying the address's suggestion that they "look upon the negroes as 'BRETHEN.'" Yet such expressions of antipathy were few and far between exactly because Irish Americans interpreted the slavery question as not one of race but of states' rights.[40]

The editors of the Dublin *Nation* took sides with the Irish Americans against O'Connell. Repeal relied on American dollars and the threat to England on the world stage of a muscular, coherent United States. Antislavery threatened both. Taking the lead from their Irish American cousins, the *Nation* opposed immediate abolition on the grounds of law and citizenship. Instead of rejecting or qualifying their transnational ideals of universal freedom, they deracialized the American slavery debate, making it a strictly national question of states' rights and domestic institutions that, however repugnant, ought to be sorted out by the Americans themselves. "Aye! notwithstanding the slavery of the negro, America is liberty's bulwark and Ireland's dearest ally," reminded the *Nation*. "Ireland laments and condemns the slavery which England planted in America" and would "exult at its abolition in all the States . . . but she knows that its abolition, however possible and right, is difficult and dangerous." Repeal must not conflict with friends in the United States, urged the *Nation* in 1844, including southern slave owners, "whether right or wrong." Irish nationalists were pledged to their own political independence and nothing else.[41]

The international transmission of individual copies of newspapers among the readers themselves played an important role in this transatlantic debate. Opinions expressed in the press frequently cited speeches, editorials, and letters that had been either read in a copy of a newspaper sent across the ocean or clipped and reprinted in a local paper. Irish abolitionists such as R. D. Webb, Richard Allen, and James Haughton maintained constant communication with the leading lights of Bostonian antislavery. In a letter to the Reverend Samuel May Jr., Haughton thanked his correspondent "for an occasional Newspaper" and mentioned having "reciprocated kindness with you in the same way, & for a similar purpose, to let you know that your short visit to us lived in our remembrance." If newspapers were sent as friendly gestures between friends and fellow activists, they also served more practical purposes. By "the Liberator & Standard, I get regular accounts of the progress of the Anti-slavery agitation among you," explained Haughton, "& by the same medium you learn of our labors in the cause." The Young Irelanders' opposition to antislavery embarrassed these Irish philanthropists. When George Thompson asked for sample issues of the Dublin *Nation*, Haughton replied that he was not a regular subscriber, "but whenever I get a copy of it, I will take pleasure in forwarding it to you." The paper "is conducted with spirit but not *always* in the right spirit," warned Haughton. "Its writers have little feeling about human brotherhood." Haughton's correspondence with Boston abolitionists illuminates the steady transmission of ideas and news through a transatlantic network of newspapers.[42]

Eager to internationalize their political campaign, the Young Irelanders described British imperialism as a problem that transcended the boundaries of individual nation-states. England's worldwide perfidies against people of color were held up as pertinent case studies of the very problem facing the Irish Celts. From a practical standpoint, they could do so because adopting an anti-imperial stance over Afghanistan, China, and even Amerindians could only help the Irish cause. The slavery debate, by contrast, presented a threat to the Repeal movement, which relied on the financial, moral, and political support of Americans, some of whom owned slaves. As a result, the Young Irelanders' transnational perspective on imperialism contrasted with their narrow approach to slavery. The latter was a constitutional matter for the Americans to figure out for themselves. In sum, the Young Irelanders were not one-dimensional racists. They were savvy politicians whose attitudes toward people of color were as flexible, pragmatic, and at times as hypocritical, as their discourse on Celts and Saxons. O'Connell's hard-line approach to abolitionism, however noble, had failed to acknowledge the diversity of the transnational Irish community he was addressing.

Division, Rebellion, Exile

The year 1845 was, therefore, a time of division within the Repeal movement. O'Connell's "Eagle Speech" had drawn the ire of many followers. His simultaneous hints toward a federalist resolution of the Repeal question also irked Irish separatists. The impending split between "Young" and "Old" Ireland finally exploded during a boisterous two-day meeting of the Repeal Association in July. The crisis crested when Meagher delivered a speech in which he refused to disclaim the morality of violence. The performance earned him the nickname "Meagher of the Sword," which he proudly carried around the world for the rest of his life. "Abhor the sword? Stigmatise the sword?" he shouted. "No, my lord, for in the passes of the Tyrol it cut to pieces the banner of the Bavarian, and through those cragged passes cut a path to fame for the peasant insurrectionists of Innsbruck. Abhor the sword? Stimatise the sword? No my lord, for at its blow, and in the quivering of its crimson light, a giant nation sprang up from the waters of the Atlantic, and by its redeeming magic, the fettered colony became a daring, free Republic." When John O'Connell stormed the stage, dragging Meagher from the lectern, Smith O'Brien and most of the Young Irelanders walked out of the hall. Daniel O'Connell responded by banning the Dublin *Nation* from all LNRA outlets. Each reading room mustering £10 per annum toward the Repeal Rent was entitled to a weekly subscription of a pro-Repeal newspaper, and the *Nation* had been by far the most popular. O'Connell, declaring the Young Irelanders treasonous to the cause of Ireland, now made it an offense to buy, read, lend, or borrow the *Nation*. When one enthusiastic O'Connellite declared his intention to burn a copy of the *Nation*, the Liberator dryly reminded him that he would have to buy it first.[43]

After several months of drift, the split in the Repeal movement was formalized in January 1847 with the formation of the Irish Confederation by Smith O'Brien, Duffy, Meagher, Mitchel, McGee, O'Gorman, and their various supporters, including radical Catholic priests such as John Kenyon and C. P. Meehan. Almost immediately, the slavery question plagued the fledgling organization when new member James Haughton echoed O'Connell's refusal to accept "the blood-stained contributions of American slaveholders." A direct response soon came from the pen of Father Kenyon, the fiery priest of Templederry, County Tipperary. Kenyon ignored the entire question of whether slavery was right or wrong, simply asserting that "flinging back bags of dollars over the Atlantic ocean into the pockets of these very slaveholders, enriching them at our present expense, is such an Utopian remedy for the supposed evil as only homoeopathists could countenance." The debate continued in the columns of the *Nation* throughout the spring. When Haughton raised the issue again in April, the audience shouted him down, calling "Three cheers for America" and "Repeal! We want no slave lecturing here." Haughton, who had left O'Connell's LNRA because it lacked freedom of speech, resigned from the Irish Confederation soon after. The Young Ireland refusal to couch American slavery in transnational terms was as resilient as ever.[44]

Davis's pluralist dream of a union between Celts and Saxons was picked up and carried forward by the Irish Confederation, who saw in such inclusive language a potential wedge between themselves and the more sectarian, populist nationalism of O'Connell's Old Ireland. Thomas D'Arcy McGee led the attack with an article in the *Nation* entitled "Popular Fallacies about Irish History," which complained that there was "no popular fallacy . . . more common in Ireland than that the early Irish . . . were all of one race— all Milesians." In fact, he argued, the Irish people had always been a heady mix of Normans, Britons, Celts, and Saxons. It was ignorance of this fact that stood at the root of all modern divisions among the people. At a meeting of the Irish Confederation later in the week, McGee pledged that the new organization would embrace diversity. "Placed on the western verge of Europe," he said, "our island has been the field, as it were, over which Providence has scattered many races." This heterogeneity called for the freedom of speech denied by the LNRA. The Irish natural environment remained important to Duffy as well. "Separate Irish Nationality from Ireland, and it must perish," he editorialized in the *Nation* in April 1847. "As well might you make a bird live and sing in the depths of the sea, or a fish live on the solid earth, as do this."[45]

Presbyterian John Mitchel's writings from this period also reflected the dream of racial unity in Ireland. "I am one of the Saxon Irishmen of the north," he told an assembly of Repealers in 1845, "and you want that race of Irishmen in your ranks more than any others . . . [for] this is our country as well as yours." Soon after his accession to lead writer of the *Nation*, Mitchel published a history book entitled *The Life and Times of Aodh O'Neill* (1845), which he dedicated to Thomas Davis. As a Saxon, he hoped that he "may be the more easily believed in disclaiming the base intention to exasperate Celtic Irish against Saxon Irish, or to revive ancient feuds between the several races that now occupy Irish soil, and are known to all the world besides, as Irishmen." Ireland's deadliest foes, he concluded, were not the Saxon inhabitants of the island but rather "the foul fiend of English imperialism." The moral of Mitchel's story was clear: "that at any time it only needed Irishmen of all bloods to stand together—to be even *nearly* united—in order to exorcise that fiend for ever, and drive him irrevocably into the Red Sea."[46]

Thomas Francis Meagher continued to drive home the theme of regeneration. Confident of a new dawn in Irish nationality, Meagher told the Irish Confederation's first meeting in the Rotundo in January 1847 that "a new race of men now act in Ireland—men who will neither starve as victims, nor serve as the vassals of the British Empire." The resurrection of the people had reawakened the ancient Irish essence or "spirit," which was rooted not in science but in the history of the people. "The ruins that ennoble, the scenes that beautify, the memories that illuminate, the music that inspires our native land," he told the crowd, "have preserved it pure amid the vicious factions of the past, and the venal bargains of later years." The national spirit, "rooted in our hearts," he concluded, "is as immovable as the altar of the Druid, pillared in our soil." This regeneration of the people, coupled with recognition of their mixed heritage, should imbue the people with political strength. The "intermarriage of race in Ireland," argued Duffy in mid-January 1847, was the basis for Irish nationality. They were "brothers in blood and in their physical and intellectual nature," he argued. "Why not brothers in the common cause of all Ireland—self-government?"[47]

The movement for Repeal hit its nadir in mid-1847. The Irish Confederation, dogged by violent mobs of O'Connellites, still struggled to establish itself. The LNRA was not much better off. Under the crushing weight of the Famine, the weekly Repeal Rent had dwindled from being counted in thousands of pounds to being counted in tens of pounds. When Daniel O'Connell died in Genoa while on a pilgrimage to Rome, much of the national outpouring of grief over his death was aimed at the Young Irelanders. The Dublin *Pilot* claimed O'Connell had been pushed to the brink by Young Ireland's treason, "THEN BURST HIS MIGHTY HEART!" The prospects for Repeal worsened as the year progressed. John O'Connell's Irish parliamentary party collapsed. Deaths around the country mounted during the worst phase of the famine. Sporadic violence pockmarked the countryside. Instead of famine relief, the British government introduced a coercion bill. It began to look to some of the Young Irelanders as if the grounds for defensive violence were becoming apparent. A revolutionary coterie headed by Mitchel and Devin Reilly soon developed in opposition to the more conservative leadership of Duffy and McGee. In December 1847, Mitchel ended his connection with the *Nation* and seceded from the Irish Confederation to form what Richard O'Gorman wryly referred to as "Infant Ireland." With the help of others, he founded a new weekly in Dublin entitled the *United Irishman,* which enjoyed immediate success with a circulation of around 5,000. The paper allowed Mitchel to espouse the radical rhetoric that he claimed Duffy had prohibited him from publishing in the *Nation*.[48]

In the wake of the February 1848 uprising in France, Ireland was seized by revolutionary excitement. "All over the world," exulted Duffy, "from the frozen swamps of Canada to the rich corn fields of Sicily—in Italy, in Denmark, in Prussia, and in glorious France, men are up for their rights." The *Nation* and the *United Irishman* competed with each other for the soul of an impending Irish revolution. "Two years of famine have swept into the grave one million of our race. . . . our foreign Government is but a Club of Grave-diggers," exhorted the *Nation*. "Ireland's necessity demands the desperate remedy of Revolution." An Irish Confederation assembly on March 21, 1848, complete with the kind of brinkmanship language of violence with which O'Connell had bluffed his way to Clontarf, attracted as many as 20,000 people. In a flash, the government struck back. Mitchel was arrested for publishing inflammatory articles in the *United Irishman*, while Smith O'Brien and Meagher were remanded in custody for provocative speeches. Although the juries failed to convict Meagher and Smith O'Brien, Mitchel was not so lucky. In May, a packed jury found him guilty according to the new treason felony act, and he was sentenced to fourteen years' transportation. He was immediately whisked away to Spike Island in County Cork and from there to Bermuda, where he began to serve his sentence abroad.[49]

Following Mitchel's transportation in June 1848, things moved quickly toward insurrection. Two parallel organizations formed. The first reunified the Young and Old Irelanders into a peaceful, constitutional political party called the Irish League. The second, consisting of Duffy, Meagher, Dillon, O'Gorman, Kenyon, Martin, and Devin Reilly, was a secret collective dedicated to planning a rebellion. Smith O'Brien, unaware of these plans, headed down to the countryside in July 1848 to tour the southern organization of Confederate Clubs. In mid-July, the government arrested Duffy, Martin, and one of their associates, a talented young medical student and journalist named Kevin Izod O'Doherty. Habeas corpus was suspended on July 22, and the *Nation* was suppressed six days later. Under the threat of imminent arrest, Smith O'Brien and his lieutenants, including Terence Bellew McManus, Patrick O'Donohoe, James Stephens, and John O'Mahony, decided that open rebellion was the most honorable course available to them. Supported by a fluctuating crowd of ill-armed peasants and interested onlookers, their anticlimactic rebellion occurred on July 29 when they besieged forty policemen in a farmhouse in Ballingarry, County Tipperary. Unwilling to burn the house down, Smith O'Brien retreated before government reinforcements arrived. He, Meagher, and several others were arrested soon after. The Young Ireland rebellion of 1848 was over.[50]

During the second phase of the Young Ireland movement, Irish nationalist racial discourse continued to perpetuate the same contradictions that the first phase had. While predicating their argument for independence from Britain on an ethnic solidarity that reified irreducible differences between Celts and Saxons, they simultaneously perpetuated a paradoxical dream of civic pluralism, which sought to unify Catholic Celts and Protestant Saxons in Ireland. Though the argument was useful in the short term as a practical political instrument, the inability to reconcile this paradox constituted the main failure of Young Ireland's nationalist rhetoric. They were also hampered by the reignition of the slavery debate, which undermined repeated claims of common humanity with colored victims of oppression around the world. At the same time, the second period strengthened the intra- and international network of newspapers that would, in later years, play such a key role in the lives of Ireland's migrants. The two-sided sword of ethnic/civic nationalism would also serve them well as they negotiated their new lives and identities abroad.

Conclusion

In the early decades of the nineteenth century, social relations were profoundly affected by the expansion of international capitalism as mass migration within and between nation-states forced people to rethink the boundaries of their imagined communities. Europeans responded by using a grab bag of methodologies drawn from the natural and social sciences to develop a picture of society predicated on race and nation. Immutable physiological differences, the theory ran, bubbled to the surface in distinctive linguistic, psychological, and religious patterns that resulted in what Augustin Thierry called a "spirit of unending contradiction" between Celts and Saxons. Having drawn national borders around these races, Europeans believed that the role of the modern nation-state was to effect the perfect balance between "l'esprit et les lois" of the country. For Irish nationalists in the 1840s, this language of Celts and Saxons was a practical instrument for legitimating their political project. It was, however, a tricky device riddled with paradoxes and ambiguities. On the one hand, the rhetoric of race justified the national campaign for political independence from England. On the other, it was equally effective at underlining the sectarian differences within the Irish nation. When the Great Famine hit, it released a tsunami of

Irish out-migration, which overran the shores of distant lands. As they settled into their new worlds, these migrants sought to resolve the tension
between their *esprit* and *les lois* of their new lands. They, and the people
they met, used the multivalent language of Celts and Saxons to settle the
debate.[51]

Those leaving Ireland in the mid-nineteenth century did so armed with a
tradition over half a century old of using print culture to justify their inclusion in the polity. Newspapers, pamphlets, handbills, and posters were part
of Irish nationalism long before Davis and company sold the first copy of the
Nation in October 1842. The Young Irelanders' success partly lay in the way
they consolidated this network's connections across the island and abroad.
Throughout the 1840s, Irish nationalists situated the essential differences
between Celts and Saxons in a chronological perspective that emphasized
timelessness. The thousands of speeches, cheers, homemade banners, editorials, poems, letters to the editor, and history lessons that drove this message home were all found, week in, week out, in the columns of the popular
press. One did not have to attend an assembly or share Sunday dinner with
the Clique to get the point. No wonder, therefore, that a contemporary referred to the paper's readership as a "permanent monster meeting." The
weekly rag was a place for the Irish to congregate virtually on a regular
basis. As famine and exile scattered these people overseas, their popular
press—and identity—expanded accordingly.[52]

IN THE TEN YEARS following the outbreak of the Great Famine in 1845, well
over 1 million Irish men and women migrated abroad. The Young Irelanders
were part of that global exodus. Charged five times by a government anxious to convict the brains behind the *Nation*, Duffy saw the prosecution's
case fall apart each time, and in April 1849 he was finally released from
prison. Some of his former confederates, suspicious of his court tactics and
good luck, later nicknamed him Charles "Give-In" Duffy. He reestablished
the Dublin *Nation* in September 1849. The other leading Young Irelanders
were exiled in various ways. Several, including John Blake Dillon, Richard
O'Gorman, Thomas Devin Reilly, P. J. Smyth, and Thomas D'Arcy McGee,
escaped to the United States. Others were not so lucky. John Martin and
Kevin Izod O'Doherty, who had established newspapers to replace Mitchel's
suppressed *United Irishman*, were convicted of treason felony in August
1848 and sentenced to ten years' transportation. They were sent to Britain's
penal colony in Van Diemen's Land, southern Australia, on board the
Mountstewart Elphinstone, arriving in late 1849. Smith O'Brien, Meagher,

McManus, and O'Donohoe were convicted of high treason in October 1848. Their death sentences were commuted to transportation for life, and they were shipped to Van Diemen's Land on board the *Swift*, which departed Dublin in July 1849 and arrived in Australia in late October. These six "State Prisoners" were joined in April 1850 by John Mitchel, who was sent there after almost dying in a prison-hulk off the coast of Bermuda. Life in Australia would give the Irish a new perspective on the breadth of the Celtic race.

CHAPTER TWO

"A Lone, Lone Spot in the Far Southern Seas"

The Irish Race in Australia, 1848–1855

[handwritten: Intro/hook/thesis/roadmap]

In August 1848, Young Irelanders John Martin and Kevin O'Doherty left Ireland on board the *Mountstewart Elphinstone* to serve their ten-year sentences in Van Diemen's Land. Almost a year later, William Smith O'Brien, Thomas Francis Meagher, Patrick O'Donohoe, and Terence Bellew McManus sailed on the British war brig *Swift* to begin their life sentences in Australia. The prisoners were treated as gentlemen and, though guarded, were assigned manservants and allowed relative freedom both above and below deck. Reading material played an important role during the course of the 16,000-mile journey. "I took out my bundle of the United Irishmen & Felon & I read over one or two of my own articles," diarized Martin, "& so brought on a conversation about Confederation Affairs with O'D[oherty]." On the other ship, Smith O'Brien read aloud from his collection of books, which included Von Ranke's *History of the Popes*, Homer's *Odyssey*, and Words-worth's poetry. Arriving in Van Diemen's Land on October 27, 1849, after an average-length journey of 108 days, the men on board the *Swift* were immediately struck by the scenery. Meagher was particularly impressed by the willingness of local Irish, despite the threats of armed sailors, to paddle their little boats close enough to shout welcoming cheers to the exiles. "In all these incidents, slight and fleeting as they were, we saw at once the evidence of a kindly feeling towards us," he wrote to Duffy back in Dublin, "and somehow we felt as though a few warm whispers of the old Irish heart at home were floating through the air."[1]

This chapter examines Irish racial discourse in the Australian colonies during the five years that the Young Irelanders spent there as "state prisoners." Juxtaposing the private and public writings of these exiles with the opinions of Irish Australia's main weekly newspaper, it reveals the early in-

[handwritten: letters papers]

klings of global nationalism. On the one hand, finding themselves in a society united not by nationalism but by settler colonialism, Irish Celts portrayed themselves as hearty pioneers entirely suitable for membership in this far-flung British settler society. On the other hand, global nationalism's edge of ethnic solidarity, which situated these migrants spatially among contemporary Irish Celts abroad, remained strong. As it had in Ireland in the 1840s, the international spread of the Irish popular press fostered the construction of this new identity. As copies of the weekly rag circulated among Irish people in remote locations, their ideas about themselves shifted as well. An "Irish Celt" living in Australia aptly summarized this phenomenon when, after reading an article in his local paper that had originally been published in the Dublin *Nation*, he rattled off a letter to the editor. "The [Dublin] *Nation* is quite right when it asserts that Celtic hearts universally turn homewards at Christmas," he wrote in April 1855. "In the wild bush of Australia, where the Irish shepherd is tending his flock, remote from civilised life and surrounded by uncouth aborigines, even there, in those wild, barbarous regions, the sentiment of patriotism seems burnt into his heart." A worldwide Irish nation was beginning to take shape.[2]

Economics and Society in the Australian Colonies

Following the loss of its American colonies in the early 1780s, the British government sought to shore up its position elsewhere by establishing a penal colony in the South Pacific. In 1788, the first fleet arrived with a handful of free settlers and a cargo of over 700 prisoners, mostly petty thieves from the slums of London. Over the next eighty years, Britain transported approximately 160,000 convicts to labor in the new Australian colonies. While some were retained by the administration to build roads and government buildings, the majority were, until 1840, assigned to families of free settlers and colonists. In exchange for their labor, convict workers were given food and shelter. After years of good behavior, they could earn a ticket-of-leave, which allowed them to live independently and sell their labor on the free market. Those who finished their sentences were termed "emancipists," while insubordinates and repeat offenders were sent to work at notorious jails in Macquarie Harbour, Maria Island, and Port Arthur. By the mid-nineteenth century, a fierce debate was raging over the transportation system. Many free settlers demanded its abolition, whereas powerful pastoral interests sought to maintain it as a source of cheap labor.

Thanks in large part to pressure from the Radicals in Britain, who equated transportation with the slave trade, the imperial government agreed to stop sending prisoners to New South Wales in 1840. Van Diemen's Land, a small island off the southern coast of the mainland, became the main penal colony until 1853. After that, all convicts were sent to Western Australia until the program was given up for good in 1868.[3]

As the economy bloomed in the first half of the nineteenth century, the Australian standard of living rose as well. Between 1820 and 1860, the Australian gross domestic product per capita trebled, allowing the colonies' comparative level of income to surpass even such economic powerhouses as the United States and the United Kingdom. Stimulated by the growing British Empire's insatiable appetite, pastoral agriculture provided the main engine for economic growth. Thousands of convicts, energetic free settlers, and new technologies flowed into the colonies as wool products and foodstuffs flowed out. Wealthy British investors and subscriptions to public loans financed infrastructure. As colonial policies began to emphasize market relations over coercion, writes Stuart MacIntyre, a settler society "characterised by high rates of literacy, general familiarity with commodities, productive innovation, and impressive adaptation" evolved. There was also, however, a strong conservative strain in colonial society. Until midcentury, much of the land across eastern Australia was held under license or extended lease. Yet vast tracts remained under the control of a relatively small collection of several thousand pastoral landowners, many of whom had increased their holdings by squatting, without legal title, on previously unclaimed land. This "squattocracy" smacked of a feudal elite, and throughout the middle decades of the nineteenth century, increasing the number of land proprietors by "unlocking the land" was, along with the anti-transportation movement, the biggest social issue facing Australia's governors.[4]

These drives to reform landholding and stem the convict tide went hand in hand with the desire to democratize the colonial constitutions. The gold rush of the early 1850s had a profound effect on this process. In 1851, a former California Forty-Niner, Australian-born Edward Hargraves, noticed geological similarities between southeastern Australia and the western United States. His discovery of gold that year sparked one of the greatest rushes in human history. From New South Wales, the frenzy soon spread to the infant colony of Victoria, whose population grew sevenfold between 1851 and 1861, from 77,000 to 540,000, and whose capital, Melbourne, soon rivaled Sydney as the main city of the colonies. At its peak in 1858, there were 150,000 men working on the Victorian "diggings." As the producer of more than 30 percent of the world's gold in the mid-nineteenth century, Victoria played a critical role in the financial power of the British Empire by allowing the government to adopt the gold standard for its currency. The gold rush also changed the face of colonial society. In just two years, more free settlers arrived in the colonies than the total number of convicts transported there over the previous seventy years. Between 1851 and 1861, the Australian non-Aboriginal population nearly trebled, from 430,000 to 1,150,000. The new population created vast markets for local and imported products, railways and telegraph lines sprawled across the land, and steamships shortened the distance between Europe and the colonies.[5]

This rapid development played a key role in the advent of limited self-government. By 1852 it had become, declared the minister for the colonies, "more urgently necessary than heretofore to place full powers of self-government in the hands of a people thus advanced in wealth and prosperity." Between 1842 and 1851, partly elected legislatures replaced government-appointed councils. Constitutions for representative governments in the colonies were drafted and enacted in New South Wales, Van Diemen's Land, and Victoria (1855), South Australia (1856), and Queensland (1859). Universal manhood suffrage soon followed. Under Australia's limited self-government, each colony's London-appointed governor was essentially a constitutional monarch who acted on the advice of representative colonial parliaments. The colonies retained some jurisdiction over domestic affairs, but London reserved the right to veto any law and completely controlled external relations.[6]

The fortunes of Australia's Irish immigrants were closely tied to all of these developments. Between 1815 and the outbreak of the Famine in the mid-1840s, Australia's Irish moved, writes one historian, "from margin to mainstream." While there were a few Irish in military, colonial, and clerical positions, most of the earliest Irish arrived in chains. In 1791, the first convict ship sailed direct from Ireland to Australia when the *Queen* left Cobh with 133 men, twenty-two women, and four children on board. In total, approximately 50,000 Irish (almost 25 percent of the total number of transported convicts) were sent from Ireland and England to the mainland Australian colonies between 1791 and 1867. Of these, Van Diemen's Land received 14,492 prisoners of Irish birth (20 percent of the total number of prisoners transported there) between 1803 and 1853. Upon emancipation, these convicts provided the basis for an Irish community in the colonies. In the early decades of the nineteenth century, less than a thousand free settlers came from Ireland. The long distance, great financial cost, and stigma of convictism dissuaded many Irish from choosing the Antipodes over safer bets in the United States and British North America. Those Protestants and Catholics who did come tended to have greater financial security and a wider range of skills.[7]

The Irish who migrated to Australia during and immediately after the Famine built on the foundations laid by these earlier pioneers. The Antipodes never experienced the torrent of impoverished Irish migrants that flocked across the Atlantic after 1845. Between 1851 and 1855, only 53,801 Irish emigrants made their way to Australia and New Zealand, relatively inconsequential numbers compared to the 740,216 and 104,844 who immigrated to the United States and British North America, respectively, during the same time period. Due to the small number of convicts, those free Irish settlers who did migrate to Australia in the 1840s and 1850s experienced relatively low levels of bigotry and opposition from the settled British population. Indeed, Malcolm Campbell has characterized the Irish position in Australia in the mid-nineteenth century as "a curiously strong and influential one." As original members of the European occupation that had begun only a half century earlier, "Irish ex-convicts and free settlers had carved a satisfying niche in colonial life, beneficiaries of the liberal political and religious policies of successive colonial administrations and the colonies' insatiable demand for labor." Scattered across an economically successful agricultural landscape, the Irish were insulated from the nativist animosity their compatriots faced in Britain and America.[8]

This was the society into which the Young Ireland state prisoners arrived in 1849. As gentlemanly political prisoners rather than common criminals, all six men were spared labor duties upon arrival in Van Diemen's Land and were offered the comparative liberty of tickets-of-leave. By giving their word to both forgo any escape attempts and to remain within their assigned districts, they were afforded freedom of travel and residence. All but Smith O'Brien accepted the offer. After having their physical descriptions carefully recorded, they were conveyed to their respective districts. Within a few weeks, Martin, O'Doherty, and Meagher had discovered a point of land bordering their three districts at which they could meet without breaking their paroles. Located at a neck of land between Lakes Crescent and Sorell was a "small, cozy, smoky bit of a log-hut" whose sole reading materials consisted of "a tract upon Foreign Missions, and two columns of a *Sunday Observer*, bearing a remote date." Here the men would meet once a week, usually on Mondays, to break the loneliness of exile. While the cabin's owner, a shepherd named Cooper, cooked up hearty meals, the exiles rambled "along the shores of the lake, talking of old times, singing the old songs, weaving fresh hopes among the old ones that have ceased to bloom." These meetings enabled Meagher and Martin, whose districts were more remote, to acquire comfort items brought by O'Doherty, who lived in the town of Oatlands. In January 1850, Meagher urged his friend to "bear the saddle-bags in mind, and the ale, and plenty of shot, and powder, and a back-gammon box."[9]

Unlike the others, John Mitchel had been committed to fourteen years' transportation on board the *Dromedary* hulk (a floating prison) off the coast of Bermuda. Concerned that his worsening asthma might make a martyr out of him, the government decided to transfer Mitchel to a more healthful location. After prolonged stops in Pernambuco and the Cape of Good Hope, he was eventually sent to Van Diemen's Land, where he accepted a ticket-of-leave in April 1850 and moved into the Bothwell cottage of his childhood friend and fellow Young Irelander, John Martin. The following Monday, the two friends braved a long ride through bad weather to meet Meagher and O'Doherty at Cooper's cabin on Lake Sorell. Meagher was shocked by Mitchel's poor physical appearance. "When I saw him first," concluded Meagher, "I thought that, with him at all events, the exile was for life." Mitchel's own account of the reunion was bittersweet. As the men exchanged greetings in that dark, wet, foreign land, "I know not from what impulse, whether from buoyancy of heart, or *bizarre* perversity of feeling," he diarized, "we all *laughed* till the woods rang around; laughed loud and long, and uproariously." After so long at sea, Mitchel found himself "two years in arrears of Irish history," and in a letter reminded fellow exile Meagher of the importance of the printed word. "This is to apprize you that I carefully inquire for all Irish newspapers, & parts of such, of the last two years' dates to get *news,*" insisted Mitchel. "Martin has some, but tells me that you have, or had, far more, containing reports of trials &c. all which is new to me—but that you are in the habit of lighting cigars with them or putting them to more ignominious uses. Now, pray consider this postscript as a kind of 'Injunction' in Chancery *to stay waste.* Let not a shred of printed paper be wasted henceforth till I have learned all I can of modern Irish history." Mitchel knew what Meagher had taken for granted: the printed word was their connection to the wider Irish world.[10]

Newspaper Circulation in Australia

Since the founding of the *Sydney Gazette* in 1803, the popular press played a critical role in the life of the Australian colonies. As integral members of an international market, Australian farmers and merchants used the press to connect with distant buyers, peruse the latest statistics on supply and demand, and keep abreast of imperial policies. Yet the press was always more than an economic instrument. Exchange and subscription agreements with European and American newspapers, aided by innovations in steam printing and transportation, allowed Australian editors to clip, reprint, and reinterpret news and opinion from abroad. The press also connected colonists across the Antipodes, strengthening bonds of voluntary association and drumming up support for campaigns on land reform, opposition to transportation, and self-government.[11]

By the mid-1850s, there were five dailies operating in the colonies, including the *Sydney Morning Herald* and the Melbourne *Argus*. "Since the discovery of gold on both sides of the Pacific Ocean, a new field for the newspaper Press has been opened," declared the *Herald* in April 1854. "The power exercised by the Press at home [in Britain] is acknowledged to be great; but in new countries, where everything has to be created, its power may almost be regarded as absolute." The *Herald* situated itself in a global network of communication and exchange. "In California and in the Australian Colonies, in the British settlements in China and in the Indian Seas; in Central America and in those parts of South America where English or Americans have taken up their abode," it editorialized, "newspapers have sprung up like mushrooms." Previous scholars have underestimated the degree to which the Irish in Australia used the popular press to maintain their own independent connections to the rest of the world. One historian has recently argued, for example, that news from home traveled through London and "arrived in the colonies filtered and sanitized, containing little to excite the passions of the local Irish population." This interpretation is not without merit, given Young Ireland exile John Martin's complaint to a friend back home that the "news of Ireland extracted from the English papers into the papers of this Colony . . . [is] generally very meager and unsatisfactory." Yet close examination of personal correspondence and the newspapers themselves suggests that the Irish succeeded in using the popular press to maintain strong connections with their compatriots at home and abroad.[12]

Founded by the Scottish-born W. A. Duncan in August 1839 as the champion of "the civil and religious principles of Catholics," the *Australasian Chronicle* served as a surrogate newspaper for Irish Australia through the 1840s. The Irish got a journal of their own in June 1850, however, when the Catholic priest John McEncroe founded the Sydney *Freeman's Journal*. Born in Cashel, County Tipperary, McEncroe was ordained at Maynooth in 1819.

Three years later, he volunteered to join Bishop John England on his American mission, where he was impressed by the older man's energy and liberalism and by American democracy. When Bishop England founded the *United States Catholic Miscellany*, America's first Catholic weekly newspaper, in Charleston, South Carolina, in 1822, he hired McEncroe as its editor. The editorship allowed the young priest to experience the potential power of the newspaper business. After a brief return to Ireland, McEncroe left again in 1832 to become the official chaplain of Irish Catholics in Australia. He soon became known around Sydney as an aggressive populist. He worked tirelessly for various benevolent societies while advocating self-government, the abolition of transportation, and land reform. McEncroe's experience with the *United States Catholic Miscellany* convinced him that the Irish in Australia needed a similar organ, and in June 1850, he founded the Sydney *Freeman's Journal*, presumably with help from the Church in New South Wales. Within a few weeks, the paper had developed a network of agents across the six colonies of Australia.[13]

The new weekly's strong identification with Irish ethnicity reflected deeper divisions operating at the time within the Catholic Church in eastern Australia. For most of the nineteenth century, the papacy had tacitly agreed that Englishmen would control the Catholic hierarchy in Australia, and since the late 1830s, English Benedictines, a monastic order within the Catholic Church, had dominated the New South Wales mission. By the early 1850s, their leader, Archbishop John Polding, was seeking papal approval for the formal integration of the archdiocese of Sydney and the Benedictine order. Father McEncroe was one of the most vocal opponents to the plan. In a letter to the Propaganda Fide in Rome, McEncroe explained that national antipathies between the Irish and the English constituted a severe threat to the continued growth of the Church in eastern Australia. The majority of incoming Catholics were Irish people who associated England with oppression and tyranny and would not accede to an English hierarchy, he argued. Moreover, while missionaries from Ireland were willing to go to Melbourne and Adelaide, where there were Irish bishops, none would go to Sydney to serve as assistants to Benedictine monks led by an Englishman. The Catholic community in eastern Australia, McEncroe warned, would fall into Protestantism, irreligion, or worse. His letter to Rome, which played a role in the papacy's decision to reject Polding's proposal, exposed the very real divisions bubbling under the surface of the Catholic Church in the Australian colonies. It also explains why McEncroe's new weekly newspaper identified so strongly with Irish Catholicism. A new readership was growing day by day.[14]

McEncroe's newspaper was O'Connellite in tone. Like the *Boston Pilot*, it had explicitly copied the title of a pro-Repeal Dublin weekly, and promised to do its best "to render the paper worthy of the *name* it bears; and . . . make it imitate the spirit and character of its namesake and model in Dublin, as nearly as circumstances will permit." Influenced by the tolerant tenor of Australian society, the *Freeman's Journal* was resolved to stand for Catholics without being ultramontane or sectarian. The paper promised to fill its columns with material "which must affect the hopes and fears of the whole community, not only Priest and Layman, but we may even say—Catholic and Protestant." As Irish Australia's mainstream weekly periodical, the new paper prided itself on offering its readers both "copious and authentic news from our suffering but faithful Fatherland" and "correct intelligence regarding the state and progress of Catholic affairs throughout the world." Father McEncroe's experience in the United States with Bishop England had shown him how effectively the popular press could maintain communication among far-flung Irish communities. He immediately established reciprocal exchange and subscription agreements with other Irish newspapers to keep his readership in touch with the global currents of Irish discourse. The *Freeman's Journal* allowed the Irish in Australia to remain part of the same international newspaper network as the Dublin *Nation*, the *Boston Pilot*, and others. The weekly press kept Ireland's worldwide migrants connected.[15]

Soon after arriving in Van Diemen's Land, Young Ireland exile Patrick O'Donohoe founded his own weekly periodical. A man of humble means, he successfully petitioned the authorities to allow him to make a living in Van Diemen's Land's main port, Hobart Town, even though he was disgusted by the moral tone of the busy port. The people "do nothing but eating, drinking, whoring, and backbiting," he complained to fellow exile O'Doherty, and their newspapers "are the vilest rags on the whole globe." While his fellow Young Ireland prisoners believed their elevated status held them in "too respectable a light" for public life, O'Donohoe was poor and had no choice. On January 26, 1850, the first issue of the *Irish Exile and Freedom's Advocate* entered the global currents of the Irish popular press. The new journal adopted many tricks of the trade. It appeared on Saturdays, when workers were usually paid, and at a price they could afford. O'Donohoe also employed selling agents and established exchange agreements with other journals. "Newspaper proprietors in this and the Sister Colonies," he reminded his readers every week, "will have a copy of each paper regularly posted in Exchange for their Journals." Another recurrent ad insisted that

"Masters of Vessels, while in harbour, may have a copy of the 'Exile' upon leaving their names at the Office" and thanked them for furnishing the *Irish Exile* "with the latest papers of the ports they have left, as well as any occurrence of interest at sea." O'Donohoe also subscribed to the Dublin *Nation*, which Duffy had reestablished in September 1849, and combined this with a file of the original one from which to draw editorials and poetry. Such strategies allowed even tiny publications like his, with barely any capital, to remain part of the Irish global popular press.[16]

The efforts of these editors were not the only connection to the outside Irish world. Individual copies of imported newspapers also circulated freely among the exiles themselves. While imprisoned at sea from 1848 to 1850, John Mitchel was forbidden to have any intercourse with the crew and convicts on the ship, save the captain and the highest officers. He was also prohibited from having any connection with public affairs, which was interpreted to include access to newspapers. He found it "a violent provocation" to see newspapers arrive by the monthly mail and pass "from hand to hand amongst the guards and mates," for there was "a whole month's history of Ireland in them." Still, newspapers and periodicals did manage to leak into his cell, "percolating through the strangest capillary tubes." A man "cannot be sealed up hermetically in a hulk," wrote Mitchel in his diary, "and I am not to be fourteen years in utter darkness." Before leaving Ireland, he woke up one morning to find "the *United Irishman* of yesterday in my cabin. The sixteenth and *last* number." There were obviously friendly guards on board. Another evening "as I sat at my window, looking drearily out on the darkening waters, something was thrown from the door of my cell, and lighted at my feet." It was a London paper, recently arrived via the Halifax mail. Mitchel carefully hid it until the cell was locked for the night. When all was safe, he lit a candle "and with shaking hands spread forth my paper" to read the news of Smith O'Brien's conviction. Though consigned to a tiny cell on a floating prison in the middle of the ocean, Mitchel was in touch with the pulse of Irish life.[17]

Editors in Ireland, as well as the readers themselves, also played important parts in making the Irish in the Antipodes a part of the global network of newspaper circulation. Indeed, the state prisoners established a circulatory system of newspaper sharing among themselves, which allowed them to remain part of the fabric of Irish international politics. O'Doherty's position in a bustling port made him especially well positioned to gather newspapers for his fellow prisoners. "Have you received any new or Irish newspapers?" asked Smith O'Brien in October 1852. "Does your friend Dr. Smith ever receive

American newspapers? If so I should feel obliged if he would occasionally let me see some of those which arrive." Duffy was a far more reliable source for Irish papers. Soon after reestablishing the Dublin *Nation*, he began sending two copies of every issue to the prisoners, care of Smith O'Brien. Each week he sent "one direct to the colonies to take its chance of reaching you; the other to Mrs. O'Brien to be forwarded as opportunity offered." On the first anniversary of the new *Nation*, Duffy sent out a huge batch of newspapers to the prisoners in Australia. "Three months ago I sent you a file of the *Nation* up to that time," he told Meagher in a letter dated September 1850. "I now send you three complete files of the first year. One for yourself, one for Martin, and one for McManus." In case the issues he had been mailing to Smith O'Brien had not reached him, "pray lend him one of these," continued Duffy. "You will find in it the best history of my year's work." Newspapers sent from home were living works of history.[18]

In Van Diemen's Land, Smith O'Brien served as the heart of an exchange system of newspapers among his fellow prisoners and friendly neighbors "for whom," he told his wife in September 1852, "I keep a sort of circulating library." He was a stern librarian. O'Doherty, who often missed Monday meetings, was equally guilty of failing to promptly pass on newspapers, leading Smith O'Brien to constantly remind him of his duties. After receiving a fresh batch of Dublin *Nations*, Smith O'Brien agreed to send one to O'Doherty, "but I will forward no more until you send back the former numbers which I placed in your hands about six weeks ago." O'Doherty had a responsibility to the other members of the library. "There are several persons in this neighbourhood who desire to read the Nation," reminded Smith O'Brien, "and if you do not send them back[, they] are denied of the opportunity of reading it." Smith O'Brien also wished to archive the back numbers for reference. The elder often reminded O'Doherty of the element of shared responsibility inherent in the system. "You ought to reciprocate my attention," he admonished the younger man, "by occasionally sending me any Irish or American papers that you can lay hold of." The state prisoners were not the only members of the lending library. When he sent O'Doherty two issues of the *Nation* in April 1854, Smith O'Brien reminded him to forward "them and others which will follow *with as little delay as possible* to Joseph Cahill Esq. Shooters Hill New Norfolk." Despite the trouble O'Doherty caused, he remained a part of the circulatory system of news, and for that he was grateful. "Many thanks for your promise of the Nations," he meekly told Smith O'Brien, "which to me are always welcome."[19]

Selling newspapers on the Bendigo gold diggings, 1854. Newspapers from all over
the world reached Irish migrants in Australia. Here, a vendor sells papers to men
mining for gold. *Illustrated Sydney News*, December 9, 1854.
Courtesy of the State Library of South Australia.

Being friends with one of the leading newspaper editors in Ireland certainly gave the Young Ireland prisoners an advantage, but ordinary Irish
immigrants in Australia regularly received newspapers from home as well.
When William and Eliza Dalton's servants Ned and Johanna Hogan emigrated from Munster to New South Wales soon after the Famine, they
vowed to keep in touch. "Now Dear Johana," wrote William on August 20,
1853, "write often and send the papers and I will write as often and send
you papers." The surviving correspondence between the two families indi-
cates that newspapers accompanied almost every exchange. "Your name
Shall be always dear to me, for not forgetting to write me tho in a distant
land," Eliza told Johanna. "Mr Dalton is also indebted for the Newspapers
he so frequently gets and says it must be both troublesome and expensive."
These letters make clear that the Irish in Australia and Ireland exchanged
ideas unmediated by the British government. Sometimes, the information
was economic in nature. As a prosperous Tipperary farmer, William Dalton
was interested to "see by the paper you sent me that Irish Butter Sells high
in Sydney. I wish I Could Send you a firkin of the right Sort from abbey, one
of Mrs Murnanes Make."[20]

The letters between the Hogans and the Daltons show that newspaper exchange also allowed political news and opinion to circulate freely among the world-scattered Irish. "I Send yee Newspapers with this," William told Johanna in the summer of 1853. "You will read a Speach of Docter Cahils it will remind yee of the old Country and the old religion." He later sent Ned news on the latest attempts at land reform in Ireland. "You will See by the papers I send you that wee are Seeking tenant right what wee never can get as it is imposibile to Frame one," wrote William. "You will think a [great deal] of the Thurles Meeting when you read it but will be Surprized when I tell you it was got up by the tag rag of this Country by a few village attorneys and a Skow pool of a MP." In the wake of 1848, many prosperous farmers like the Daltons were unsympathetic to the radical Young Irelanders. "You do not Say a word about your friend Smith O Brine [Smith O'Brien] did you Call to see him?" asked William in 1851. "I see by the papers that he is as mad as ever." Though they obviously disagreed on politics, these neighbors continued to exchange newspapers with each other. "I Send yee a newspaper," concluded William, "and will bee always glad to hear from yee."[21]

The international public outcry over William Smith O'Brien's imprisonment in Van Diemen's Land illustrates the degree to which a worldwide web of Irish newspapers connected the seemingly isolated Irish in Australia to the outside world. As noted earlier, of all six state prisoners only Smith O'Brien refused to accept a ticket-of-leave. "Having fully resolved to bind myself by no engagement whatever," he diarized, "I replied without hesitation [to the offer of a ticket-of-leave] that I could not make any pledge that I would not attempt to escape." The government, hoping to physically pressure Smith O'Brien into accepting parole, consigned him to solitary confinement in a tiny guarded cabin at the probation station on Maria Island. His exercise was limited to a small patch of ground directly in front of the building, his rations were those of an average convict, and he was not allowed contact with anyone except the visiting magistrate and the station's superintendent (both of whom happened to be Irish). Within a few months, the strain of the regimen began to show on Smith O'Brien's health. Lady Denison, the wife of the colony's governor, was confident that his isolation was complete. Smith O'Brien could have no grievance, she wrote a colonial official, "and *nobody to hear of it* if he had one!"[22]

In fact, Smith O'Brien's grievances sparked an international public campaign. It began with letters in Australia, but by mid-April the news had reached Britain and Ireland. While his brother Lucius raised the matter at the highest levels of the British government, letters from exiles Meagher and McManus were published in the Dublin *Nation* and subsequently reprinted further afield. Sympathetic editorials followed. In Dublin, the *Nation* criticized the "unexampled penalties and privations" and "dread agony," while the *Freeman's Journal* objected to "the system of torture" that Smith O'Brien was suffering. When rumors of his death circulated in July 1850, a correspondent to the *Boston Pilot* claimed that the British government had realized its intention "to kill him." Back in Australia, the Sydney *Freeman's Journal* joined in. "There is not an Irishman from Cape Clear to the Ganges, or from Carrickfergus to the St. Lawrence," it editorialized in October 1850, "who does not consider the vile treatment of Smith O'Brien . . . as a wanton insult to Ireland and Irishmen all over the globe." Throughout the summer and autumn of 1850, resolutions and minutes were printed and reprinted across the English-speaking world. Finally, in November 1850, under pressure from friends and enemies alike, Smith O'Brien accepted a ticket-of-leave and moved into Elwin's Hotel in New Norfolk. Soon after, a letter arrived from Dublin. "I send you a file of the *Nation* that you may see how the country regarded [your captivity]," wrote Duffy, "and that I left no end of [Ireland] unmoved by the outrage." If anything, Duffy's letter understated the global extent of the campaign.[23]

The controversy over Smith O'Brien's solitary confinement reveals the international scope of mid-nineteenth-century Irish print culture. Thanks to personal connections in Ireland and elsewhere, Irish Australian migrants like Ned and Johanna Hogan, missionaries like Father John McEncroe, and exiles like the Young Irelanders received and transmitted individual copies of weekly periodicals back and forth across the oceans. In so doing, they created a worldwide web of weekly newspapers that kept the Irish in touch with their compatriots around the globe. While much of the news arriving in the colonies was filtered through the London press, it is equally true that even the most isolated Irish received unmediated information and opinion from home. If copies of newspapers from Ireland, Britain, and the United States were the migrants' ears, then open letters back home, published in the columns of the press, were their voices. Moreover, the practice of clipping and reprinting, so critical to editors working with limited budgets, exponentially increased the audiences of such letters and articles. "Thanks for your public letter [regarding Smith O'Brien's captivity]," Duffy wrote Meagher in the autumn of 1850. The whole affair had "raised a storm of grief and indignation among his friends, which you will see by the *Nation* we communicated to the whole people."[24]

Nation and Race in Irish Australia

Historians have struggled to define a mid-nineteenth-century Australian collective identity. In 1853, a merchant declared that the people "do not in general feel Australia to be their home." The stigma of convictism, the recent arrival of many settlers, and the frenetic movement spurred by the gold rush undermined the development of a national identity. Australia was merely a collection of independent, self-governing colonies, the confederation of which into a coherent nation-state did not occur until 1901. Although inklings were evident as early as the 1890s, Australian nationalism really coalesced during and after World War I and the slaughter at Gallipoli, which provided an evocative set of shared memories and symbols. In the mid-nineteenth century, by contrast, mainstream group identity was a form of settler colonialism characterized by Anglo-Saxon pride and loyalty to the British Empire. The *Launceston Examiner* agreed when the Polish explorer and geologist Paul Edmund de Strzelecki, while visiting the Australian colonies in the early 1840s, attributed their progress to "the hardy nature of the Anglo-Saxon race." Its success abroad proved that "it does not depend on the soil either for its character or its nationality; the Anglo-Saxon reproduces his country wherever he hoists his country's flag." Even at the height of the campaign for colonial self-government, the *Melbourne Morning Herald* acknowledged that the British crown was "the keystone and pinnacle to the dome of an Anglo-Saxon empire." The *Bathurst Free Press and Mining Journal* lauded the Anglo-Saxon race's "wonderful power of adaptation to all changes of climate and circumstances." The "Anglo-Saxon type," it opined in 1851, "is fast becoming the master-type of the world's civilization."[25]

At the same time, the tolerant nature of Australian society dissuaded overt Anglo-Saxon triumphalism. In a series of essays published in 1854 under the pseudonym John Adams, the contemporary historian of the Australian colonies, John West, elucidated this civic pluralism. "The people of Australia are one people," he wrote, whose "provincial prejudices are rather reminiscences than living realities." Raised in a society far removed from ethnic solidarities, the "Australian youth talks of the nationalities of his parents," argued West, "without feeling them." A June 1854 letter to the editor of the *Sydney Morning Herald* by "Alpha" warned that "slow indeed must be our material progress if we depend alone for a supply [of immigrants] from the great 'hive' of our race." Australians "must welcome among us the myriads from Continental Europe who, oppressed by tyranny, ground down by intolerance, bigotry, or priestcraft, and doomed to slavish servitude or

starvation in the lands of their birth, are ready to fly to this far off land."
Welcoming non-Saxons added to Australia's "sinew and bone" and enabled
it to "go forward in developing and laying bare the incalculable wealth of
this wonderful continent." Even a correspondent to the conservative Sydney
Empire had to admit that "mixed races [have] ever shown themselves superior to the so-called pure races."[26]

Father McEncroe's Sydney *Freeman's Journal* sometimes echoed mainstream settler colonialism by espousing loyalty to British constitutional freedom and citizenship. In the early days, it described New South Wales as "an
offshoot of the great Anglo-Saxon stock" where "a freeman might walk
erect, and with a freeman's hand beckon to his brethren of elder and crowded
nations, to come and share his new world." It praised the 1850 extension
of the franchise to ten-pound freeholders by comparing it to the Magna
Carta. While unsure why Providence had permitted millions of acres of
productive land to lie idle for so long, it was convinced that the open tracts
of Australia were "intended as a refuge and an inheritance for the poor and
industrious surplus population of the British Empire." In justifying this loyalty to the British constitution, the *Freeman* strove to remind its readers
that the problems of misgovernment and sectarian ascendancy that had
plagued Ireland were not present in Australia. In Ireland, it editorialized,
"there was excuse—reason—for identifying ourselves with a strong agitation . . . but why . . . do we entertain the self-same views when the causes
or pretexts are removed?" Unlike in the United States, where Know-Nothing
nativism plagued immigrants, the Irish in Australia had their political
rights, physical security, and freedom of religion. In the end, land policies
were the keys to a happy population of mixed background. "Nothing but a
fair and moderate distribution of the public land among the industrious and
middle classes of society," warned the *Freeman's Journal*, "will prevent in
time such calamities falling on Australia, as have of late fallen on poor
Ireland."[27]

At the same time, the *Freeman's Journal* pulled no punches over the state
of Ireland, complaining in its inaugural editorial that never "was a land so
favoured by nature in so deplorable a state as this ill-governed country."
News and opinion directly from Ireland became a thread in the fabric of
Irish Australia, beginning in the second issue when McEncroe clipped and
reprinted an account of a meeting over land rents from the Dublin *Freeman's Journal*. The Young Ireland prisoners were also subjects of interest.
While willing to applaud their selfless struggle to right Ireland's wrongs,
the *Freeman* looked disparagingly on their rash, hopeless rebellion. The

Young Irelanders were "chivalrous but mistaken champions for their country's wrongs." Like other Irish newspapers springing up abroad, McEncroe's *Freeman's Journal* maintained loyalty to its host community without abandoning the Irish national identity that had developed in the 1840s. The journal also perpetuated the complicated racial discourse of Celts and Saxons. The Irishman in Australia should pledge loyalty to his new home, it editorialized in 1855, "without becoming a recreant of his race and a traitor to his blood—without giving the oppressors of the land of his forefathers the sweet delight of feeling that the children have hated all the father loved—that the children have despised all the father battled, perchance, bled for." Rather than strive to become "dilettante Cockneys and *quasi* Anglo-Saxons," the children of Irish migrants to Australia should memorize the five great chapters of Irish history. These included ancient Ireland's civilization, Christianity, scholarship, missionary work, and the "Celtic Race—*the* race of Ireland."[28]

Migration was an important theme in the racial discourse of the *Freeman's Journal*. The newspaper often reprinted pieces originally published elsewhere that argued that the quintessential Irish spirit survived overseas. An article written in Newfoundland on the Irish there, for example, noted "all the eccentricities, errors, vices, and virtues—the accent and very habits of the South of Ireland are to be found stamped upon the Irish portion of the population here, and upon the 'natives' born of the Irish race." The *Freeman's Journal* also argued that the experience of Irish emigrants abroad proved the falsity of the London *Times* commissioner's argument that Irish poverty was attributable to the Celt's ungovernable nature and lack of industry. "That the misery and desolation of Ireland are owing to *bad laws*, and not to any inherent vices or defects in the Celtic character," argued the *Freeman's Journal*, "is proved by the industry, comfort and contentment of the Irish when settled in those British colonies, where all, whether English or Irish, are *equal* in the eye of the laws, and where the fell spirit of class legislation or of anti-Catholic intolerance has not been introduced." In this vein, the *Freeman's Journal* eagerly clipped and reprinted from the *Edinburgh Review* a speech Paul Edmund de Strzelecki delivered before the committee of the House of Lords on the Irish Poor Law. "I saw Irishmen in the United States, in Canada, and in Australia, living as well as the Anglo-Saxons," noted Strzelecki, "acquiring their grumbling habits, and thus improving continually their condition." The *Freeman's Journal* took Strzelecki's words as "honourable testimony to the Irishman's capacity for whatever circumstances he may be placed in."[29]

While the *Freeman's Journal* liked to portray the Irish as a unique element of the big, happy Australian family, the columns of the mainstream
press indicate that relations between the Irish and their Australian neighbors were not always amicable. Between 1848 and 1850, the British government sought to relieve overcrowding in the workhouses and charities of
Ireland by sending over 4,000 Irish "orphan girls" to the colonies as domestic servants and potential wives. In a letter to the editor of the Melbourne
Argus, "Spectator" decried the program. Despite the "unbearable" stupidity
of the young women themselves, what troubled Spectator most about the
scheme were the emotions it stirred among the Irish in Australia when Protestant clergymen opposed their importation. Special meetings of Irishmen
were called where the "base and bloody Saxon was railed at in such favourite
terms as thief, vagabond, and pauper." Such outpourings of Irish national
identity threatened the fragile fabric of an Australian settler colonialism
founded on interethnic amity. "It is hoped that the various elements of the
United Kingdom transplanted to this province shall in course of time merge
into one homogenous colonial population," concluded Spectator, "and to at-
tain this it is absolutely necessary that no man should enter public life as an
Irish, English, or Scotchman, but as a colonist determined to work for the
good of the colony alone." The alternative was "a war of races." Spectator's
letter shows that the antagonistic language of Celts and Saxons still meant
something to the Irish in Australia.[30]

The letters and diaries of the Young Ireland state prisoners offer an intimate perspective on how migration to the South Pacific influenced Irish
perspectives on race and nation. The exiles' understandings of "home," for
example, changed during their stays in Van Diemen's Land. John Mitchel
had expected to find the "gardens of hell," but he soon warmed up to the
place and, on the ride back from the first Monday meeting at Cooper's cabin,
recounted looking "down over the valley of Bothwell, which already seems
a sort of home to me." Evenings spent with Bothwell's genteel society kin-
dled this further. "It gave me a sort of home-feeling," he later wrote in his
journal after one particular evening out, when he found himself, for the
first time in two years, seated in the parlor of "a most amiable and accomplished Edinburgh family." As he and Martin returned to their cottage that
night, Mitchel was "dreaming, dreaming, dreaming how blessed a privilege
it is to have a *home*." At first, Mitchel dissuaded his wife and children from
coming out, but that changed after three months in the colony. "I do so pine for
something resembling a home—something that I could occasionally almost

fancy a real home," he admitted in July 1850, "that I have written this day to Newry, inviting all my household to the antipodes." When Smith O'Brien expressed surprise that his friend intended to bring his children up as Tasmanians, Mitchel replied that the comment left him "a little hurt." "Not one hour will I, or mine, remain under the shadow of the British flag, save by compulsion," he assured his friend. "I am not indeed an Irishman of ancient race, as you are," wrote Mitchel, "but an Irishman I am. Other country I have none, & never shall have." His Irishness transcended exile.[31]

The conflicting feelings of being at home in a foreign country created a constant tension for Mitchel in Van Diemen's Land. When Jenny and the children arrived in June 1851 with domestic articles (and stacks of newspapers) from Ireland, Mitchel noted that Bothwell now had "a wonderfully homelike aspect to me, returning to it now with all these materials and appliances of home." Mitchel was approaching the lifestyle of the sturdy yeoman he had admired since childhood, and he lauded the "pure air, glorious forests, lovely rivers, a thinly-peopled pastoral country, and kind friends" they had in Bothwell. Jenny was a brave, resourceful woman who brought five children (and two servants) on a four-month sea voyage to a land she had only read about. The drive from the port of Hobart Town to Bothwell was an adventure of its own. "Minnie was quite frightened at the sight of all the great trees and mountains, no houses and no road, only a track," Jenny wrote to her friend Mary Thompson back in County Down, "but I was greatly delighted and so were the boys." Two months later, the meanings of home continued to cause friction in Van Diemen's Land. "You cannot think how busy I have been for the last month," she told Thompson, "getting settled in my new 'lodging,' for John will not have me use the word 'home' in this country."[32]

What effect did the Irish in Australia believe the natural environment had on racial attributes? Did the process of migration change races? The flexibility of Irish racial discourse prohibited consensus on the matter. In the 1840s, Irish nationality was closely tied to the natural environment of Ireland itself, but the Young Irelanders, like the Sydney *Freeman's Journal*, were continually impressed by the survival of a quintessential Irish spirit among the emigrants and exiles of Van Diemen's Land. In an open letter to Duffy that was printed in the Dublin *Nation* and subsequently reprinted abroad, Meagher assured his friend and readers that "should hearts grow faint at home" and in despair or grief give up on the hope "that once waved, like a sacred torch, on high," he wanted them to know that "here, in this strange land, and in the loneliest haunts and pathways of it . . . here upon a lone, lone spot in the far Southern Seas, there are prayers, full of confidence, and faith, and love, offered up for Ireland's cause." John Martin echoed these sentiments of respect for an immortal, essential Irishness that survived among the Irish in Van Diemen's Land. "I never believed that I was so Irish in temperament and disposition, till I was lodged in jail as a convict felon," he wrote to Smith O'Brien. It was then that he "made the happy discovery of my Irish elasticity of spirit," which, he believed, was a "merciful gift of God to save us from perishing under the afflictions of our nation."[33]

At the same time, there were those who believed that the host community's natural environment influenced the character of immigrant races. For example, an article from the *Dublin Quarterly Journal of Medical Science*, reprinted in the *Irish Exile and Freedom's Advocate* in February 1851, hypothesized on the effect of the local environment on human nature. It was no coincidence that "the American settler, no matter from what race derived, who fixes himself anywhere between the Mississippi and the Atlantic, undergoes a positive change of form and feature, as well as new habits of mind, and his offspring, born and educated anywhere throughout that tract, will be distinguishable from their kindred in the mother country." The same logic explained why the Irish had never lost the "peculiarities of thought and demeanour" that distinguished them from the English. "Nature is not to be put out of her way," it concluded, "by any devices of government or legislation." In his diary, John Mitchel reached similar conclusions. The European settlers in Tasmania tended to be "tall, straight, and handsome" but also have "the same languor that is said to characterize all the Creole races of America and the West Indies—that soft, luxurious, voluptuous languor which becomes girls rather better than the men." Mitchel attributed this torpor to the lack of electrical storms in the Australian atmosphere, and he longed for "a rattling, sky-rending, forest-crashing, earth-shaking thunder-storm" to "shoot a sharper life into blood and brain." For Mitchel, "the finest specimens of the genus are those who have been born in the northern hemisphere and who came hither as children."[34]

For the most part, however, the Young Irelanders were convinced that Irishness remained untainted in foreign lands. Indeed, the great distance from a government whose laws were so utterly at odds with the spirit of the Celts even allowed that race to excel. A family of Irish free settlers from County Cork named Connell, who had immigrated thirty years earlier, particularly struck the state prisoners. John Martin enjoyed their hospitality and found it "both very sad and very delightful to me to find in a forest at the Antipodes the warm Irish feelings and the grace and intelligence natural to the Irish character" that was, he feared, "fast being extirpated at home." He told Mrs. Connell that he wished to see "poor old Ireland inhabited by families like yours. Alas! 'tis a slave population there now, and one fast degenerating into all the vices of slavery." John Mitchel lauded the family for overcoming the obstacles of early settlement, including "a wild forest to tame—wilder black natives to keep watch and ward against—and wildest convict bush-rangers to fight sometimes in their own home." Years earlier, Mrs. Connell had single-handedly outwitted and overpowered four armed convict bandits when they raided the house. She was, remarked Mitchel, "a thorough Celtic Irishwoman" with a "Munster accent as fresh as if she had left Cork last year." As "genuine an Irish *Vanithee*, or 'Woman of the House,' as you will find in Ireland at this day," he continued, "perhaps more so; for Carthaginian 'civilisation' has been closer and more deadly in its embrace amongst the valleys of Munster than it could be amongst the wilds of the [Tasmanian] Sugar-loaf forests." Irishness did not merely survive; it excelled beyond the shores of Ireland.[35]

The idea that race remained untouched by migration was in keeping with theories elucidated by Robert Knox in *The Races of Men: A Fragment* (1850). Intended "to show that in human history race is everything," *The Races of Men* sparked an international debate over Celts and Saxons. "The fact, the simple fact, remains just as it was," wrote Knox: "men are of different races." Troubled by the role that ethnic identity had played in the 1848 revolutions, Knox echoed Augustin Thierry's belief that physiological differences between the races manifested themselves in cultural incongruence, which sparked conflict between societies. Migration was a key piece of the puzzle. "Transplant [the average individual] to another climate, a brighter sky, a greater field, free from the trammels of artificial life, the harnessed routine of European civilization; carry him to Canada," declared Knox, "*he is still the same;* mysterious fact." To understand an individual's behavior, argued Knox, "go back to France; go back to Ireland, and you will find it there: it is the race." Like the exiled Young Irelanders, Knox was arguing that racial characteristics survived the process of migration, even though he also thought that individual races were only designed to survive in their natural environments. He raised the ire of many Irish, however, when he argued for the inherent inferiority of the Celt compared to his Saxon neighbor. Some ascribed Irish misery to British misgovernment, but Knox was convinced that "the source of all evil lies in *the race,* the Celtic race of Ireland. There is no getting over *historical facts.*" By contrast, he gloried in "the march of the Saxon onwards to democracy; self-government, self rule."[36]

The debate over Knox's work spilled onto Australia's shores. On June 24, 1852, the Sydney *Freeman's Journal* reviewed George Ellis's *Irish Ethnology Socially and Politically Considered* (1852), which had been written in direct response to Knox's book. An Irish-born ethnologist, Ellis accepted the theory that the races were essentially different but disclaimed Knox's belief in Saxon superiority and in the natural antipathy between Saxons and the Celts. The Saxons and Celts, argued Ellis, "have always exhibited, and continue at this day to exhibit, in as distinct and vivid colours as ever, notwithstanding some hundred years of partial intercommunication, the most strikingly opposed mental characteristics." Freedom, government, economy, and civilization meant different things to Celts and Saxons. Ellis's main argument, therefore, was that "until the leading difference between the two races shall be clearly ascertained, and the characters indelibly distinguishing the great Celtic family shall be correctly understood, no clear principle for the improvement of Ireland can be laid down." English misgovernment of Ireland was doomed to continue as long as the managers of the British Empire failed to understand, and build legislation acknowledging, the essential differences between Celts and Saxons. The Celt's *esprit* could never harmonize with the Saxon *lois*.[37]

Later in the year, a pro-Celtic diatribe made a big splash in the press. It came from the pen of another Irish ethnologist, John McElheran, who had studied under Robert Knox in Edinburgh. In an October 1852 letter to the editor of the London *Times*, McElheran objected to the notion of "'this godlike Anglo-Saxon' whom you insultingly hawk about the world as an object of worship." The average Saxon was, wrote McElheran, a "flaxen-haired, bullet-headed, pig-eyed, huge-faced, long-backed, pot-bellied, bad-legged, stupid, slavish, lumbering, sulky boor, whose moral state is a disgrace and regret to England." By contrast, continued McElheran, the "intelligent and progressive English are Celts of 'various hues,' as ancient historians and bards described them." Toward the end of his letter, McElheran claimed that religion and science suggested that "Saxon and Celt are brothers, that degeneracy is the cause of peculiarities of race in both, and that both are capable of restoration." By describing the races in these terms, McElheran seems to have held out the possibility for their eventual amalgamation. His letter was widely reprinted in Irish papers in Dublin, Boston, and Sydney.[38]

By connecting migrants in Australia to their compatriots in faraway lands, the popular press encouraged the mid-nineteenth-century Irish to begin thinking of themselves as a global nation. As discussed earlier, the steadily increasing control enjoyed by Irish clergymen over local Catholic parishes throughout the English-speaking world during this time clearly played a role in the process. Yet the evidence presented here shows the critical influence the popular press had on this development. Contemporaries marveled at its international reach. The "surface of the globe itself, one might suppose to be covered with the books, brochures, and newspapers that have issued from the press by millions," noted one letter to the editor of the Sydney *Freeman's Journal*. Since the publication of Benedict Anderson's *Imagined Communities*, historians have understood the role print culture played in the development of modern nationalism, but most studies have limited their analyses to identities within sovereign nation-states. The Irish experience in Australia and, as we shall see, the United States shows that newspapers, and the identities they nurtured, were capable of transcending national borders.[39]

In the case of Australian immigration, it shows that while aggressive campaigns for Irish independence never gained the support they found in Boston and New York, it is also true that the Irish in the Antipodes retained material and psychological connections with their fellow compatriots at home and abroad. What was, from the perspective of the Irish in Australia, remarkable about Celts (and, indeed, Saxons) was the way in which their characteristics remained static across time and space. In fact, those who had moved to Australia were, in some ways, *more* Irish than those who had stayed home. Australia's great distance from the heart of Saxon misgovernment, figured John Mitchel, actually allowed Mrs. Connell's Irish spirit to flourish more fully than it could in Ireland. The *Freeman's Journal* agreed. The successes of the Irish abroad showed that British misgovernment, not any inherent defect in the Irish character, accounted for Ireland's problems. The Celtic *esprit* could not be reconciled with strictly Saxon *lois*, but a liberal colonial policy could easily incorporate it. Membership in a uniquely Irish global network of communication, in the form of weekly newspapers, was important in fostering this transnational identity. The Irish were evolving into a global nation.

Aboriginal Australians and European Settlement

What did the Irish in Australia think of the rapidly diminishing Aboriginal population that had lived in the area for thousands of years before the establishment of New South Wales? The British government's attitude was clear: Australia was *terra nullius*, an "empty land" whose inhabitants lacked any kind of recognizable government. No treaties were signed or compensations offered to the local natives as the rapid expansion of pastoral agriculture in the 1820s and 1830s brusquely pushed them aside. Death through violence and disease followed. Anti-Aboriginal violence was perpetuated by a combination of regular soldiers, bands of bounty hunters, and the settlers themselves, the most notorious instance occurring near the Gwydir River at Myall Creek in New South Wales in 1838. When a group of stockmen in pursuit of Aborigines who had speared their cattle happened upon a party of unarmed women and children, they dragged the natives into the bush and butchered them. Although seven of the murderers were convicted and executed, the case illustrated the lawless savagery that often accompanied the expansion of pastoral agriculture. Although it is notoriously difficult to confirm the accuracy of available statistics, one national study has indicated that between 1821 and 1850, the native population was cut in half, from 600,000 to 300,000. In the early years, many Aborigines unsuccessfully attempted to negotiate with the encroaching settlers, but by the 1830s and 1840s it was obvious that incorporating into the agricultural workforce was the best strategy. In a labor-hungry environment, many found work as stockmen, shepherds, and shearers.[40]

Attempts by the British government to force Australian settlers to treat the native population more humanely were largely ineffective. For the first fifty years after 1788, the terra nullius ethos dissuaded imperial administrators from forming a coherent government policy regarding settler-native relations. Colonists were more or less given free rein to exploit the land and manage indigenous resistance as they saw fit. The widespread bloodletting of the 1820s and 1830s, however, convinced the home government that something needed to be done. At the same time, London-based evangelical Christians founded the British and Foreign Aborigines' Protection Society in 1836. Composed of power brokers in the British Parliament, the new organization's greatest success came in 1837 when a select committee of the House of Commons found that British settlers in southern Africa, Australia, and northern America had denied local natives the "incontrovertible right to their own soil." As a result, reserves of land were set aside for Aboriginal communities in Australia during the 1830s. In 1846, the House of Commons affirmed the right of local natives to hunt. Nevertheless, most of these laws and decrees were ignored in Australian colonies. Humanitarian impulses from thousands of miles away were unable to effect real change.[41]

Chapter 1 showed that the Young Irelanders' position on people of color was often paradoxical and guided by practical considerations. While unwilling to undermine financial support for Repeal by loudly supporting

American antislavery, they also claimed common cause with dispossessed native peoples around the world, including Aboriginal Australians. It would be inaccurate to suggest that this respect never wavered. The Dublin *Nation*, like other European newspapers, sometimes published articles that depicted Aborigines in unflattering terms. In January 1845, for example, it ran a review of Charles Griffith's *The Present State and Prospects of the Port Philip District of New South Wales*, which depicted Aboriginal Australians as "hideous" cannibals who "devour all their children after the birth of the first, until it is able to follow the tribe." Nevertheless, most pre-Famine Irish nationalist rhetoric was marked by support for colored victims of oppression. In the House of Commons, Daniel O'Connell was an outspoken advocate of antislavery and Aboriginal rights. Likewise, William Smith O'Brien, who was a longtime supporter of Edward Gibbon Wakefield's plans for colonization, insisted on the fair repayment to Aborigines for land sales in Australia under Lord Stanley's 1842 emigration bill. As a member of the Aborigines' Protection Society, he seconded Daniel O'Connell's motion insisting on the "common humanity" of indigenous peoples and agreed with O'Connell's claim that whenever "the white man settled, the natives had been first banished, then pursued, and next exterminated." When O'Connell praised his national ardor, Smith O'Brien denied that there was any merit in loving his country, "as having descended from the Aborigines he considered it a duty."[42]

Confinement in Australia several years later gave Smith O'Brien plenty of time to reflect on the problem of indigenous dispossession. After reading Robert Godlonton's *A Narrative of the Irruption of the Kaffir Hordes into the Eastern Province of Cape Colony in 1834–1835* (1836), he rued that "whenever a civilized people have established themselves in the vicinity of barbarous tribes, instead of communicating to them the somewhat equivocal blessings of civilization and adopting them into an intimate and friendly association, they have carried out against them a war of extermination which has not infrequently ended in the total extinction of the aboriginal race." Philanthropic attempts to benefit the local natives seemed to have uniformly failed, whereas insurrection afforded justification for cruelty. While "the lawless violence or cupidity of the savage" played its role, Smith O'Brien ultimately laid the blame at the feet of the white settlers for whom "the name of Religion has too often been used as a pretext for . . . invasion and massacre." This troubling pattern was especially true of Van Diemen's Land, where, Smith O'Brien noted in his diary, Aborigines constituted only 38 out of the island's 70,164 inhabitants.[43]

Smith O'Brien's sympathy for the Caffirs of South Africa, the Maori of New Zealand, and the Amerindians of North America was a classic eighteenth-century view of the human in the state of nature as a noble savage. He was, for example, struck by Herman Melville's *Typee: A Peep at Polynesian Life* (1846) and *Omoo: A Narrative of the South Seas* (1847), which featured European characters shipwrecked among South Seas "savages." Beyond the pleasing natural environment of the South Seas, Smith O'Brien envied the "race well deserving to be called 'the children of nature' who live without toil and spend each succeeding day in making themselves and others happy, except when warlike enterprise calls into action the qualities of manly courage and noble daring." Though Aboriginal traditions often sanctioned distasteful practices, Smith O'Brien doubted that contact with Europeans could bring favorable change to their lives. "The Red Indians of North America—the indigenous inhabitants of the West India Islands, of Mexico, and of Peru—the Caffres of South Africa and many other races," he complained, "have derived little except demoralization and ruin from their intercourse with men enlightened by what is called superior 'civilisation.'" For Smith O'Brien, the difference between Irish and English nature was analogous to the difference between the noble savage and civilization. "I confess I like the warm frank genial social qualities which belong to Irishmen infinitely better," he diarized, "than the cold indifference the shy reserve or calculating selfishness which are too often to be found as the distinguishing marks of an Englishman."[44]

The annals of history provided countless examples of this troubling pattern of Aboriginal victimization. The sixteenth-century European conquest of the Americas, for example, released "unbridled lust, love of domination—all the worst passions of the worst men of the European world." Similarly, Irish history provided a context for understanding foreign struggles for Aboriginal autonomy. Reviewing John Mitchel's *Life and Times of Aodh O'Neill* (1845), Smith O'Brien remarked how, under the pretext of introducing civility and religion, foreign adventurers chased the native populations out of their homelands while spreading discord "founded upon the ascendancy of race over race and creed over creed." Reading Augustin Thierry's *History of the Conquest of England by the Normans* (1847) undermined the contemporary axiom of "the energy, the perseverance, the bravery which in all climes and countries distinguishes the Anglo Saxon race." Instead, an imperialist, usurping spirit had visited much misery upon Aboriginal peoples around the world. Admitting that it was not easy to see how settler/native issues could be resolved, Smith O'Brien did propose a solution. Though sympathetic to "the aborigines of every country," he did believe that sparsely populated tracts of the earth should be open to settlement by people from overpopulated nations. By dividing the land between self-governing white and indigenous communities, "the native should be at liberty if he chose to settle amongst the colonists and to adopt their habits." During his years in Van Diemen's Land, Smith O'Brien organized these and other ideas on government into a two-volume book, which he later published as *Principles of Government, or Reflections in Exile* (1856).[45]

Smith O'Brien was not the only Young Ireland prisoner to support the rights of Aboriginal Australians. When he founded the *Irish Exile and Freedom's Advocate*, Patrick O'Donohoe openly advocated the rights of both natives and convicts. "Our *highest aim*—and that upon which our eye shall ever rest," he wrote in the first lead article, "will be, to *defend every oppressed man*, whether he be *free or in chains*, and to denounce such oppression, and expose its authors *whether official or unofficial*." This was to be a paper for all races and classes. "No man in a chain-gang shall be too despicable for our attention," assured O'Donohoe, "provided his grievance be real, and that oppression of rulers, and *not* misconduct on his part be the source of his sufferings." The *Irish Exile* would "not pander to power, or shrink before oppression, but will be ready to defy tyranny in every form and in all places, and to SUSTAIN THE OPPRESSED OF EVERY CLIME, CREED AND COLOUR." To legitimate his policies, O'Donohoe reprinted articles from the original Dublin *Nation*. On June 29, 1850, he published Thomas Davis's article "Sympathy," which had originally run in the *Nation* on March 25, 1843. "We are battling for Ireland," wrote Davis; "if we conquer, 'twill be for mankind." Later in the year, O'Donohoe featured other Davis editorials, including one that referred to a national language as "a surer barrier, and more important frontier, than fortress or river."[46]

While O'Donohoe's paper was undoubtedly dedicated to supporting the convict classes, its editorials were sympathetic to Aboriginal Australians as well. He castigated an unnamed local newspaper when it described Australia as the birthright of the children of free settlers. "Wherefore do you claim this broad and beautiful island for the *'children of the originally free'*?" demanded O'Donohoe. "Where are the copper-coloured natives, with their hearts full of red blood, to whom and to whom only, this sunny land appertained? Answer that," he scorned, "ye descendants of those robbing adventurers who deprived them of their rightful heritage, squatted upon their wild mirthful homesteads, committed plunder upon a broad scale, and would, now that ye are white-washed, throw blackball at culprits of a less questionable class." For O'Donohoe, those who supported the dispossession of Aboriginal Australians spoke with the same voice, which *"even here,* gloats over the idea of having *plundered* and *starved nine millions of Irishmen* of their 'birthright.'" The Irish people's right to the land of Ireland was, like that of the natives of Tasmania, "aboriginal, and not arrived at, through, or by means of pick-locks, long passages, and black vaults."[47]

This sympathy, rooted in an Irish self-identification as dispossessed natives, found expression in the Sydney *Freeman's Journal* as well. As in most contemporary newspapers, the columns of the paper occasionally featured unflattering articles on the exotic habits of "savages" around the world, usually reprinted from travel books. More often, however, native victims of imperialism were frequently the subject of heartfelt, if rather patronizing, sympathy in the *Freeman's Journal*. There was not a man "who has a proper sense of the rights of human nature whether savage or civilized," it asserted in 1851, "that will not recoil from the scenes of suffering and destruction brought on the 'Aboriginal races' of this country, by our squatting and depasturing system." Like Mitchel and Smith O'Brien, the *Freeman* saw English imperialism as crueler than the French, Portuguese, or Spanish versions. The most noteworthy aspect of "Anglo-Saxon Colonisation," it argued, "is, that wherever England has undertaken the work of colonization, *there* the Aboriginal races, the Lords of the Soil, have almost totally disappeared in the course of a few generations!" Examples from around the world proved the point. While "'might' may prevail over *right,"* the paper reminded proimperialists, "the Almighty Father of every portion of the human race will, in his own good time, take vengeance, even in this world, of those states who have thus trampled on the common rights of humanity."[48]

The limits of the *Freeman's* empathy for people of color were demonstrated when the importation of Asian workers threatened the European-Australian labor force's wages. A lack of agricultural laborers had always plagued the colonies, and the problem was compounded when young men fled to the "diggings" following the discovery of gold in 1851. In July 1852, the *Freeman* considered this labor shortage the "all absorbing question at present." Some large, landowning "squatters" attempted to fill this labor gap by importing cheap "coolies." The *Freeman* opposed the strategy on several grounds. In one of its few elucidations of white supremacy, it argued that those who advocated "importing coolies, Cannibals, or Chinamen" ignored "the injustice and degradation that would be thus committed on the Christian white men, against whom they were as it were, to be placed in competition." At least emancipated convicts were "of our own kindred and Creed—they have fallen and may be reclaimed, but the others are *heathens* of whose conversion or reformation the most distant hopes cannot be entertained." Although willing to admit that such a policy contradicted "our boasted philanthropy and . . . our repeated invitations to the people of all nations to come and settle down amongst us," the *Freeman's Journal* ultimately felt that coolies would threaten the Australian Christian community. There was also a thread of settler guilt over the dispossession of the Aboriginal populations. The *Freeman* wondered whether "this influx of a vicious and idolatrous race [was] like 'Retributive Justice' on us for our cruel treatment of the harmless and simple-minded Aborigines of New Holland?"[49]

Pre-Famine Irish nationalism's close identification of the people with the soil of Ireland encouraged some midcentury Irish living in Australia to express support for those whom they considered fellow Aboriginal victims of settler colonialism. Native dispossession was a problem transcending time, space, and skin color. The Irish, Caffirs, Maori, Peruvians, Amerindians, and Aboriginal Australians had all suffered the same fate throughout the modern era. Nor was "white civilization" the apex of human life. While he saw a certain inexorability in the white man's progress, Smith O'Brien also believed that there was much to be said for the uncivilized life of "savages" even if, regrettably, the meeting of civilized and uncivilized often resulted in the eradication of the latter. As it had in Ireland, however, this affinity for fellow indigenous peoples was limited by practical considerations. While the Sydney *Freeman's Journal* saw common cause between the dispossessed of Ireland and other countries around the world, the importation of coolie laborers tested the limits of this universality. Here, the problem was rephrased from broadly universal to strictly national terms—as a practical threat to a society founded on free labor and Christianity. Irish racial discourse in Australia was as complicated and uneven as it had been in Ireland.[50]

Departures

The Young Irelanders' departures from Van Diemen's Land were more piecemeal than their arrivals. Irish American financial support played an important role in the first four cases. Terence Bellew McManus escaped in March 1851, soon after his release from a probation station for breaking his parole but before his ticket-of-leave was renewed. A year after marrying the daughter of a free settler in February 1851, Thomas Francis Meagher resigned his ticket-of-leave and escaped the island, leaving his wife and infant to follow. Patrick O'Donohoe escaped in early 1853 without having resigned his parole. The Irish Directory, an organization formed in New York by 1848 Irish exiles, had facilitated all three escapes, and in January 1853, it sent an exiled veteran of the 1848 rebellion named P. J. Smyth to Van Diemen's Land with cash and orders to facilitate further escapes. With Smyth's help, John Mitchel walked into his local police station on June 9, 1853, resigned his ticket-of-leave, and galloped off into the surrounding bush on horseback with constables close on his heels. Five and a half weeks later he sailed incognito to Tahiti, where he awaited a ship to take him to America. Finally, in May 1854, news arrived in Van Diemen's Land that the British government had granted conditional pardons to the three remaining Young Ireland prisoners. They could live anywhere in the world, bar Ireland or Britain. O'Doherty went to try his luck on the gold diggings, while Martin and Smith O'Brien prepared to return to Europe.

The news of these pardons ignited great rejoicing among the Irish in Australia. The farewell addresses, steeped in the language of an ethnic solidarity that seemed to transcend time and space, repeated the glorification of Smith O'Brien's genealogy that had characterized similar addresses in Ireland in the 1840s. A resolution by the residents of Victoria hoped that "you may live yet to witness and enjoy the permanent regeneration of your own, your native land." An address by the Irish in Sydney wished him "a speedy Return to the Land of *Your Illustrious Ancestors*" and hoped Providence would "smile upon you for the remaining Years of your Chivalrous life." Speaking at the meeting at which the Sydney address was adopted, Father John McEncroe espoused the global nationalism that had characterized the *Freeman's Journal* under his editorship. On the one hand, McEncroe appealed to ethnicity. "The allusion in reference to the ancestry of Mr. O'Brien was justified by the fact, of which they were no doubt all aware," declared McEncroe, "that O'Brien was a lineal descendant of the immortal King, Brien Boru. (Great Cheering)." On the other hand, he argued that what was really at work in Ireland was British civic pluralism. "All that the Irish people sought previous to 1848," argued McEncroe, "was that they should be placed on the same footing with regard to national and constitutional rights and privileges as the other peoples which constituted the empire." It was to that end that "the men whom they assembled to honour risked and partially forfeited all that is near and dear to man. (Cheers)."[51]

The state prisoners' replies expressed a mix of ethnic solidarity and civic pluralism as well. Martin thanked the Australians for their hospitality, noting that from "people of all races, sects, parties, and classes in the island I have received kindness, or at least civility." He promised not to hold the Tasmanians' loyalty to Britain against them, for he supported any government that the people respected. "While I vagabondise through the crowded cities of Europe and America," he concluded, "I will remember with affection the kindly brown woods of Tasmania, which have often almost charmed my melancholy away." Smith O'Brien's responses repeated the metaphor of an Irish Celtic nature allowed to flourish when not stunted by English misgovernment. He was delighted to have found that the Irish "retain in this hemisphere, those features of the national character—those noble impulses—those generous emotions—those genial susceptibilities—which I have been elsewhere accustomed with loving pride to extol as the attributes of our race." The Irish in the Australian colonies had given "a practical refutation to the calumnies which appeared in English papers regarding the Celtic race," and he was glad to see that "there were reporters now present who would convey to the world" the opinions being expressed that night. The popular press gave every meeting a global audience, and Smith O'Brien knew it. Life in Australia had proved that Irish misery was rooted not in the character of the Celts but in the political institutions that misgoverned them. As he left for Europe, Smith O'Brien rued that his conditional pardon left him unable to return to Ireland. "I am still an exile from that home," he admitted. "I am, henceforth, a wanderer on the face of the earth."[52]

Around the time that Smith O'Brien and the others were leaving, their colleague in Ireland, Charles Gavan Duffy, began considering migrating to Australia. When Smith O'Brien settled in Brussels after leaving the Antipodes, Duffy wrote him with queries as to the suitability of Australia as a destination. Various attempts by Duffy and his associates in Ireland to rebuild Irish nationalism and secure tenant rights had failed, and remaining in Ireland was becoming less tenable. "Day by day our prospects grow blacker," he wrote, "as if God had no mercy . . . for the Celtic race." Duffy was encouraged by Smith O'Brien's reply. The Irish in Victoria possessed "more of Genuine Irish feeling than is to be found in any great number of Irishmen . . . in Ireland." "You will find in Australia," assured Smith O'Brien, "many of our fellow countrymen whose noble and generous natures have not yet yielded to any corrupting influences but who have sought to maintain in their own persons that independence of spirit which we endeavored in vain to infuse into the institutions of Ireland." Reflecting on the exodus of Irish to all corners of the world over the previous ten years, Smith O'Brien admitted that what "may be the ultimate aim of Providence in dispersing throughout the world so large a portion of the Irish race (not less than two millions) who might have lived happily in their own land under the protection of a good domestic government is a question which to me at least is inscrutable." Satisfied with Smith O'Brien's assessment, Duffy sailed with his family to Australia on October 8, 1855, having admitted in one of his last *Nation* editorials that there was "no more hope for the Irish Cause than for the corpse on the dissecting table."[53]

Conclusion

This chapter has demonstrated the early evolution of global nationalism among those Irish who migrated to eastern Australia in the early 1850s. As they had in Ireland before the Famine, weekly newspapers played a critical role in the construction of this new identity. Uniting the Australian Irish with their compatriots in other countries, the international popular press constituted a transnational public sphere through which new ideas about race and nation circulated. The articles, editorials, and letters printed (and endlessly reprinted) in periodicals around the world continually reiterated the portrait of an Irish Celtic community that was both timeless and global. This was not a static set of one-way relays but a dynamic international network of exchange—a virtual meeting place where the Irish could assemble once a week to debate and define information and identity. Whether contributing to the uproar over Smith O'Brien's solitary confinement, reviewing the latest ethnological scholarship on Celts and Saxons, or reporting on meetings over land reform in Tipperary, the pages of the press offered the Irish in Australia a place to build and consolidate their transnational imagined community.

This Irish global nationalism, which was predicated on the dichotomy of Celts and Saxons, featured a flexible blend of both ethnic solidarity and civic pluralism. Despite the presence of large numbers of people of color in eastern Australia, a Celtic, as opposed to white, racialism dominated Irish Australian discourse in the early 1850s. The Irish remained more Celtic than white because, despite the relative amicability of the host society, the biggest threat to Irish inclusion in the colonial polity came from above (the Saxon Protestant mainstream) rather than below (Aboriginal Australians). At the same time, migration to the other side of the earth introduced a spatial aspect to what had previously been a primarily chronological phenomenon. Whereas in Ireland before the Famine, the Celtic race was a timeless community closely tied to the island's natural environment, migrants to

Australia like John Martin delighted "to find in a forest at the Antipodes the warm Irish feelings" that were "fast being extirpated at home." Meagher similarly assured Duffy that the Irish spirit survived in that "lone, lone spot in the far Southern Seas." The next chapter examines how the idea of a global nation played out on the other side of the earth, among the Irish living in the antebellum United States.

AFTER A THREE-WEEK WAIT in Tahiti following his escape from Van Diemen's Land, John Mitchel joined his wife and children on the passing ship *Julia Ann* and sailed with them to San Francisco. As they crossed the Pacific, he commented in his diary on a troubling phrase that he had been hearing a lot lately, which suggested that Irish mass migration to the United States was creating "a new Ireland in America." The phrase conveyed no meaning to his mind. "Ireland without the Irish—the Irish out of Ireland— neither of these can be *our country*." Yet all was not lost. "I believe in moral and spiritual electricity," he wrote. "I believe that a spark, caught at some happy moment, may give life to masses of comatose humanity; that out of the 'exodus' of the Celts may be born a Return of the Heracleidae." John Mitchel was full of hope for the next chapter in the epic drama of the Celtic race even though, as he knew from reading Irish American newspapers, the United States was proving an inhospitable environment.[54]

CHAPTER THREE

Battling the Anglo-Saxon Myth

Irish Identity in the Antebellum
United States, 1848–1861

Following the failure of 1848, several key Young Irelanders fled to New York City. On a Sunday in May 1857, after ten years of exile in the United States, one of those escapees, Richard O'Gorman, sat down to write a letter to his former mentor, William Smith O'Brien. The years had been good to O'Gorman. He and Dublin *Nation* cofounder John Blake Dillon had established a successful law practice in Manhattan and done well for themselves. "I love, most of all the quiet of my own home, when the day's work is done, and the luxury of having my wife and children around me," wrote O'Gorman. "Still, I remember my old home and there comes sometimes a sting, and I dream of old times. But I shake it off soon. It's all useless. There is no going back for me. I have staked too much here to think of another change. In the rest of my life, I am American." O'Gorman admitted to having been a poor correspondent, but the international tentacles of the Irish popular press had allowed him to follow Smith O'Brien's progress, and he could assure his friend that "I have read every word you have spoken." Before quitting, O'Gorman commented on how the Irish in America were faring overall.

> The Destiny of our Race is to me utterly mysterious. In so much mental and physical vigour, elasticity & adaptability must have a Destiny to fulfill. There seems to me nothing in the Irish nature to indicate a worn out, a moribund Race. The moment it touches this soil, it seems to be induced with miraculous energy for good and evil; so that something Irish is prominent every where, and you have to praise or blame, to bless or curse it, at every turn. My own belief is that this northern continent will fall into the hands of men whose

composition will be four-fifths Celtic. The Descendants of the Puritans—the Saxon Element, is physically deteriorating and will soon have done its work. A softer, more genial generation of men will be needed. More capable of enjoyment, more artistic than the Yankee; and our Celtic blood will just supply the want.

For O'Gorman and his fellow Famine-era Irish Catholics, their Celtic racial heritage strengthened their claim to American nationality.[1]

This chapter examines the contours of Irish American racial discourse between the arrival of the first Young Irelanders in the late 1840s and the outbreak of the Civil War in 1861. Historians have long debated the nature of Irish American nationalism. In the mid-1960s, Thomas N. Brown held that it reflected the immigrants' collective desire to prove their suitability for American democracy. In later years, Eric Foner saw it as a dimension of working-class radicalism. More recently, the received wisdom among American historians is that the Irish facilitated their assimilation by cutting their ties with home and adopting a white identity. "In becoming white," wrote Noel Ignatiev, "the Irish ceased to be Green." This chapter challenges that truism by showing that American Anglo-Saxonism constituted a greater threat to these migrants than any alleged lack of whiteness. Rather than seek to become Saxon, however, Irish immigrants expanded the boundaries of American citizenship by depicting themselves as members of what one exile termed a proud and noble "world-wide race" of Celts. The Celts' democratic impulses were, they claimed, locked in a timeless transnational struggle with the same oligarchic Anglo-Saxons who had opposed the American War of Independence. Aided by the Democratic Party, antebellum Irish Catholics pledged dual loyalty to their home and host communities. Like its Australian counterpart, this Irish American identity was both transcendent of, and rooted in, the nation-state. While imbued with an ethnic solidarity based on race, there was an equally important strain of civic republicanism at work, which lauded the Irish Celts' place in the American nation. As ever, a worldwide web of printed words remained critical to the construction and dissemination of this Irish global nationalism.[2]

Migration, Slavery, and Citizenship
in the Antebellum United States

Irish people had been migrating to the North American colonies since the seventeenth century, but the economic and social crises accompanying the end of the Napoleonic Wars sparked a new surge that continued throughout the nineteenth century. The cessation of hostilities in 1815 brought a sudden drop in demand that depressed the values of agricultural and manufacturing exports. Ireland's rapidly expanding population, augmented by unemployed soldiers, felt the pinch of chronic underemployment and a series of poor harvests. Many responded by moving to North America. Between 1815 and 1818 alone, some 35,000 Irish people established patterns that continued over the next several decades in spite of periodic cyclical downturns in the U.S. economy. In the thirty years between Waterloo and the outbreak of the Great Famine, approximately 1 million men and women migrated across the Atlantic Ocean toward, in the words on one contemporary, "countries where the productive powers of man were better rewarded than they are in Ireland." Around half of these emigrants were Catholics from the north and east of Ireland, coming from middling classes of artisans, small farmers, or wage laborers. In the United States, they found work on the margins of a market revolution whose bourgeois social relations were very different from those they had known in Ireland.[3]

The steady stream of transatlantic Irish migration established in the wake of 1815 became a flood following the outbreak of the Great Famine in 1845. As successive harvests of the potato failed completely or partially, excess mortality multiplied. Between 1845 and 1855, as many as 1 million people died as a result of starvation and disease, leading many of the survivors to panic and flee "the hand of death, which is now stalking abroad and entering the door of every peasant in the country." Of the 5 million people who immigrated to the United States between 1830 and 1860, almost 40 percent were Irish. In the 1850s alone, 989,834 Irish came to the country. This mass movement left an indelible demographic mark on the northeastern urban landscape. By 1870, Irish-born inhabitants constituted at least 20 percent of the population in nine cities across New England, New York, and New Jersey. Stimulated by these new communicants, the American Catholic Church grew under Irish-born New York archbishop J. J. Hughes. Hundreds of churches were built, thousands of priests either trained or imported from Ireland, parochial education founded, and greater centralized discipline instituted. Irish American nationalism enjoyed a similar boost. In the pre-1845 period, Irish identity had been fissured by the religious and regional differences that characterized the early nineteenth-century society from which the migrants came. Thanks in part to the arrival of the Young Ireland leaders and the growth of a secular Irish American weekly press, however, a strident nationalism was steadily spawned among Irish American immigrants.[4]

The Irish who arrived in the United States found themselves in a boisterous, contradictory polity in which freedom and skin color were inextricably entwined. While willing to admit European immigrant men onto its voter rolls, American democracy excluded men of color. In the late eighteenth century, southern states such as Virginia, Georgia, and South Carolina explicitly forbade blacks from voting, but throughout the nineteenth century even the northern states slowly limited or eliminated black participation in elections. In 1821, the New York Constitutional Convention raised the property qualification for black voters while simultaneously eliminating all such tests for whites. Black voting was completely eradicated in Pennsylvania in the 1830s. By the eve of the Civil War, there were only five states (all in New England) in which African Americans enjoyed the same voter status as whites. Skin color also played a critical role in restricting economic independence. There were 4 million enslaved African Americans in the South, while free blacks and other racial minorities struggled to fully exercise economic independence. In the Northeast, many were mired in low-paying, unskilled jobs and domestic positions. Along the western frontier, where federal law restricted blacks' access to the public domain, apprenticeship and indentured servitude, which had ceased to employ whites since the early nineteenth century, continued to hold Amerindians, Mexicans, and Chinese in states of semibondage until midcentury.[5]

Thanks to profound similarities between the economic plights of blacks and the immigrant Irish in the antebellum era, it has become a virtual truism in American historiography that the Irish had to "become white" in the United States. Radically overrepresented in menial, unskilled, and insecure jobs, while their female counterparts worked as domestic servants, male Irish and black workers both experienced hostility from prospective employers who associated them with indolence, stupidity, and moral laxity. Forced to do "nigger work" like unloading freight and digging ditches, they occupied the lowest rungs of industrial American life. Building on the similarities between Irish and African American economic positions in the industrial North, scholars in the 1990s began using "whiteness" as a way to understand mid-nineteenth-century Irish immigrant identity. The Irish integrated into the American industrial economy, the theory ran, by becoming virulent white supremacists and thus dissociating themselves from African Americans. In *The Wages of Whiteness*, David Roediger summarized the argument when he wrote that the logic of white supremacy "had particular attraction for Irish-American immigrant workers, even as the 'whiteness' of these very workers was under dispute." Later, Noel Ignatiev's *How the Irish*

Became White argued that "the Catholic Irish, an oppressed race in Ireland, became part of an oppressing race in America."[6]

By narrowly focusing on the lowest rungs of northern industrial society, the whiteness school offered a colorful but ultimately unsatisfying picture of Irish American racial status. True, many Irish in the North were stuck doing dead-end, distasteful jobs. In the South, however, where being on the wrong side of the color line could mean a lifetime of servitude, the Irish were undoubtedly white. There is no evidence that Irish immigrants were ever "black" enough to be considered candidates for slavery. Out West, the Irish enjoyed full upward mobility, while blacks, Amerindians, and Mexicans labored in various states of semifreedom. The argument that the Irish needed to become white also ignores the right to vote. The Naturalization Acts of the 1790s, which declared that "any alien, being a free white person, may be admitted to become a citizen of the United States," rendered the Irish, but not African Americans, eligible for citizenship. Later, the Jacksonian tide of white manhood suffrage lifted the Irish boat as much as that of any other European immigrant or native-born male. Though certain New England states sought to reduce the power of Irish immigrants by instituting a brief waiting period between naturalization and voting, many western states actually offered them the vote even *before* they became citizens. "In a country where the right to vote had become intrinsic to understandings of freedom," concludes Eric Foner, "it is difficult to overstate the importance of the fact that white male immigrants [like the Irish] could vote almost from the moment they disembarked in America, while blacks, whose ancestors had lived in the country for centuries (and Indians, who had been there even longer), could not."[7]

While the antebellum Irish were not discriminated against on the basis of their skin color, their Roman Catholicism did stoke nativist fears that, in the words of John Higham, "some influence originating abroad threatened the very life of the nation from within." Catholics had been a part of American society throughout the colonial and early Republic eras, but the massive influxes that accompanied the Great Famine and the Mexican-American War stoked fears that these immigrants' fealty to the pope might outweigh their loyalty to the Republic. Roman Catholicism and American democracy were, in the minds of many nativists, quite simply incompatible. Beyond the stigma of moral depravity that Protestants had attached to popery since the sixteenth century, Catholicism's authoritarianism seemed incongruent with American democracy's emphasis on individual freedom. The Catholic Church's centuries of cooperation with feudal monarchies in Europe strengthened this association. With the sectional division between North and South widening throughout the 1850s, antipopery seemed to offer many native-born Protestants a platform for national unity. Visits by Catholic dignitaries such as Archbishop Gaetano Bedini combined with volatile public debates over Catholic schools and church property to fan the flames of American nativism. Membership in militant populist organizations such as the Order of the Star-Spangled Banner increased rapidly, reaching its political acme in 1854–55 when the Know-Nothing Party got eight state governors, three city mayors, over a hundred congressmen, and thousands of local officials elected to public office.[8]

In comparison to the Australian colonies, therefore, the United States in the middle decades of the nineteenth century was much more hostile toward Irish immigrants. Many believed that free labor and slave labor, the economic bases of North and South, could not coexist in a single nation. Desperate to unite this "house divided," Americans strove for common ground with their fellow native-born. Immigrants, with their foreign languages and strange notions, seemed to import new threats to an already imperiled institution. The fact that most of the newly arriving Irish Catholics were unskilled, landless laborers forced to compete with blacks for work on the wharves and canals of the United States also undermined their position in society. The Irish could vote, own land, and participate in the free market because they were white, but this does not negate the fact that their lowly economic status fed into the discrimination. Irish immigrants' Catholicism also deepened nativist animosity toward them. The authoritarian, monarchical, and supposedly immoral nature of the Church, nativists alleged, rendered its adherents ill fitted for the sturdy individualism of American democracy. In coming to grips with this discrimination, however, the antebellum Irish had a powerful weapon of their own: the printed word. And in the Young Ireland exiles, they had an experienced coterie of writers and editors dedicated to using the weekly newspaper as a "vigilant corrector" against the "daily supply of falsehood" that accosted them.[9]

The Irish American Weekly Press

Most of the Young Irelanders who escaped in the wake of 1848 made their way to New York City. Perhaps the highest-ranking member to do so was Thomas D'Arcy McGee, who arrived in September 1848. Financial help from admirers soon allowed McGee to found a weekly newspaper, and on October 28, 1848, less than six weeks after his arrival in the United States, he sold the first issue of the New York *Nation*. He devoted the new periodical to "Ireland and her Emigrants" and declared as its prime object the "combination and elevation of the world-wide [Celtic] race." It joined the *Boston Pilot*, New York *Freeman's Journal*, and, later, Patrick Lynch's New York *Irish-American* as the community's leading voices in the late 1840s. When Thomas Francis Meagher and John Mitchel escaped from Van Diemen's Land a few years later, they too came to New York and founded Irish American weeklies. In January 1854, Mitchel established the *Citizen* and, later in the decade, the *Southern Citizen*, while Meagher started the *Irish News* in April 1856. In an age of "personal journalism," editors like these co-created with their readerships a platform for the construction and dissemination of information and identity. Connected to other Irish weeklies in Ireland, Britain, the United States, British North America, and Australia, the journals offered a place for Irish people to virtually assemble once a week. For the Irish in the United States, the weekly consolidation of an international imagined community helped to counteract American nativism.[10]

The expansion of the Irish American press was part of the broader growth of American journalism in the late eighteenth and early nineteenth centuries. In 1783, there were only thirty-five newspapers published in the United States, all of them east of the Appalachian Mountains. By 1833, there were 1,200, spread as far as the Mississippi River, and by 1860 the number had reached 3,000 from coast to coast. Technological advances facilitated this expansion. The Fourdrinier machine produced paper that came out as one long, continuous sheet. Steam-driven machines replaced the hand-operated flatbed presses run by slaves and indentured servants. These new "lightning presses," characterized by revolving cylinders with type mounted on them, allowed printers to produce folded newsprint faster than ever before. As specialization increased, the editor replaced the printer as the ideological prime mover of each given journal. In the 1830s, men like Benjamin Henry Day and James Gordon Bennett founded "penny press" publications such as the *New York Sun* and the *New York Herald*, which aimed to increase circulation and advertising numbers by publishing stories of sex and violence. Though dedicated to giving "newsboys something to yell about," these dailies were decidedly sympathetic to the Democratic Party. In April 1841, Horace Greeley gave the Whigs a voice in the penny press when he founded the *New York Tribune*. Partisanship was part and parcel of the business, and editors scoffed at what Greeley referred to as "gagged, mincing neutrality." This was especially true of immigrant editors, who saw themselves as advocates for their beleaguered communities.[11]

Before the late 1840s, Irish American weeklies were a fragile and scattered bunch. Plagued by limited readerships and by squabbles among cantankerous editors, most survived only for a year or two. The majority of early Irish American periodicals such as the *Shamrock, or Hibernian Chronicle* (founded in 1810), *Globe and Emerald* (1824), and *Irish Shield and Monthly Milesian* (1828) were primarily political in focus, but the most popular, New York's *Truth Teller* (1825), was explicitly Catholic. Yet at a time when the *New York Sun* claimed a daily circulation of 10,000, even the *Truth Teller* could boast only 3,000 a week in 1833. Nevertheless, its popularity encouraged others, and for a decade between the mid-1830s and the mid-1840s, the number of Catholic journals increased from six to fifteen. Papers such as the Cincinnati *Catholic Telegraph* (1831), Philadelphia *Catholic Herald* (1833), *Boston Pilot* (1838), New York *Freeman's Journal* (1840), and Pittsburgh *Catholic* (1844) appeared to, as Bishops Francis Patrick Kenrick and John Baptist Purcell put it in 1833, "explain our doctrines, protect our feelings, and increase our devotion." Overall, however, the Irish American press before 1848 was a struggling enterprise with a limited readership. The Great Famine radically altered this situation in two ways. First, the tens of thousands of immigrants streaming into the country monthly provided a vast new market. Second, the exiled Young Irelanders brought a wealth of newspaper experience and radical republicanism that changed the face of the Irish American press.[12]

When Thomas D'Arcy McGee founded the New York *Nation* in October 1848, his years of familiarity with the transatlantic Irish press allowed him to foster the international connections that were so critical to the success of weekly periodicals. Three years before joining the Dublin *Nation* in 1845, McGee had migrated from Ireland to Massachusetts, where, at only nineteen, he briefly edited the *Boston Pilot*. In that position, he managed reciprocal exchange and subscription agreements between the *Pilot* and other newspapers across the United States, Britain, Australia, and Ireland. When he founded the New York *Nation* years later, McGee immediately reestablished those international connections. He envisioned a transatlantic circulation for his new periodical and advertised job opportunities for agents "in all Towns and Cities in the [American] Union, the British Provinces, and Ireland." Taking another lesson from his experiences with the *Boston Pilot*, McGee simultaneously published the paper in three American cities (New York, Boston, and Philadelphia) to avoid the onerous postal levies charged on newspapers carried more than thirty miles. The title of the new weekly was also designed to draw transnational connections between the Irish at home and abroad. It was meant as "an American sequel to the [Dublin] Nation," explained McGee, "to supply its place as far as possible" and to "resemble the old as far as it is in our power to imitate so exalted an original." Like the *Pilot* in Boston and *Freeman's Journals* in New York and Sydney, McGee had explicitly copied the name of an established newspaper from home to lend authenticity to his diasporic one.[13]

While the New York *Nation* reflected the international scope of the newspaper business, it was also susceptible to the internecine quarrels that plagued the immigrant press. Though a practicing Catholic, McGee got in a fight with the powerful bishop of New York, Irish-born "Dagger" J. J. Hughes, when he intemperately used the columns of his new newspaper to blame the Catholic hierarchy for the failure of 1848. In a series of letters published in the New York *Freeman's Journal,* his unofficial mouthpiece, Hughes replied by accusing McGee of belonging to "an Irish tribe whose hearts have apostasized from the honoured creed of their country, but whose lips have not yet mustered the bad courage to disavow the faith of their fathers." The deathblow came when Hughes urged that "every diocese, every parish and every Catholic door should be closed against the [New York] *Nation.*" While Hughes attacked McGee's anticlericalism, the competing secular nationalist Irish paper, the *Irish-American,* assailed him for being too critical of the Irish in America. Caught between the Church and the radical republicans, McGee's newspaper collapsed. Income from advertisements and subscriptions dwindled to a trickle, and by the middle of 1850 the paper was no longer financially viable. In June 1850, McGee closed the New York *Nation.*[14]

Transatlantic personal connections also played an important role in the development of the new Irish American press. Chapter 2 showed that Charles Gavan Duffy stayed in close contact with the prisoners in Van Diemen's Land by sending them batches of newspapers and publishing their open letters. He also stayed in close correspondence with McGee and tried several times to convince him to return to Ireland and rejoin the staff of the Dublin *Nation.* Though the threat of arrest had diminished, however, McGee was defiantly "bound to our outcasts." "Seven months ago I entered this city with £11 in my purse," he told Duffy in May 1849; "since then I received 5,000 dollars, all of which has been sunk, as it came in," into the New York *Nation.* When the paper collapsed in 1850, McGee considered returning to Dublin, but a group of sympathizers encouraged him to accept their financial support and found a new weekly periodical in Boston. On August 31, 1850, just two and a half months after the issue of the last New York *Nation,*

Masthead, *American Celt* (Boston), 1850. By employing the word "Celt" and featuring an image of a young woman in Ireland looking hopefully across the Atlantic, Thomas D'Arcy McGee ensured that his new weekly newspaper drew symbolic connections between the Irish at home and abroad.
American Celt (Boston), September 28, 1850.

the *American Celt* rolled off the printing press. Reciprocal agreements with newspapers in the United States and overseas were reestablished. McGee also ingratiated himself to the Catholic hierarchy. His new prospectus promised to "commence on a clean tablet, with fresh pencils," and leave behind the "controversies . . . errors and omissions of the past." This pleased the clergy but annoyed his former confederates. Fellow exile Richard O'Gorman told Smith O'Brien that McGee had "long since repented of his connection with that infidel Young Ireland Party of 48" and become "a pious Catholic."[15]

Soon after arriving in New York from Van Diemen's Land in May 1852, Thomas Francis Meagher was drawn into conflict with the Catholic press. "To this land I came as an outcast, to seek an honorable home," he told the crowds that welcomed him, "as an outlaw to claim the protection of a flag that is inviolable." He hoped the United States would long prosper, "gathering into the bosom of her great family the children of all nations." Meagher was far less enamored with the Irish American Catholic press. "I declare to God!" he complained in a January 1853 letter to Duffy, "I have found infinitely more bigotry and intolerance in this country, amongst our countrymen, than ever I was sensible of in Ireland." He even awarded preeminence to "the 'American Celt'—McGee's paper," which, along with others like the New York *Freeman's Journal* and the *Boston Pilot*, was guilty of "doing incalculable mischief—lowering the character—encouraging the vices, and diseasing the strength of Ireland in this republic." To stem this tide, Meagher, Dillon, and O'Gorman entreated Duffy to help them found a new weekly in New York "to spread good seed, where weeds and poisoned plants have been thickly set—to build up a great Irish power." They hoped to base the new paper on the ideals of Thomas Davis and the old Dublin *Nation* while, given its American audience, "somewhat more fully generalizing the Irish cause." Meagher's plan fell through, but it was given new impetus later in the year when the indefatigable John Mitchel, having escaped from Van Diemen's Land, arrived safe and sound in Manhattan.[16]

Within a month of arriving in New York, Mitchel founded a weekly newspaper entitled the *Citizen*. The prospectus, which was reprinted as far away as Sydney in the *Freeman's Journal*, was cosigned by his friend Meagher, who left almost immediately on a lecture tour and never played a major role in the newspaper. From his office on Spruce Street, Mitchel immediately established the usual reciprocal exchange agreements with Irish newspapers at home and abroad. The columns of the *Citizen* show some of the ways in which the new weekly circulated overseas. Within a couple of months, H. Searson, a "General News and Periodical Agent" located on Capel Street in Dublin, was advertising himself on both sides of the ocean as the *Citizen*'s Dublin agent. Searson had established a reputation as an agent of Irish American papers, having peddled McGee's New York *Nation* in 1850. In reply to a letter from a reader in Ulster, Mitchel wrote that while Irish readers could presently subscribe only through either Searson in Dublin or the New York office, Mitchel was "quite as anxious as you that we have an agent in Belfast." In the United States, the *Citizen* circulated through domestic channels. James Markey's Citizen House on 499 Pearl Street, New York, claimed to "have constantly on hand a good supply of the choicest Ales, Liquors, and Segars" as well as reading rooms "kept well supplied with Irish and American Papers." Newsagents like Abbe and Yates on Ann Street and William Busteed in Harlem also advertised in the columns of the *Citizen*. Outside large metropolitan areas, traveling agents, often working on behalf of several newspapers at the same time, garnered subscribers in small towns and rural areas. In May 1854, Captain P. G. Coghlan was appointed "to collect subscriptions for the 'Citizen,' and to establish local agencies in the South."[17]

When Meagher finally founded his own New York weekly newspaper on April 12, 1856, his *Irish News*, which he dedicated to "the Irish at home and abroad," stayed true to the New York Democratic policy of supporting states' rights while staying neutral on slavery. From 1856 until the outbreak of the Civil War, the *Irish News* was one of the most important voices in the Irish American community. As with its predecessors, the new journal relied heavily on connections with the homeland. Its staff was drawn from the ranks of unemployed Irish journalists such as James Roche, an experienced Irish newspaperman who had formerly edited the pro-Repeal *Kilkenny Journal*. Fellow Young Ireland exiles John Savage and Richard J. Lalor worked as subeditors, while P. J. "Nicaragua" Smyth acted as the paper's Dublin correspondent. Old confederates such as Duffy and Smith O'Brien were encouraged to contribute articles and letters. While primarily targeted to the Irish in America, the paper maintained a readership in Ireland. "We have regularly mailed several hundred copies to our agent, Mr. Plasto, of 144 Upper Abbey street, Dublin," Meagher noted in the business columns of the paper, "and likewise to our friend Mr. Condon, of Waterford, for sale and distribution as specimens." If Plasto or Condon were inconvenient, the New York office was willing to "regularly send a copy of the News to any part of Ireland, on receipt of subscription at the rate of 16 s[hillings] sterling per annum." In North America, Meagher's traveling agents included Timothy Edward Hughes, J. J. Conway, and H. McCawley, who was authorized to collect subscriptions for the *Irish News* "throughout the Canadas."[18]

In a country where only 9 percent of the population lived in cities containing over 25,000 people, traveling agents crisscrossing the towns and villages in search of subscribers were critical to the extension of a newspaper's subscription list. The potential for graft was great, however, and all newspapers had to deal with a certain amount of loss due to dishonest agents, most of whom either took batches of newspapers and sold them without returning the profits to the main office or collected cash subscriptions from unsuspecting readers and ran. "Of all bad men preserve *us* from a bad Agent," McGee editorialized in the *American Celt* in November 1850. "The evil he does to others is incalculable, while he himself usually gets off scot free." Editors struck back by publishing the names of dishonest agents. Just a few weeks after declaring McCawley its agent for the Canadas, the *Irish News* had to suspend his authority, not having heard from him since he left. Likewise, in February 1857 the *Irish News* had sent a William Boyle in California 5,550 copies "for which we have not received a single cent." Three months later, the *Irish News* stepped up the pressure. "Mr. Boyle has not yet paid us a cent of $192.50, which he owes us," it warned. "If we don't hear from him, with it, by next steamer, we shall instruct our friend, Mr. Emmet, to proceed against him." Certain con artists made a name for themselves in the business. "As to Charles Doorly, of Wooburn, we apprehend he is an incorrigible Swindler," Meagher editorialized in May 1857. "He has been so frequently denounced by the *Boston Pilot, Irish American*, and ourselves, that those who permit him to defraud them hardly deserve better." Readers who refused to pay their subscriptions were another thorn in the side of every paper. Caught between the desire to maintain high circulation numbers and the need to stop giving the paper away for free, editors often sent newspapers to recalcitrant nonpayers in colored wrapping paper as a gentle reminder. When times got tough, they drew a harder line. In the very last issue of the New York *Nation*, McGee claimed that nonpaying subscribers "now owe us for '49 and '50 *over three thousand dollars*," and asked "every honest man among our Subscribers . . . [to] discharge his debts to us." The same problem plagued the New York *Irish News*. "Scattered from Ireland to California there are probably near 1,000 such friends who thus keep us out of pocket some $2,000," it editorialized in June 1860.[19]

While some readers exploited gaps in bookkeeping and policing to more or less steal copies of their favorite weekly papers, editors needed to treat these readers carefully, for they played an important role in the international circulation of newspapers. As we have already seen, personal correspondence between Ireland and Australia often included copies of the local rag. The same was true of the Irish in the United States. "Do you get the *Citizen* regularly?" John Mitchel's wife Jenny wrote to her friend Mary Thompson in Ireland. "It has been sent to you every week. Your name was the first on my list of friends." These exchanges had tangible effects on the circulation of Irish American papers. In response to a letter from a reader in April 1854, John Mitchel said he was "well pleased to hear that you 'have sent from six to eight *Citizens* every week to friends of the Old Cause' in Ireland. It certainly is the most effectual means of circulating the paper there." Mitchel had an agent in Dublin and was seeking other agencies around the country. "The greater portion of our Irish circulation, however," he admitted, "consists in the transmission of *Citizens* from this country to individual friends in Ireland." The revolutionary potential of these transmitted newspapers was not lost on the readers themselves. "Would it not be well to call your subscribers' attention to the fact," a reader named Sarsfield wrote to Mitchel, "that if they would send the *Citizen* to their friends in Ireland, it would give as much publicity to the doctrines it teaches as if it was published there, and stir up the ancient fire against our enemies." The editors themselves, always eager for back issues of newspapers for reference, also encouraged readers to forward any copies of papers they had lying around. "WANTED. For Love or Money," advertised the New York *Nation* in its first issue, "A file or back numbers of the Dublin Nation since its commencement." Similarly, the *Irish News* implored its subscribers for local reports of Saint Patrick's Day celebrations. Readers were more than passive acolytes. They were active apostles in the international circulation of the Irish popular press.[20]

Tensions that had been simmering between Mitchel and Duffy since the former had left the Dublin *Nation* in late 1847 came to the surface in April 1854 when Duffy published an intemperate attack on his former colleague in the Dublin *Nation*. The open letter, which was widely reprinted abroad, accused Mitchel of having dishonorably broken his parole in his escape from Van Diemen's Land, before expanding into a broader assault on Mitchel's character. He was, charged Duffy, a man who "had denied and denounced many things, but discovered nothing." Mitchel had "great demagogic force of expression, but of independent thinking or creative faculty not a jot." Duffy's attack found few supporters and even threatened to split the staff of the Dublin *Nation*. By contrast, many flew to Mitchel's defense. In Ireland, Father Kenyon called Duffy's charge "a manifestation of about as childish spite as a man can fancy." In San Francisco, Mitchel's fellow Australian escapee, Terence Bellew McManus, bitterly regretted "the suicidal—nay Criminal—*personal war* that is still waged among my countrymen." In his defense of John Mitchel, New York *Citizen* assistant editor John McClenahan touched on the international scope of the Irish and their press. Duffy's "naked, unsupported assertion" contradicted what everyone else knew as truth. "The facts of the case published in all the Australian journals agree in every particular, and have never been contradicted," wrote McClenahan. "They have been copied into the Irish and American newspapers," he concluded, "and have not been called in question by any one." Duffy's charges contradicted what a global community had read on the matter.[21]

News and opinion about the Young Ireland exiles maintained connections between the Irish in Australia and the United States even after their escape from Van Diemen's Land. During their imprisonment in Tasmania, McGee had used the columns of the New York *Nation* to keep his readers abreast of their story. "We ask that it shall be read aloud in all places of general resort among [Irish people]," he editorialized, "and that those into whose hands it comes will disseminate it among those who have not seen it." It was up to the readers themselves to spread the news by transmitting copies of individual newspapers. Throughout the 1850s, Irish American papers regularly reprinted clippings of Irish news from Australian periodicals.

"There is no portion of the globe that does not bear the impress of Ireland's genius," editorialized the *Irish News* in 1857. From the far shores of the United States, it was delighted to see Irishmen in the Antipodes assisting "in lifting the Southern Cross above the Union Jack." Following the Young Ireland escapes, Irish Australian editors had their own opinions of the exiles in America. As a Catholic journal in a British colony, the Sydney *Freeman's Journal* was perturbed by their republican speeches, which were printed and reprinted in Irish, American, and Australian papers. "The sincere friends of Ireland all over the globe," it rued in April 1855, "have too much reason to deplore the hair-brained and reckless career of the self-conceited and infatuated 'Young Ireland' party." Dissimilar political environments in the United States and Australia dictated different reactions to the Young Irelanders, but the popular press rendered them a global phenomenon. Even the Sydney *Freeman's Journal* had to acknowledge that Meagher's name and talents had lately been "the subject of much public notice and of national rejoicing . . . on both sides of the Atlantic and Pacific Oceans. In a word, his has become a name of 'World wide celebrity.'" The editors and readers of the Irish popular press made sure of that.[22]

Thanks in part to the massive number of new readers, along with a handful of energetic and ambitious young editors, the Irish American press enjoyed a renaissance in the 1840s and 1850s. The hundreds of thousands of Irish people landing on American shores were accustomed to supporting a vibrant print culture that expressed their sense of isolation, exile, and bitterness toward Britain. Moreover, Young Ireland leaders like McGee, Meagher, and Mitchel had established reputations for themselves in Ireland in the early 1840s as both principled leaders and effective propagandists, which transferred easily to the United States, where their republican credentials earned them accolades from immigrants and the native-born alike. Given the intensity of these personalities and the stakes at play, it comes as no surprise that nasty editorials sometimes sparked fisticuffs in the streets. Michael Doheny threw Thomas D'Arcy McGee down a flight of cellar steps when he saw him in the street in November 1849. Five years later, Meagher reacted to a libelous editorial in the New York *Freeman's Journal* by assaulting its author with a cowhide riding whip (and almost getting shot for his efforts).[23]

Though many Irish American editors and writers hated each other, their weekly periodicals shared many traits. Each and every issue of the antebellum Irish American press reprinted articles, editorials, poems, and letters that had been originally published in overseas newspapers. This, combined with the constant circulation of individual copies of newspapers and the steady transatlantic migration of people, facilitated the international transmission of news and opinion. "During the year just ended," editorialized the *Boston Pilot* in January 1855, "one million five hundred and fifty thousand copies of the Pilot were printed and circulated all over the world!" Agents and readers could, and often did, pilfer copies of their favorite journal. Others took the money and ran. Nevertheless, despite the risk associated with using foreign and traveling agents, Irish American papers continued to employ them, because the agents, along with the readers, were critically important cogs in the international circulation of the Irish press. And the popular press remained Irish America's greatest weapon in the struggle against American nativism. A transatlantic campaign in the columns of the British and American press had built in the minds of many people the myth that Irish Celts were an inferior race. "Anglo-Saxon energy, Anglo-Saxon civilization, invincibility, and manifest destiny have been paraded in every sea and on every shore, and rehearsed in every language," lamented the *Irish News*, "until a great portion of the human race acknowledged its inevitable supremacy." It was up to Irish Celts, and their popular press, to defeat "the myth styled Anglo-Saxonism."[24]

Battling the Saxon Myth

In 1839, the Massachusetts lawyer and politician Robert C. Winthrop exulted at the sight of "this Atlantic seaboard . . . settled by colonies of the Anglo-Saxon race!" His comment reflects the transnational scope of the exclusivist racial nationalism that Irish immigrants faced in the antebellum United States. The mass migration of Irish "Celts" in the mid-nineteenth century played a critical role in the simultaneous rise of international Anglo-Saxonism. Whereas the Australian colonies, for a variety of reasons discussed earlier, featured a gentler form of this racial identity, its American manifestation bore, writes L. P. Curtis, "a remarkable resemblance to Anglo-Saxonist patterns of thought in England." This version was deeply antagonistic toward what one antebellum American observer called the "trouble and annoyance" caused by the recent "influx of hordes of Celts." The transatlantic popular press facilitated this transnational Anglo-Saxonism. In England, newspapers like the London *Times* lauded the Anglo-Saxon race as "the most prolific, the most spreading, the most adventurous, the most ambitious, the most versatile, the most daring, the most persevering, the wealthiest and most powerful people under the sun." Many American newspapers agreed. In 1849, the *Christian Intelligencer* described the Saxon as "the most intellectual, most moral, most considerate, and mightiest being on the globe." The evidence lay in Great Britain, which "has been rising, like a balloon" and "is looked up to as the admiration of all nations." The United States was part of the same growth. "We are the same as they are in substance: and our conquests are the same," claimed the *Christian Intelligencer*. "They are Saxon there: we are Saxon here."[25]

The identification of American nationalism with Anglo-Saxonism dated to at least the late eighteenth century when Thomas Jefferson proposed putting "Hengist and Horsa, the Saxon chiefs from whom we claim the honor of being descended," on the Great Seal of the United States. Jefferson associated English Saxonism with the seventeenth-century Parliamentarian struggle against royal absolutism and, later, with the Whigs versus the Tories, as if, writes Nell Irvin Painter, "liberal and reactionary parties had existed from time immemorial, perpetuating themselves immutably, one generation after the other, as though coursing through the blood." The English writer Sharon Turner's *History of the Anglo-Saxons* (1799–1805) was greeted with acclaim in the United States, and a Philadelphia edition was published in 1841. By 1853, Ralph Waldo Emerson was declaring that it was "right to esteem without regard to geography this industrious liberty-loving Saxon wherever he works—the Saxon, the colossus who bestrides the narrow Atlantic." On both sides of the ocean, many feared that Celtic migration would despoil the centuries-old Anglo-Saxon heritage of freedom and self-government. For nativists, who were opposed to Catholic and radical elements entering the country and distressed by the sight of their country being rent in two by slavery, Anglo-Saxonism provided a transcendental basis for national unity. Their blood, not their skin, threatened the Irish in America.[26]

Though a white identity undeniably played some role in how Irish immigrants thought about themselves, the fear of Anglo-Saxonism, imported from Ireland but shaped by the process of migration, dominated Irish American nationalism. The matter was highlighted in July 1854 when Orestes Brownson used Anglo-Saxonism to defend the proposition that the foreign-born be denied suffrage. The *Pittsburgh Catholic* wished his article had "been free from the contest about races, and the disgusting cant about Anglo-Saxon, Anglo-Norman, and Anglo-something-else," while the New York *Truth Teller* derided his perpetuation of "the humbug of Anglo-Saxonism." James A. McMaster's New York *Freeman's Journal* mocked the "the old hackneyed one about the Americans being 'Anglo-Saxons.'" American society was "a curious, but, we think, not undesirable mixture of the various nationalities that have contributed to form them," and the *Freeman's Journal* rued the fact that Brownson was attempting "to join in turning us all into 'Anglo-Saxons,' when we are no such thing." If anything, the American character was more Celtic than Saxon. John Mitchel similarly rejected Brownson's brand of American nationalism, which required "something more than obedience to law—namely, a submissive demeanour in the presence of one's native American superiors, and a conformity 'to the character of the Anglo-American race.'" There was nothing "Anglican" about the American Constitution, Mitchel argued. Immigrants could promote their ethnic solidarities as long as they did not contradict the duties of citizenship.[27]

The skirmishing over Brownson's article was not an isolated event. Throughout the antebellum era, Irish immigrants consistently decried American Anglo-Saxonism. They did not disagree with periodicals like the *American Whig Review* when it editorialized in September 1851 on the "great influence of race in the production of national character." They did, however, challenge its subsequent claim that American society had been shaped exclusively by Anglo-Saxon language, laws, manners, and customs. In 1849, Thomas D'Arcy McGee used the columns of the New York *Nation* to castigate such "Anglo-Saxon Slang" as "criminal, canting, flippant, puffed-up ignorance." The following year, he recognized that the international popular press was facilitating this phenomenon. "The same parrot cry echoes daily in dozens of editorials from the *Sun, Herald,* and *Tribune* here [in the United States]," wrote McGee in May 1850, "and from the *Times, Chronicle,* and *Standard* in London." When he founded the *American Celt* later that summer, he continued to assault American Anglo-Saxonism. "In choosing the name this paper bears," explained McGee in the inaugural issue, "we meant to adopt the opposite side of a popular theory, namely: that all modern civilization and intelligence—whatever is best and most vital in modern society, came in with the Saxons or Anglo-Saxons." The name Celt was meant as an antidote for this poison. "When 'the Anglo-Saxons' cease to claim America as their exclusive work and inheritance," McGee exhorted, "we will cease using the term *Celt*—but not sooner."[28]

McGee's fellow exiles emphasized the connection between the Anglo-Saxon myth and Know-Nothingism. Nativism was "unconstitutional, un-American, [and] un-Republican," argued John Mitchel, because it denied that a variety of "hardy races of diverse origin and faith" peopled America. Its roots lay in the bad old days in Ireland when Saxons mistreated Celts with impunity. "Thus, in a servile and altogether *provincial* spirit," Mitchel declared, "Americans strive to emulate that nation which oppressed them, which strove to crush them, and which still hates, fears, and despises them, and in the very point wherein that nation is least of all worthy of imitation." Throughout the antebellum era, many Irish-born Protestants of various denominations allied with nativists under the auspices of organizations such as the American Protestant Association, which they had dominated since its founding in 1842. In this context, many believed that the struggle between Celts and Saxons had carried across time and space to continue in nineteenth-century America where, Meagher wrote, "Know-Nothingism, Plug-Uglyism, and Abolitionism, joined with Irish Orangeism" to attack the Irish Celt. It was the duty of every democratic American "to put down this overgrown English lie." After all, the "Irish laborer, the brawny Atlas, who bears the new world, literally upon his shoulders, is the most faithful conservator of our institutions, because he knows that they are his protection to the steps by which his son may rise, like Jackson, to be the scourge of the common enemy of mankind." Anglo-Saxonism, and its cat's-paw, nativism, transcended space and time.[29]

In denying that the legal code, customs, and language of the United States were an Anglo-Saxon inheritance, Irish Catholic immigrants frequently countered that, in fact, America's republicanism was a Celtic inheritance, born of the immemorial struggle between freedom and tyranny. Driven to the American colonies by misgovernment and oppression, wrote Meagher, it was the Celts' "democratic antipathies . . . against the Gothic, brutish George, [which] produced the American Revolution." William Erigena Robinson, an Irish Presbyterian immigrant and a New York lawyer, considered it absurd to suggest that American laws and religion were strictly Anglo-Saxon. "The Anglo-Saxons had no law, save that Might makes Right," he told an Irish American audience in the autumn of 1857, "and no religion, save Paganism, till they came into contact with Celtic civilization." Others felt that the Irish Celts' history rendered them particularly well suited for American democracy. "True to freedom as the magnet to the pole," claimed John Mitchel in 1854, "there is no section of the foreign population who so truly appreciate Republican institutions as the Irish, because there is none that has suffered so much from the cunning despotism of oligarchy." At the fifth annual assembly of the St. Patrick's Society of Brooklyn in March 1854, Mitchel told the guests that the "more faithful Irishmen we are, the better Americans we shall make."[30]

Many of these words and ideas borrowed from the work of the famed Irish-born ethnologist John McElheran, the leading theorist of transatlantic

Celtic racialism at this time. After gaining notoriety in 1852 for his sparkling defense of the Celt in a letter to the London *Times* (see chapter 2), McElheran reappeared in the United States in the mid-1850s with a new book and lecture series for an American audience. These works essentially expanded on the argument that it was Celts, not Saxons (whom he called "the outer rind of humanity"), that had bequeathed America its national character. To illustrate and popularize his arguments, McElheran conducted colorful lectures before packed halls in various cities. One such lecture, titled "The Physiognomy of the American Race," was delivered to a "completely occupied" Tabernacle Hall in New York in October 1856. A correspondent's report of the lecture, published in Meagher's *Irish News* the following Saturday, gives a feel for McElheran's entertaining style of lecturing: "Upwards of one hundred large cartoons of the human head and face were cleverly used [by McElheran] in support of his position that the strongly marked Yankee physiognomy is absolutely and purely Celtic," explained the correspondent. "Great interest and laughter was excited. A sketch of a Paddy with a short pipe and battered hat was unmistakable. The Doctor removed his pipe, clapped on him a goatee, and, presto he was a Frenchman. Away with the beard and his military cap, and there stood revealed the noble features and brow of Washington. . . . [McElheran] observed, that climate alters some things, but not the type. The lecture gave great satisfaction." McElheran's cartoons used popular science to effectively portray the founding fathers of American democracy as Celts. Less obvious was the transnationalism inherent in his lectures. McElheran's argument that the Celt's characteristics transcended time and space was an important element in the developing notion of the Irish as a global nation.[31]

With thousands of Irish migrating abroad throughout the late 1840s and the 1850s, many Irish Americans believed they were witnessing the birth of a new global community. When Thomas D'Arcy McGee founded the New York *Nation* in 1848, he dedicated his new paper to "Ireland and her Emigrants" and held as its goal "the combination and elevation of the worldwide race." The first premise of the paper's nine-point "National Creed" was belief "in the Irish race, one and indivisible," and its motto was Edmund Burke's adage that defined a nation as "a moral essence, not a geographical arrangement or a distinction of the nomenclator." It was "no longer a dead kingdom but a living race we serve," explicated McGee, not "the nation as it was or is, on Irish soil, but the indestructible 'moral essence' of Burke's definition we labor for." The motif found its way into McGee's poetry as well. In August 1850, "A Salutation to the Celts" described an international community:

Hail to our Celtic brethren, wherever they may be,
In the far woods of Oregon, or o'er the Atlantic sea—
Whether they guard banner of St. George in Indian vales,
Or spread beneath the nightless North experimental sails,
One in name, and in fame,
Are the world-divided Gaels.

When he founded his *Citizen* in 1854, John Mitchel described the new Irish nation in similar terms. "Our nation is scattered abroad like the Jews and trampled at home," he editorialized in March 1854, "as no people, or tongue, or nation, Jew or Gentile, ever was before them."[32]

What united this worldwide race? The multivalent nature of global nationalism prohibited an agreed set of tenets. Instead, it served as a rhetorical device to suit times and places. Following the failure of 1848, for example, an embittered and exiled McGee asserted that hatred of the British Empire united all Irish people. "This is our only point of union, our only national bond," he editorialized in June 1849, "the one great popular passion of which the Irish race . . . are [presently] capable." Following his release from Van Diemen's Land, William Smith O'Brien similarly argued that the British government had made a mistake when it drove the Irish from their native land. "Even the attempts which were made to annihilate the Irish race have augmented its power," he argued, and Irish people were now "dispersed over the whole world." Each community contributed to "the aggregate strength and influence of the Irish nation," which would one day overwhelm its enemy. Although the Irish in Australia would not have been willing to espouse such Anglophobia, it did serve as a useful rhetorical tool for many Irish elsewhere. Anti-British rhetoric often filtered into Meagher's public utterances too, but he also liked to suggest that their historical memories connected the Irish around the world. "The national festival of the Irish race is at hand," he told his readers on the eve of Saint Patrick's Day, 1857. "Once more, over the wide earth, the heart of the old race returns to the land of its first love . . . towards the beautiful mother who, in the shadow of the gray cathedrals and towers, wears the ancient crown of emerald." Global nationalism meant different things to different people in different times and places.[33]

As an annual event not tied to a specific spot on the map, Saint Patrick's Day offered a moment around which to rally the Irish international community. In March 1861, for example, New York *Irish News* editor Richard J. Lalor took his readers on a virtual tour that followed the dawning of Saint

Patrick's Day on various Irish communities across the globe. Lauding the transnational sprawl of the Anglo-Saxon race, Daniel Webster had once boasted that the English morning roll call was heard around the world. "We in turn may as truly and emphatically say that the drum and challenge of our Tutelary Saint roll also round the world to the spirit-stirring air of St. Patrick's Day in the Morning," countered Lalor. "For the brave old Celtic Apostle has his drum as well as St. George." Others saw the practical applications of international communion. "In India, in Polynesia, all through America," argued McGee, Saint Patrick's Day "should be kept sacred by us. The sense of having even one day in the year on which, by a common impulse, all our widely scattered race, can give themselves up to national thoughts, refined and elevated by a religious sense of duty," he noted in 1849, "is a bond of sympathy and strength we cannot afford to give up." For McGee, the Irish nation's most important possession was "the individual character of the scattered, uncemented Irishmen of the Earth." On March 17, each and every year, Irish people were reminded that they shared a "Hereditary Cause, which never can be abandoned as hopeless, while a thousand true men of our race, are found upon the Earth."[34]

The Irish in Ireland were also bearing witness to the rise of global nationalism. In a Dublin *Nation* editorial that was subsequently reprinted in the United States and Australia, Duffy pondered the psychological effect of mass migration on the world-scattered Irish nation:

> For those thousands upon thousands who have, by so singular a
> destiny, abandoned Ireland and sat down to create a new Irish Nation
> beyond the Ocean, the pains and difficulties of the Exodus have then
> some alleviation. There is that mysterious bond which triumphs over
> time and region; that intense patriotism which dwells like a second
> soul in the heart of our race; that pure and heroic attachment to their
> beautiful Religion, which in the Woods of the West as in the home-
> steads of their new land makes them so pious and trustful; that
> miraculous spell of kith and kin, yearning affection for their own
> blood, which made poverty joyous and taught the rude hut to shine
> brighter than the palace; that confidence in the resurrection of their
> country and in their destiny to aid it; and now, added to these, the
> presence of the glorious young Patriot [Meagher] who typifies the
> wrongs, the patriotism, the genius, and the glory of their beloved Erin.

The worldwide reprinting of articles such as this illustrates that these transnational ideas enjoyed transnational circulation. Some even believed that

the overseas Irish were more Irish than those who stayed at home. Following his release from Tasmania, Smith O'Brien opined that the Irish in Australia and America "cherish towards Ireland feelings more intensely national than those which at present prevail in this country." Duffy found the same when he migrated to Australia in the late 1850s. In a letter to John Blake Dillon, he expressed ambivalence over moving from one Irish community to another. "There is I am sorry to say no place under the sky of heaven where I would live with so little satisfaction as in the dear old country," he wrote in April 1858. "But there is a nation growing up here [in Australia,] which is more Irish than the remnant at home; and which I can serve with almost as much zeal as if I had got a portfolio from a Government formed by Thomas Davis on the banks of the Liffey."[35]

In ways that were reminiscent of the pre-Famine nationalism described in chapter 1, Irish American global nationalism's strength lay in its flexibility. National allegiance was an especially hot topic in the antebellum United States. Vociferous charges of treason and disunion scarred the public debate over slavery. Nativists, fearful that Catholicism and despotism had warped the hearts and minds of incoming foreigners, challenged the notion that immigrants could ever be truly faithful to American democracy. To resolve the tension inherent in being dually loyal to both *l'esprit* of the Celtic race and *les lois* of the communities they lived in, Irish migrants in the United States combined ethnic solidarity and civic republicanism. The concept worked because people believed that ideologies, like races, transcended time and space. Some, like John Blake Dillon, thought that Irish immigrants should appeal to Americans strictly on the basis of transcendental republicanism. "If you were to tell an American that Celts ought not to be ruled by Saxons, he would say you are either mad or drunk," he wrote to his wife. "But if he should see a people struggling to overthrow a dear and a bad Government, and to replace it by a good and cheap one, he would give a dollar to help them." Despite Dillon's aversion to ethnic solidarity, most Irish Americans sought to interweave it with civic republicanism, and agreed with Thomas D'Arcy McGee that the "distinct existence of the Irish race on this continent is, for the present, necessary for them and for America's greatness."[36]

John Mitchel similarly struck a balance between ethnic and civic nationalism in his first major address in the United States, titled "The Position and Duties of European Refugees." Delivered before a large crowd in the Boston Music Hall on December 28, 1853, it was reprinted in Irish newspapers around the world. "Citizenship (of what Commonwealth soever it be) is a clear and precise idea," he explained. "The citizen, as a citizen, belongs absolutely and exclusively to the State—that is to say, to the community which protects him, which gives him civic privileges, rights and power, which guarantees to him the secure exercise of them by its laws, which guards the sacredness of home, and the quiet enjoyment of the fruits of his industry; that community has a clear title to his sole and undivided allegiance. . . . It would be simply treason towards the Commonwealth if he should pay more regard to the national claims or necessities, to the rights or to the wrongs of any other land—even the land where his mother bore him and where his father's bones are laid—than to those of the new country whose nationality he has voluntarily chosen to take upon him." Yet loyalty to America did not require that immigrants forget their native lands. Mitchel was particularly enthusiastic about ethnic militias. For the Irish, such "national reminiscences" as green uniforms, banners, and the names of Irish saints, kings, and heroes sparked the "memory of ancient glory" in the hearts of Irish American militias, thus rendering them more effective defenders of their new homes. He urged his audience to "act in the affairs of our native country and interest ourselves in her movements and her destinies precisely so far as a native-born citizen may properly do, as an American, and no farther. There is the simple rule." For Mitchel, American republicanism was strengthened by the ethnicity of its European immigrants.[37]

By doggedly espousing a form of dual loyalty that combined ethnic solidarity and civic republicanism, Irish American immigrants helped to legitimate a pluralist vision of American nationalism shared by some native-born citizens. Key similarities between Irish American and native-born speeches on Celts and Saxons suggest that the former informed the latter to some degree. Speaking at an assembly of Baltimore Irish immigrants in 1853, the governor of Maryland, Enoch Louis Lowe, propagated the idea that Irish Celts were a constituent element of the American nation. "Let us remember that we [Americans] are not Saxons, Celts, nor Anglo-Saxons," he said in a speech that was clipped and reprinted in the Irish newspapers in the United States, Ireland, and Australia, "but that every nation of Europe has contributed its blood to the formation of our great amalgamated race. . . . We are altogether *American!*" Others explicitly endorsed the blend of ethnic solidarity and civic republicanism that Mitchel and his friends espoused. In a Saint Patrick's Day address, G. W. Gerard claimed to hold the highest opinion of immigrants who venerated their homelands. The man who "turned his face from his native soil, or forgot the ashes of his domestic hearth or would speak of the bones of his father and mother with perfect coldness and indifference," he concluded, "could not ever make a good American citizen." Irish ethnic solidarity could translate into American civic loyalty.[38]

Despite these pluralist voices, it is indubitable that the hostility Irish American immigrants faced shaped the development of their version of global nationalism. Historians agree that Catholicism, which American nativists associated with immorality and despotism, was one of the main bases on which much anti-Irish hostility stood. Yet the editorial columns of the antebellum Irish American popular press reveal how deeply threatened they felt by the "Anglo-Saxon myth" then being propagated by the mainstream media on both sides of the Atlantic Ocean. A fear of their "unwhiteness" barely registers in these articles. Rather, Irish editors felt challenged by the belief that the United States' laws, customs, and manners were the inheritance of a transnational Anglo-Saxon race. In ways similar to those being simultaneously expressed by their compatriots in Australia, the Irish in America met this supranational threat with a supranational response, which portrayed Irish Celts as an international community joined by blood, customs, and history. This kind of ethnic solidarity was effective at reconstituting and maintaining the imaginary ties disrupted by mass migration, but it did little to convince native-born Americans of their suitability for citizenship. To achieve this, the Irish simultaneously picked up on the pluralist rhetoric of American republicanism: the United States was a racial mosaic to which the fiercely loyal Irish were perfectly fitted. The Irish Celts were, in sum, a global nation capable of expressing dual loyalty to both home and host. The slavery debate tested that twofold fidelity.

The Slavery Debate in Transnational Perspective

In late November 1853, the Dublin abolitionist James Haughton publicly addressed Thomas Francis Meagher with a transatlantic open letter in which he encouraged Meagher and his fellow Irish Americans to disavow black slavery. As advocates of human liberty, the exiled Young Irelanders must stand up for the rights of the enslaved, Haughton reasoned, or risk becoming "a participator in these wrongs." While Meagher's reply was cautious and noncommittal, his colleague John Mitchel used the second issue of his weekly *Citizen* to reply to "our pertinacious little friend" with "a little plain English." "We are not abolitionists; no more abolitionists than Moses, or Socrates, or Jesus Christ," he insisted. "We deny that it is a crime, or a wrong, or even a peccadillo, to hold slaves, to buy slaves, to sell slaves, to keep slaves to their work, by flogging or other needful coercion . . . and as for being a participator in the wrongs, we, for our part, wish we had a good plantation well-stocked with healthy negroes in Alabama." Mitchel's editorial provides fodder for the truism, popular among many American historians, that the Irish "became white" by vehemently supporting slavery. A closer look at the affair, however, complicates this interpretation. "I detest and abhor the slavery of an African negro, a Hill coolie or any coolie," wrote fellow Forty-Eighter Michael Doheny in an open letter to the American press the following week, "precisely as I detest and abhor the slavery of a white Irishman. The pretenses, called arguments, that are heard on the inferiority of race and distinctions of color, I utterly repudiate and stigmatize as fraudulent, barbaric, brutal, and contemptible." A sizable number of Irish Americans agreed. Later in the month, Mitchel conceded to having received "about thirty" letters criticizing his "Alabama Article," and when he sold the newspaper a year later, in part due to weak circulation numbers, he admitted that the editorial had "swept off ten thousand readers at one blow." The kerfuffle over Mitchel's article shows that a full understanding of antebellum Irish immigrant identity must situate their opinions on slavery in broader chronological and transnational contexts than previous historians have offered.[39]

When viewed in a wider context, Mitchel's and Doheny's opinions appear as part of a tradition of ambivalence over slavery among the transatlantic Irish. Chapter 1 showed that white supremacy did not play a significant role in the defeat of Daniel O'Connell's campaign to intertwine Repeal with American antislavery. J. J. Hughes opposed O'Connell's 1842 abolitionist address "not precisely because of the doctrines it contains" but because of their having come from a foreign source. Ten years later, while editing his weekly *American Celt*, McGee replied to a letter from a correspondent who had demeaned a recent antislavery comment published in the Dublin *Nation*. "Our Correspondent surely does not *approve* of Slavery!" wrote McGee in January 1851. "But if our correspondent thinks that leading Irish Politicians should avoid all allusion to Negro Slavery in this country, we entirely agree with him. It gratifies England, it weakens Ireland, and it hurts the feelings of some of our best friends." Even John Mitchel's attitude toward slavery had changed over time and space. While anchored off the shore of Pernambuco on his way to exile in Tasmania in July 1849, Mitchel saw slaves selling oranges from small boats. He surveyed them in earnest, he diarized, "for before this day I never saw a slave in his slavery." While the blacks he saw were "fat and merry, obviously not overworked nor underfed," Mitchel was, nevertheless, unimpressed. "I do not pretend I altogether like the sight of these slaves," he mused. "If I were a rich man I would prefer to have my wealth in any other kind of commodity or investment." Less than five years later, he was clamoring for an entire plantation.[40]

The fact that Mitchel's Alabama Article was elicited by an open letter from a Dublin correspondent reminds us that the Irish debate over slavery was always a transatlantic one. Words, ideas, and memories from Ireland played a critical role in how Irish Americans thought about the subject. Despite O'Connell's failure in the mid-1840s, Haughton publicly called on the Young Irelanders to repudiate slavery soon after their mass escape in 1848. McGee responded that although abolitionism "may be very comprehensive and very exalted," it was the task of Irish nationalists "to liberate their own slaves, not to travel across the Atlantic for foreign objects of sympathy." One month later, he explained the difference between Repeal and abolitionism. "Ireland is geographically a nation, struggling with another nation, England," argued McGee, while "the negroes are a caste *within* this nation." The American question, therefore, was "essentially local and democratic," while the Irish debate was "essentially international and physical." As had its Dublin predecessor, the New York *Nation* deracialized the question by portraying it as a uniquely American problem of states' rights rather than a universal question of oppression. When Haughton pressed the point in William Lloyd Garrison's *Anti-Slavery Standard*, McGee reminded him that Haughton had resigned from the Irish Confederation in 1847 "because out of fifty Irish Nationalists," he could not find one to second "that black hobby of yours." Yet McGee's opposition to antislavery did not translate into white supremacy. "We believe in no fatalism of blood," he editorialized that same year. "We believe that God has scattered his natural gifts pretty equal among all men—and has not opened his hand wider to the Planter than to the Negro who holds the horse at the planter's door."[41]

In a lecture he delivered to the citizens of Richmond, Virginia, in June 1854, Mitchel told them that "the violent storm of censure" that his Alabama Article had elicited from one part of the country was matched by the "generous recognition and warm approval, which it found in another part." American press reactions to his proslavery stance reflected the sectional divide at large. The *Richmond Dispatch* lauded him for having "taken up the cause of the South in a den of abolition wolves," while the Charleston *Courier* defended him against those who "are jealous of that freedom of speech which does not coincide with their ideas of progress and reform." The Louisiana General Assembly passed a resolution praising him for his "able defence in the midst of a fanatical opposition" of those constitutional rights "which are calculated to unite and harmonise the diversified interests of the country." Abolitionists excoriated the Irish exile. The *Liberator* called Mitchel a "moral reptile," while the *Boston Investigator* depicted him as an out-of-touch foreigner whose support for slavery was "very far from being the American sentiment, generally, upon this subject." His most vehement opponent was the Reverend Henry Ward Beecher, who published a series of public letters on the matter in the New York *Independent*. Mitchel was a hypocrite who, by espousing freedom for the Irish but not for the Africans, had fallen "from the category of men persecuted for asserting the great doctrines of human rights, into the position of pitiful caitiff." In his several responses to Beecher, Mitchel attributed abolitionism to English meddling in American affairs. Did Beecher really believe that "the exterminators of Ireland, the roughshod riders of India, the armed speculators of Chinese lives, sincerely wish for the liberty of any being, anywhere under the sun?" demanded Mitchel. Anyone who cared could see "what the devotion of our Anglo-Saxon brethren to the cause of the negro really means. It means mischief. It means eternal antagonism to this republic."[42]

Years later, John Mitchel reflected in his memoirs that antebellum Irish Americans "had but little interest, one way or the other, in negro-slavery." Although the subject still awaits a full-length study, a brief survey of the press suggests that Irish Americans were divided on the matter. Many, perhaps most, followed the northern Democratic line of neutrality and were thus reticent to discuss Mitchel's Alabama Article. When they did broach the subject, most offered gentle disapproval. The *Pittsburgh Catholic* believed that "strangers and refugees must be excused from intermeddling in a native question," while the *Boston Pilot* explicitly cited the Catholic Church as "the only abolitionist society which ever accomplished any good." The secular *Irish-American* distanced itself from Mitchel's sentiments. "Irish-Americans are not advocates of, and do not stand up for, the institution of Slavery, its wrongs and evils," it declared a week after Mitchel's article. At the same time, Mitchel's enemies used his proslavery stance to undermine him. "No wonder you want a plantation of slaves," sniped Archbishop J. J. Hughes in August 1854; "you're an Irish [Protestant] Orangeman and we all know how accustomed they are to oppressing people." Mitchel was no more an Orangeman than was Hughes himself, but the slavery debate provided the archbishop with an opportunity to drive a confessional wedge between the Presbyterian Mitchel and his Catholic readership. Others supported Mitchel. In an open letter to James Haughton from New Orleans, exiled Forty-Eighter Joseph Brenan declared that the Irish peasant's "hat is without a crown, its pocket without a halfcrown, and altogether it is infinitely more slavish than the slaves of New Orleans." Haughton should be ashamed, Brenan concluded, for assailing "the best men of the Irish race, because they will not bear false witness against a country of their adoption and their pride, to gratify universal Mollycoddledom."[43]

In the immediate wake of Mitchel's article, the *New York Tribune* suggested that his opinions reflected those of the Irish American community at large. Fellow Young Irelander Michael Doheny vehemently retorted with an open letter in which he repudiated as "fraudulent, barbaric, brutal, and contemptible" the "pretenses, called arguments, that are based on the inferiority of race and distinctions of color." He maintained the position throughout the 1850s. "It will be said," he told an audience at Hermitage Hall two years later, "that your fellow-citizens of the Celtic family are animated with an inveterate dislike of the Negro." Yet this was a "caricature" manufactured by "the twin cants of Anti-Catholicism and 'Anti-Slavery.'" At the same time, Doheny attacked the "false, fraudulent, and cowardly" creed of abolitionism that aspired to cripple the South. How dare such hypocrites charge that the Irish were proslavery because they would not join the ranks of abolitionism? In an open letter to the New York *Irish News*, which had supported his Hermitage Hall speech as a "sound Democratic effort," Doheny employed Irish history to undermine the *New York Times*' claim that there is "nothing that [an Irishman] hates like a Negro." This was a perversion of the fact, Doheny argued, that slavery was unknown in ancient Ireland. "Not so the Anglo-Saxon—the real Anglo-Saxon," he countered; "he was himself a slave, bound to the soil." In a letter to Smith O'Brien written a couple of years later, Doheny returned to the subject. Since coming to America, he had never "for a moment abandoned the principles which claim equal rights and equal freedom for all men" nor made a speech "in which I have not distinctly disavowed any desire to approve of African slavery." Doheny's tussle with the New York press reminds us that the tradition of tarring all Irish immigrants with the brush of white supremacy goes back to the antebellum era itself.[44]

Press reactions across the political spectrum in Ireland largely opposed Mitchel's proslavery position. In an 1858 letter to a friend, Mitchel rued that "judging from the sort of sentiment entertained towards me by my own closest friends in Ireland, I fear that I must infer you think me (as the rest do) either crazy or depraved." One of the few willing to defend his friend was Father Kenyon, who publicly argued that Mitchel's opinions were such "as the truest lover of liberty . . . may lawfully adopt." More generally, in the context of public opinion within the British Empire, which had abolished the slave trade and slavery itself in 1807 and 1833, respectively, most Irish editors attacked Mitchel. The *Belfast News-Letter*, Ulster's leading Conservative journal, scorned Mitchel's "awful blasphemy," while Duffy's Dublin *Nation* derided "your *escapades* in the *Citizen*, on *Slavery*." The Liberal Presbyterian *Banner of Ulster* declared that "the frightful immorality of [slavery is] as much detested in Ireland as in New England." Echoing Beecher, the Unionist *Dublin Evening Mail* felt that Mitchel's "blasphemous brutality" unmasked his hypocrisy as "a champion of the oppressed." The *Anglo-Celt* thought it left Mitchel "inconsistent with the principles of his own avowing, and opposed to the opinions of the majority of mankind." James Haughton echoed O'Connell's belief that migration changed men's hearts. "Verily, the atmosphere of slavery is corrupting," he wrote in a public letter published in the summer of 1854; "it paralyses all who willingly breathe in it, and expels every manly feeling from hearts that may have long beat responsive to every noble sentiment of our nature."[45]

Disapproval came in the form of personal correspondence from readers in Ireland as well. Family friend Mary Thompson found it "hard to reconcile" Mitchel's republicanism with his proslavery position. He replied that he found her opinion "*incomprehensible*." "Does it not occur to you to inquire," he asked, "whether in other ages, & even so late as the age of our fathers, those two sets of sentiments, now called irreconcilable, were not in fact constantly reconciled"? "My dear lady," he warned, "beware of the Nineteenth Century." When Thompson countered by pointing to the atrocities detailed in Harriet Beecher Stowe's *Uncle Tom's Cabin*, Mitchel replied that the representations of slave life in "that very clever book" were simply untrue. Mitchel's wife, Jenny, also found herself having to defend John's proslavery position to friends in Ireland, assuring Mary Thompson that she hated the topic "because it has vexed you and another dear friend of mine." She told Thompson, "Nothing could induce me to become the mistress of a slave household." Yet it was not the threat to black slaves that Jenny abhorred. "My objection to slavery is the injury it does to the white masters," she wrote, while mindful too that manumitted slaves were "very helpless when left to themselves, suffer miserably, and die off quickly." Jenny was disgusted by the inhumanity of abolitionists, one of whom argued that, as she paraphrased it, "we must get rid of these blacks, their places must be filled by honest white labour, and the quickest way to exterminate them is to give them their freedom." "Now what do you think of that?" asked Jenny.

The Mitchels' correspondence with Mary Thompson shows that the slavery debate was a private as well as a public affair.[46]

On the other side of the world, the Sydney *Freeman's Journal* shared the aversion to slavery then popular across Ireland and the British Empire at large. While it politely ignored Mitchel's Alabama Article, the "unnatural, demoralizing, and debasing 'peculiar Institution'" was a popular target of the journal's editorials in the mid-1850s. "The term 'Slavery' grates harshly upon the Christian's ear, in the 19th century," it argued in 1853, "and brings before the mind associations repulsive to the best feelings of our nature, and abhorrent to the dictates both of reason and Religion." Reaffirming its belief that all men are equal and entitled to freedom, the paper was disgusted to record that there were nearly as many slaves in the United States as there were inhabitants at the time of the signing of the Declaration of Independence. American slavery was founded on the "same sordid spirit of *self-interest*" that had established the convict transportation system and now sought to import cheap coolie labor into the Australian colonies. It also divined similarities between proslavery and American anti-Catholic nativism. While one "grasps the 'sable children of Africa' in the bonds of slavery, the other seeks to retain the fair-faced and free-born emigrants of Europe as vassals and *quasi* bondsmen to the Native-born Americans." Throughout the 1850s, the *Freeman's Journal* reprinted articles and news from English and American newspapers of fugitive slaves and antislavery fund-raisers while propping up Catholic antislavery by reprinting Pope Gregory XVI's 1839 apostolic letter, which denounced the slave trade. Far removed from the heat of battle yet constantly in touch with its progress, the Sydney Irish were free to portray American slavery as part of the universal problem of oppression.[47]

After quitting the New York *Citizen* in December 1854, Mitchel and his family spent an unsuccessful winter living in rural Tennessee before moving to Knoxville. At first, Mitchel attempted to make a living on speaking tours, but he soon tired of the circuit and agreed to cofound a pro-southern weekly newspaper with the mayor of Knoxville, W. J. Swan. In October 1857, the *Southern Citizen* appeared on newsstands. Convinced that "the most elevated, the happiest and the *freest* negroes . . . are those few millions of them who live in bondage," the new paper held that "the Institution of Negro Slavery is a sound, just, wholesome Institution; and *therefore*, that the question of re-opening the African Slave Trade is a question of expediency alone." Mitchel's opinions echoed those of the Virginian controversialist

George Fitzhugh, whose *Sociology for the South; or, the Failure of Free Society* (1854) had argued that the abolition of the slave trade had contributed to the rise of a planter oligarchy by rendering slaves unaffordable to all but the wealthiest of planters. Back in Ireland, even Father Kenyon objected to Mitchel's latest promulgations. "*Why?*" retorted Mitchel. To enslave Africans "is impossible or to set them free either, they are born and bred slaves." Despite this opposition from home, Mitchel continued to fulfill what he considered a civic duty. Slavery was the great question of the "community wherein I undertake to conduct a weekly newspaper, and where I have declared my intention to become a citizen." Over a year later, he was still gripped by this enthusiasm. "As for me, I am 'saving the South' with all my might," he admitted to his sister in April 1859, "indeed, so violently, that a greater part of the South (besides the whole North) thinks me mad."[48]

This transnational perspective on Mitchel's Alabama Article broadens our understanding of antebellum Irish opinions of American slavery. Twenty-first-century American historians tend to accept the truism, first elucidated in the 1850s, that racists like Mitchel reflected the opinions of Irish Americans at large. More careful analysis, however, shows deep ambivalence and even outright opposition to his desire for "a good plantation well-stocked with healthy negroes." The Irish debate over slavery was an international affair in which opinions expressed in Ireland, Australia, and the United States were transmitted back and forth. In this context, Mitchel's proslavery was definitely the exception rather than the rule. Operating within a British imperial context, where public opinion had been overwhelmingly opposed to slavery for several decades, editors and readers in Australia and Ireland were almost uniformly opposed. When, later in the decade, Mitchel began to advocate the revival of the African slave trade, even his most ardent supporters began to lose heart. No wonder that Mitchel's comrade John Martin diarized in 1858 that his friend "had excited the rage and grief of many thousands of his political friends against him by the course he took on the question of Negro slavery." In the United States, the majority of Irish American editors politely distanced themselves from Mitchel's remarks, while others, such as Michael Doheny, explicitly disagreed with him. There were definitely white supremacist elements within the Irish American community. Taken as a whole, however, the population was simply divided over the matter. Indeed, such were the number of Irish American opponents to slavery that, as noted earlier, Mitchel's Alabama Article cost the *Citizen* ten thousand readers. The Irish in America associated abolitionism with the evangelical Protestantism that challenged their membership in the American polity. It did not necessarily follow, however, that they supported slavery. Their greatest threat came not from the blacks below but from the Anglo-Saxons above.[49]

Conclusion

Chapter 3 has confirmed what was beginning to become apparent in chapter 2: that Famine-era Irish migrants responded to the shock of mass migration by reimagining themselves as a global nation. The antagonism they faced in the United States gave the antebellum Irish American version of this global nationalism a sharply defensive edge. Whereas the Irish in Australia were considered charter members of a developing settler colony with muted sectarian tension, those who moved to the United States in the 1840s and 1850s found themselves in a society that prided itself on its Anglo-Saxon Protestant ancestry. Their Celtic *esprit*, the myth held, was fundamentally inimical to *les lois* of American society. It was this legend, rather than their alleged lack of whiteness, that most threatened Irish immigrants. They responded by retooling the Celtic identity O'Connell and the Young Irelanders had fostered in the early 1840s. American Know-Nothings now replaced Anglo-Irish Protestant yeomen and English soldiers as the latest avatars of transnational Anglo-Saxon oppression. Unwilling to forsake the ties torn asunder by mass migration, the Irish reconstituted their group identity around the image of an international community capable of simultaneous loyalty to both the stateless Irish race and the American nation-state. John McElheran's popular lectures neatly articulated this transnational identity. While his historical arguments portrayed the Celts as perennial supporters of democracy and freedom, his humorous cartoons and interchangeable props alleged the worldwide immutability of their physiology. The Irish Celtic race, and the values for which they stood, were global phenomena.

The antebellum Irish countered nativist attacks on their suitability for citizenship by arguing that American political culture was a Celtic, as opposed to Saxon, inheritance. They also adopted a rigid loyalty to the Democratic interpretation of the Constitution, which framed the slavery debate in terms of states' rights. Finding themselves on the margins of a bitterly divided polity, most Irish immigrants adhered to civic republicanism, maintaining that the unity of the United States superseded all else, including universal freedom. This combined with the fact that their enemies, the Know-Nothings, were championing antislavery in the mid-1850s to prohibit

Irish vocal involvement in the debate. Disunionists of all stripes were the enemy. Neutrality was a harbor in the storm. Some prominent Irish leaders, such as Doheny and Mitchel, pushed the extremes of the spectrum, but most maintained a middle ground. The antagonistic response to Mitchel's Alabama Article reminds us of the dangers of uncritically adopting the claim, first espoused by bigoted Protestant evangelicals in the 1850s, that Irish opposition to abolitionism equaled white supremacy. Finally, as it had in Australia, the immigrant press played a critical role in the construction and dissemination of antebellum Irish American identity. By facilitating the transmission of ideas, it rejuvenated Irish racial discourse on a weekly basis, providing a virtual meeting place for the global Irish nation to regularly assemble. In this way, weekly newspapers enabled Irish migrants to modify transnational symbols, values, and discourses and thus chisel out a place for themselves in the United States in the years before the Civil War.

BY THE SPRING OF 1861, the original members of the Young Ireland leadership were living in different corners of the globe. Charles Gavan Duffy, who had migrated to Australia in 1855, was elected to the legislative assembly of Victoria and served as a government minister during the 1860s. Thomas D'Arcy McGee gave up the *American Celt* in 1857 and moved to Canada, where he was elected to public office the following year as a member for Montreal West. John Martin and William Smith O'Brien, fully pardoned by the British government, had returned to Ireland. John Mitchel was in Paris, having quit the *Southern Citizen* in the summer of 1859. After formally divesting himself of control over the *Irish News* in April 1859, Thomas Francis Meagher attempted to maintain his flagging career as a lecturer. Giving up, he spent most of 1860 in Central America as legal counsel for a railway speculator, but he returned to the United States in January 1861, resolved to maintain neutrality over the growing tension between North and South. With the outbreak of the Civil War, however, he and his fellow immigrants were forced to decide what role the Irish race would play in the national struggle.

CHAPTER FOUR

"Scarce a Battlefield from the North Pole to the South"

Irish Celts in the American
Civil War, 1861–1865

The ongoing debate in the United States over whether the Republic should be founded on slave or free labor exploded into war when the guns of the South opened on the federal arsenal of Fort Sumter in Charleston Harbor on April 12, 1861. Three days later, Abraham Lincoln issued a call for 75,000 volunteers to preserve the Union and overthrow the Confederate States of America, based in Richmond, Virginia, under Jefferson Davis. As rebels defending their homes against centralized authority, the Irish living in the South found it easy to justify their support of the Confederacy. Irish Americans living north of the Mason-Dixon Line, however, were in more difficult waters. Before Fort Sumter, Thomas Francis Meagher had maintained his antebellum allegiances, telling a friend that his sympathies were entirely with the South and expressing annoyance when his father-in-law, an ardent Republican, referred to the Confederates as a "set of rebels." "You cannot call eight millions of white freemen '*rebels*,' sir," snapped Meagher in reply; "you may call them '*revolutionists*,' if you will." When hostilities commenced in mid-April, however, Meagher encouraged his fellow Irish immigrants to save the Union. "The Republic, that gave us an asylum and an honorable career—that is the mainstay of human freedom, the world over—is threatened with disruption," he declared. "It is the duty of every liberty-loving citizen to prevent such a calamity at all hazards. Above all is it the duty of us Irish citizens, who aspire to establish a similar form of government in our native land. It is not only our duty to America, but also to Ireland." The Civil War was part of a transnational struggle for democracy. And the Irish had their part to play.[1]

This chapter examines how Irish people in the United States, Ireland, and abroad interpreted Irish participation in the American Civil War. It argues that, thanks in part to extensive worldwide press coverage of the conflict, the war solidified the Irish sense of themselves as an international community. There were, as before, two aspects to this wartime global nationalism. The first was an ethnic solidarity, which portrayed Irish Celts as a race of universal soldiers whose storied reputation for bravery and honor had been earned on countless battlefields across time and space. By emblazoning their battle flags with transnational symbols of Celtic racialism, many of which had been popularized at O'Connell's monster meetings in the early 1840s, Irish Americans painted an inclusive portrait of American nationalism, which challenged Anglo-Saxon hegemony. The second side of Irish global nationalism portrayed the war as part of a transnational ideological struggle. Their new homes, whether north or south of the Mason-Dixon Line, were universal torches in the dark, shedding the light of civic republicanism across America and the world. "We'll trample on all tyrant laws," declared a wartime poem by an Irish soldier. "Hurrah for the old land and the new!" As it had during the previous decade, the Irish popular press played a critical role in this process. By transmitting printed words, weekly periodicals facilitated an international Irish conversation that wended its way into the camps, marches, and bivouacs of the Irish at war.[2]

Minorities in the Armed Forces

The Irish were the second-largest foreign element in the Union forces, behind German Americans. Relatively few Irish immigrated to the United States in 1861 and 1862, but the combination of crop failures in Ireland and the U.S. government's $500 enlistment bounty led to a dramatic increase in each of the next two years. This boost, along with the large preexisting Irish American population, meant that roughly 140,000 men of Irish birth fought for the Union, with about one-third of them enlisting in New York City and its vicinity. Their motivations were many and varied. Some wanted to maintain for future generations the asylum they had found in the United States. Others, especially the underground Fenian Brotherhood, hoped that Irishmen trained in military arts would later overthrow English power in Ireland. Many others enlisted out of basic economic need or the thrill of adventure. Most, to one degree or another, aimed to challenge nativist prejudice and prove their loyalty to the United States. For Charles G. Halpine, author of the popular wartime series *The Life and Adventures . . . of Private Miles O'Reilly*, the goal of the fighting Irishman was "the full equality and fraternity of an American citizen." "Ugly and venomous as was the toad of civil strife," argued Halpine, "it yet carried in its head for the Irish race in America this precious, this inestimable jewel." While varied in their reasons, most agreed on what they were not motivated by: the emancipation of black slaves. Archbishop J. J. Hughes made this clear in October 1861 when he said that while the Irish were happy to fight for the Union, they would "turn away in disgust" from a war against slavery.[3]

The Irish were not the only minority represented in the federal armed forces. Throughout the 1840s and 1850s, more than 4 million Europeans immigrated to the United States, and by 1860 almost one-quarter of the white population living in the northern states, and one in nine of all white Americans, were foreign-born. This stream of immigration continued during the war years, and following the federal occupation of New Orleans in April 1862, the North's control over America's ports meant it could funnel all potential new recruits into the Union forces. Of the 2 million white men who fought for the Union, approximately 25 percent were foreign-born immigrants, leading Sergeant W. M. Andrews of the First Georgia Infantry (Regulars) to grumble that the "Confederates are now fighting the World." Black soldiers and sailors also played important roles in the Union war effort. Almost 179,000 African Americans served in the federal armed forces, constituting approximately 9 percent of the total number of Union troops. For the first year and half of the conflict, the U.S. Army had rejected recruitment applications from blacks, but military expediency and ideological dedication to emancipation led Lincoln to reverse that policy in the final Emancipation Proclamation. From January 1, 1863, onward, African Americans were recruited into the federal army. For many, the significance of the moment could not be overestimated. Black soldier G. E. Hystuns, who served in the Fifty-Fourth Massachusetts Volunteers, believed that arming African Americans would obliterate "that semblance of inferiority of our race, which cruel Slavery has created."[4]

Irishmen also fought for the Confederacy. Coming from one of the most densely populated countries in Europe, those Irish who migrated to the South in the late eighteenth and early nineteenth centuries often found its vastness and isolation disconcerting. They compensated by clustering in rural communities, towns, and cities, and by organizing themselves into labor enclaves on the bustling wharves and expanding railroads of the South. These gangs of unmarried men, accustomed to hard work and harder living, easily translated into antebellum militias that subsequently provided the cores of ethnic Irish companies in the army when war broke out. The Emerald Guard of the Thirty-Third Virginia, for example, was composed chiefly of Irish workers who had followed the Manassas Gap Railroad into the Shenandoah valley. New Orleans was to Confederate recruiting what New York was to the Union. On the eve of the war, approximately 85,000 Irish people lived in the eleven states that would become the Confederacy, with another 95,000 in the three border states. Historians have debated how many of them fought for the Confederacy. In a letter to the Dublin *Nation* at the height of the conflict, John Mitchel gave an estimate of 40,000. Recently, David Gleeson has adduced that this number was far too high but that Irish participation was still impressive. "If one accepts, say, 20,000 as a reasonable compromise," Gleeson argues, "it would mean an enlistment rate just over 50 percent among the eligible Irish in the South, which is still fairly remarkable." The Irish rallied in significant numbers to defend the Confederacy.[5]

A variety of other European ethnic minorities joined the Irish in the ranks of secession. Of the 5.5 million whites living in the eleven rebel states, roughly 4–5 percent (250,000) were foreign-born. When war broke out in April 1861, many European immigrants fled north. Some doubted the legitimacy of Confederate secession, while others, particularly Germans, supported the abolition of slavery. Those who chose to remain did so for a variety of reasons. Many unskilled laborers recognized that their slightly elevated position in society was precariously balanced on the maintenance of slavery. Others did it for the income. Still others saw the South's struggle for independence as part of a broader universal fight against centralized government. "The Southern Confederacy being very difficult of access," wrote Austrian visitor Fitzgerald Ross, "the foreigners who have taken service here have all been impelled to do so by their sympathy with the cause, which is in truth a noble one." Others saw military service as a way to prove their loyalty to their new home and thus reap the fruits of full citizenship. Finally, many were simply conscripted into service by a government desperate for personnel. According to the Confederate draft law of March 1862, immigrants could eschew the draft or earn a discharge if they could prove that they had not taken, nor ever intended to take, citizenship. Many exploited the loophole, but tens of thousands of others stayed to play a significant role in the Confederate armed struggle.[6]

In the North and the South, anti-immigrant discrimination was undoubtedly a part of military life as well. The fact that so many Irish had voted against Lincoln in 1860, for example, led some to question their loyalty to the Union. Many Yankee prudes objected to the willingness of some foreign-born officers to allow their soldiers to break the army's prohibition of alcohol. Charges of anti-Irish discrimination were heightened in the summer of 1862 when an Irish-born veteran of the Mexican-American War, James Shields, was passed over for promotion to a major generalship. The New York *Irish-American* expressed the "indignation felt by every Irish-American at the manner in which the brave and patriotic General Shields has been treated." The Irish were not the only ones to feel they were discriminated against in the armed forces. Many Germans felt, for example, that former Baden officer August Mersey had been denied promotion to colonel by nativist politicians and officers who were envious of him. Carl Uterhard, a physician in the Union medical corps, believed he was incapable of rising to the rank of division surgeon because "Americans have an aversion against all Germans and neglect them everywhere." Nativist discrimination against the foreign-born was rooted in a mix of factors. Some feared the foreign-born would engage in subversive activities, whereas others doubted that their dual loyalties could withstand the pressure of war. Conservative Americans found German abolitionism distasteful, while liberal natives were disgusted by Irish anti-abolitionism.[7]

Despite the discrimination with which ethnic minorities had to contend, the fact remains that the Civil War, especially in its early years, was a low point in the history of American nativism. In his classic study *Strangers in the Land*, John Higham attributes this shift to the immigrants' willingness to flock to the colors. "The war completed the ruin of organized nativism by absorbing xenophobes and immigrants in a common cause," wrote Higham. "The clash that alienated sections reconciled their component nationalities." Indeed, many native-born Americans, on both sides of the sectional divide, encouraged military manifestations of ethnic pride. Parades celebrated the creation of ethnic regiments, ladies' organizations donated silk flags embroidered with a combination of ethnic and American symbols, and native officers lauded the fighting spirit of European soldiers. The historian Christian Samito has even uncovered examples of native-born officers falsely claiming Irish heritage. Germans were celebrated for their skills in engineering, artillery, and regimental music. Brigadier General Joshua Chamberlain fondly remembered how a German band under his command "came over to reciprocate the smiles of heaven by choice music, ministering also to our spiritual upgoings." Irish bravery on the battlefield melted the hardened hearts of many nativists in the Confederacy as well. General Richard Taylor, a former Know-Nothing and a commander in Stonewall Jackson's

Shenandoah valley campaign, appreciated the hearty cheers he heard "from half a hundred Tipperary throats" on one particular occasion, and admitted that "my heart was warmed to an Irishman since that night."[8]

The majority of Americans on both sides of the sectional divide endorsed ethnic pride within the ranks as a mode of recruiting soldiers and maintaining morale. In the North, this was especially true during the early years of the war. Immigrants had energetically responded to Lincoln's original call and were disproportionately represented in the three-month regiments. The public delighted at the sight of orderly lines of men marching out of Manhattan in the spring of 1861 under flags and banners featuring ethnic symbols and commanded by foreign-born officers dressed in flamboyant uniforms and shouting orders in a variety of languages. While African American military service was sidelined, the brave performances of German and Irish soldiers fighting under exiled European Forty-Eighters such as Ludwig Blenker and Thomas Francis Meagher underlined the foreigners' dedication to saving the Union. The same was true of the Confederacy, where ethnic enclaves of unmarried immigrant men working on the wharves and railroads of the South easily transformed into units of foreign-born fighters. This realization that European immigrants were playing a critical role in the prosecution of the war reached the highest levels of government. When the governor of Pennsylvania, Andrew G. Curtin, complained in September 1861 that the Irish were recruiting for an ethnic regiment in his state, the War Department replied that "in this grand struggle no effort must be relaxed to secure the full and earnest sympathy of all nationalities." For Irish immigrants, the war was an opportunity to showcase the Celts as a global race of soldiers engaged in a transnational struggle for freedom and democracy.[9]

The Irish Celts at War

Irish American patriotism was at boiling point when Meagher raised a company of Zouaves to join Michael Corcoran's famous Irish regiment, the New York Sixty-Ninth. Fellow exile Michael Doheny was moved as he watched the men march past cheering crowds on April 23, 1861. "Every heart bled, every eye was wet, every face was flushed, every bosom palpitated," he gushed. "The highest passions of the Celtic race were stirred to their very depths." After a few months stationed at Fort Corcoran on Arlington Heights, the regiment marched into Virginia, where they fought at the first battle of Bull Run at Manassas on July 21, 1861. The "elasticity and enthusiasm of their race seemed to pervade [the Irish soldiers] thoroughly," wrote Meagher enthusiastically, there not being one man "who did not feel that the honor of his race and of its military character was staked that hour upon the conduct of the 69th." Bull Run was a disaster for the federal forces, but Meagher and his men earned wide respect for their bravery in controlling the retreat. President Lincoln soon granted Meagher permission to begin recruiting troops for an entire brigade, consisting of several regiments, and by the end of 1861 the "Irish Brigade" was ready for service in the Army of the Potomac with Meagher as brigade commander. After the early flush of enthusiasm, however, Irish support for the war effort steadily drained during the summer and autumn of 1862 as the brigade suffered heavy casualties at Fair Oaks, Gaine's Mill, and Antietam. In the wake of their suicidal charge at Fredericksburg in December 1862, many in the community agreed that Irish soldiers were being "slaughtered like sheep, and no result but defeat."[10]

By marching beneath flags emblazoned with both Irish and American nationalist symbols, the brigade encapsulated the blend of ethnic solidarity and civic republicanism that characterized the Irish American brand of global nationalism. David Power Conyngham, a staff officer and later a New York *Herald* war correspondent, described the brigade's Irish flag as "of a deep rich green heavily fringed, having in the centre a richly embroidered Irish harp, with a sunburst above it and a wreath of shamrock beneath." Speaking at the flag dedication ceremony, Irish American jurist Charles P. Daly compared the South's secession to Irish history. "This green flag, with its ancient harp, its burst of sunlight, and its motto from Ossian, in the old Irish tongue," he explained, "conveys more eloquently than by words how [Irish] nationality was lost through the practical working of that doctrine of secession for which the rebellious States of the South have taken up arms." Other Irish regiments in the federal forces marched under American and Irish flags as well. The Massachusetts 9th Volunteers' flag featured an Irish harp strung with red, white, and blue strings and a motto that read: "As aliens and strangers thou didst us befriend, as sons and true patriots, we do thee defend." When the governor of Massachusetts, John Albion Andrew, presented the Massachusetts Twenty-Eighth Regiment with a similar flag, its commander, William Montieth, assured him that the men would be inspired by both the American stars, which "shall illumine our onward march to victory," and "the flag of Old Erin . . . whose magical tones recall to mind the deeds of by-gone days." The flags symbolized the Irish race's global, timeless struggle for liberty.[11]

In his recruitment speeches, Meagher continually reminded his audiences of the Irish Celtic race's long-held worldwide reputation for military strength and valor. Irish exiles had served at Cremona and Ramillies during the War of Spanish Succession, and a brigade of Irish volunteers had fought for Pius IX and the Papal States in Italy in 1860. The most commonly cited example, however, harkened back to the battle of Fontenoy in eighteenth-century France. There, in 1745, a daring bayonet charge by a brigade of Irish exiles fighting in the French army had turned the tide of an important battle against the English. Fontenoy and other past exploits of Irish Celtic heroism were regular fixtures in Irish American martial rhetoric. The phrase "Sixty-Ninth, remember Fontenoy" was embroidered on the regiment's main flag. Legend has it that when his horse was shot out from under him at Bull Run, Meagher jumped to his feet, waved his sword over his head, and shouted, "Boys! Look at the flag and remember Ireland and Fontenoy." Meagher liked to remind his soldiers of the "glorious legacy bequeathed to them from a long line of military ancestors, dating . . . as far back as five centuries." It was up to the nineteenth-century Irish, wherever they found themselves, to uphold that tradition of excellence. "The Irish race questions not the potency of the laws or the fastness of the cause in which they are engaged," he declared, but "stand by the flag, which they have sworn to defend." Irish fealty transcended both time and space.[12]

Irish supporters of the Union effort often portrayed Ireland's campaign for political independence from Britain and the American fight against secession as parallel struggles in an international fight for freedom. Indeed, the Fenian Brotherhood, which had been founded in New York in 1858 with the goal of overthrowing English rule in Ireland, believed that the Irish in America should use the Civil War as a training ground for an eventual Irish American invasion of Ireland. Units, or "circles," of Fenians openly operated in the militaries on both sides of the Mason-Dixon Line. Meagher often reiterated this Fenian dream. "To-day it is for the American Republic we fight," he told his troops; "to-morrow it will be for Ireland." Writing to the editor of the New York *Irish News* from Fort Corcoran in July 1861, an Irish soldier expressed similar sentiments. Should England formally recognize the Confederacy, it was the duty of every good Irish American to recross the Atlantic and return to Ireland armed with American guns and military training. "PJR" hoped that remembrance of the "accumulated wrongs of seven centuries" would "nerve their arms to strike for the liberty of their native land, and smite to the earth the accursed Sassenachs, the violators of the rights and liberties of every people with whom these Saxons have ever had any intercourse!" In an open letter to B. S. Treanor, Meagher wrote that Irish immigrants must defend the United States against England, "a power which has been, as all the world knows, the inveterate enemy of our race—of its happiness and liberty at home—of its success and good name abroad." The Irish race's patriotic responsibilities knew no borders.[13]

The image of Irish Celts as a timeless, global nation of soldiers served Irish American public opinion in bad times as well. The Irish Brigade suffered relatively high casualties at the Battle of Seven Pines (Fair Oaks) in May 1862, its first major engagement after Bull Run. By the time Meagher returned to New York two months later to replenish his ranks with new recruits, editorials in the Irish American press were complaining that the brigade's numbers had been disproportionately thinned through overmarching, underfeeding, and exposure to greater danger and illness than most other military units. Meagher addressed the matter head on by admitting that they had done a disproportionate amount of fighting. "Well, whose fault is that?" he demanded. "If Irishmen had not long ago established for themselves a reputation for fighting, with a consummate address and a superlative ability; if it had not long ago been accepted, the world over, as a gospel truth, that Galway beats Bannagher, and Bannagher beats the devil . . . you may depend on it, the Irish Brigade would not have had any more fighting to do than any one else." The Irish Celt's reputation spanned the history of the earth. The loss of Irish life "on the battle-fields of the New World, transmits the military reputation of our race," he explained, "and so redeems, by a page of honest valor, the contemporary history of a people from whose political scepter, in the ancient palace, the pride and power seem to have passed away." As a nation of universal soldiers, the Irish must be prepared to endure the loss of life and limb in defense of their old and new homes.[14]

Honorable military service also offered the Irish a golden opportunity to overcome nativism. At a recruiting speech delivered at Boston Music Hall in September 1861 and subsequently reprinted in Irish papers overseas, Meagher explained that the gusto with which "the adopted citizens of the United States, German as well as Irish," had bounded into the conflict undermined antiforeign attitudes in America. Standing in the heart of a city whose Boston Brahmins had for so long insulted Irish Catholic immigrants, Meagher confidently declared, "Know-Nothingism is dead." The Civil War was allowing the Irish immigrant to stand proudly before his native-born fellow soldier, "look him straight and sternly in the face, and tell him that he has been equal to him in his allegiance to the Constitution." Here in the

United States, where "the genius of his race" could finally, fully bloom, the Irishman found his rights restored. Some native-born Americans objected to the use of ethnic units in the military on the grounds that the maintenance of Old World solidarity within the ranks undermined American unity. Meagher rejected the idea. An "Irishman never fights so well as when he has an Irishman for his comrade," he told his audience in Boston, because if an Irish soldier fell, he would do so "into the arms of one of his own faith and blood." Fellow Irishmen could then attest that "he died in a way worthy, not only of that cause in which he fell, but of the country that gave him birth." In times of trouble and strife, ethnic solidarity was "a natural, a beautiful, a generous, and a useful prejudice." Ethnic solidarity paradoxically strengthened civic republicanism.[15]

When Ambrose Burnside took over command of the Army of the Potomac in November 1862, he determined to push through Fredericksburg, Virginia. There, on the banks of the Rappahannock River, Confederate forces under General Robert E. Lee, including a small number of Irish immigrants, were dug into the hills above and behind the town. Meagher's brigade, tasked with a full frontal charge of the seemingly insurmountable Confederate lines, had it the worst. Insistent that the brigade go into battle under "the colors of their Fatherland," Meagher instructed that each man put a sprig of evergreen boxwood in his cap. The brigade's suffering that day has entered the pantheon of Irish American legend. It lost 45 percent of its manpower, including fifty-five officers killed or wounded. The Sixty-Ninth Regiment alone lost 112 of the 173 who marched into battle. Brigade chaplain Father William Corby later described the battlefield as "simply a slaughter-pen." Legend has it that cheers for the bravery of Meagher's brigade went up among the Irish soldiers in the Confederate lines on Marye's Heights, and when the Irish kept coming, one commander is reputed to have complained to see "those damn green flags again." The Irish-born London *Times* war correspondent William Howard Russell reiterated Irish global nationalism in his reflections on the day. "Never at Fontenoy, Albuera, or at Waterloo, was more undaunted courage displayed by the sons of Erin," he wrote. The brigade "pressed on to death with the dauntlessness of a race which has gained glory on a thousand battle-fields, and never more richly deserved it than at the foot of Marye's Heights on the 13th day of December 1862."[16]

In the wake of Fredericksburg, the Irish American community in the northern states found solace in the image of themselves as a soldierly, global nation. On January 16, 1863, a requiem mass in honor of the brigade's dead was celebrated at St. Patrick's Cathedral in Manhattan. At the service, Meagher's friend and fellow Young Irelander, John Savage, read a poem he had written for the occasion:

> Proud beats the heart while it sorrowing melts
> O'er the death-won fame of these truthful Celts.
> For the scattered graves over which we pray
> Will shine like stars on their race alway.
> . . .
> And oh! what doth build up a nation's weal,
> But courage to fight for the truths we feel!
> And thus did these braves, on whose graves we wait,
> Do all that make nations and races great.

The ambiguity in Savage's poem about which "nation" the Celts had fought for is noteworthy. Celtic identity could operate interchangeably within both Irish ethnic solidarity and American civic republicanism. After repeatedly failing to gain rest and recruits for the Irish Brigade, Meagher resigned his command in May 1863. To remain in charge of a brigade that, for all intents and purposes, had failed to exist, he explained in his letter of resignation, would threaten "the military reputation of a brave old race" and risk inflicting "sorrow and humiliation upon a race who, having lost almost everything else, find in their character for courage and loyalty an invaluable gift." After a final address to the officers and soldiers of the brigade, Meagher walked tearfully past the ranks one last time, shaking hands with each and every soldier.[17]

The Irish in the South also employed the discourse of Celts and Saxons to make sense of their role in the Civil War. Unlike the Irish in the North, however, whose Celtic pride scuffled for equality with American Anglo-Saxonism, the southern Irish found that many native-born southerners shared the notion of being racially distinct from the Saxon North. Building on Robert Knox's *The Races of Men* (1850), many southerners began seeing themselves as members of a Norman—as opposed to Saxon—race, and therefore part of the wider Celtic race. Robert Knox had derided the Celts as feudal aristocrats, but Confederate apologists embraced the idea by eagerly portraying themselves as an honorable, conservative race of Cavaliers. By the time war broke out in April 1861, many southerners identified themselves as a warrior race whose bravery, loyalty, and honor would carry the day. "We are socially and politically as distinct a people from the North, as from France or England," explained the *Richmond Examiner*. "The people of the South belong to the brave, impulsive, hospitable, and generous Celtic race; the people of the North to the cold, phlegmatic Teutonic race." Writing in the *Southern Literary Messenger* in late 1863, Dr. Stuart used demographic statistics and historical evidence to show that "our Southern progenitors [maintained] . . . an undeviating antagonism to the people and the principles identified with 'Anglo-Saxonism.'" European Celtic immigrants had tended to "seek fraternity in the South," Stuart argued, while "the Saxonish, or Northern peoples of the European continent" followed "a similar course of preference, for a *kindred* cause, toward the North."[18]

John Mitchel loudly agreed that the sectional divide represented a broader struggle between two separate racial nations. In May 1854, following his first trip to Virginia, he reflected that he had begun "to understand fully now, what I had partly suspected before, that dwelling on this land of the United States there are two nations, not one only; and that the two are separated not more sharply by a geographical line than by their institutions, habits, industrial requirements, and political principles." Three years later, he wrote to his old friend in Ireland, Father Kenyon, that the division between the northern and southern states reflected the difference between Ireland and Britain that Young Ireland had championed in the 1840s. He saw in the institutions, tendencies, and aspirations of the South "a special hostility to the British system" that was "founded on essential differences in the two types of human society." The South was "trying one form of civilization, and with signal success; England has tried another (I should say *the* other), and is shortly going to ruin." Mitchel's goal was "to promote the success of the one" and the failure of the other. While he was living in Paris during the first year of the Civil War, this two-nation theory remained. "The North and South are two nations, as much as France and England," he wrote in an open letter to the editor of the Dublin *Irishman* that was reprinted in the Irish American press; "their civilizations rest on different bases; their systems revolve around different centres."[19]

Mitchel often used the racial discourse of Celts and Saxons to express this two-nation theory. "In race, then, being Celtic," he wrote John Martin in 1858, "the South is a new Ireland; her rival another England. Can you wonder that I am a Southerner?" Dissatisfied with living in Europe while war raged in America, he crossed the Atlantic and slipped, incognito, through Union lines to Richmond, Virginia, where he was promptly hired as editor of the Richmond *Enquirer*, Jefferson Davis's semiofficial organ. Though dedicated to the Confederacy, Mitchel stayed in touch with the outside Irish world through open letters to the popular press. In an 1863 letter to the

Dublin *Nation* that was subsequently reprinted in Irish papers overseas, Mitchel described the sectional conflict in terms that Irish nationalists would appreciate.

> One gratifying fact is, that Confederates now universally repudiate "Anglo-Saxonism." The British, indeed, by way of paying them a compliment, claim them as Anglo-Saxons; but they politely decline the honour. The word has disappeared from the Confederate press; and there is nothing inculcated more persistently than the fact, that separation from the Yankees was necessary (amongst other reasons) by reason of the difference of *race*. We consider ourselves here rather to belong to the "Latin races," and claim kindred with the Celts. The large proportion of French and Spanish, as well as of Irish, Scotch, and Welsh blood in this Southern country, justifies the doctrine; and accordingly the whole Confederate people hail with joy the establishment of French power in Mexico. France is regarded as our natural ally, and the unfriendly course of England towards the confederacy has aroused a much more profound aversion towards that people amongst Confederates than exists amongst the Yankees.

The ageless, boundless battle between Celt and Saxon was alive and well in the war-torn United States. While Mitchel's Celtic discourse was undoubtedly tailored to fit the prejudices of his international Irish audience, it is indubitable that he was trying to shape southern identity as well. Troubled by the South's cozy commercial relationship with Great Britain, Mitchel was seeking to undermine Anglo-Confederate sympathies.[20]

Though Mitchel was eager to nurture Celticism within the Confederacy, his letters to the outside world simultaneously tried to suggest that the Irish in the South had forgone ethnic solidarity and thrown themselves entirely behind loyalty to the Confederacy. The Irish soldiers of the South were fighting "for their homes, and property, and life against invaders," he wrote; "*they* are in their duty, and are driven to arms by as strong and imperious a necessity as ever impelled Switzers to fight the Austrians at Sempach." The Irish in the Union forces, by contrast, were "guilty parties to the foulest crusade of modern times—to desolate the homes of a people who have never wronged them, and a large proportion of whom are their own kindred." Unlike the Yankee Irish, declared Mitchel, the Irish in the South did not march under ethnic symbols. "Nobody has the right to unfurl the colors of Ireland in a war of invasion and plunder and coercion," he exhorted, and the southern Irish "have never pretended to mix up their native country in the struggle."

They "indulge in no Fontenoyism; they flaunt no Sunbursts; they display on their banners no Round Towers, Wolf Dogs, or Crownless Harps," he continued, "but go ahead quite simply, under the Stars and Bars of their adopted country, to defend their own homes and hearts from a host of greedy invaders." Mitchel was attempting to subordinate ethnic solidarity within Confederate civic nationalism.[21]

Despite Mitchel's claims to the contrary, it is clear that the Irish of the South, like their compatriots in the North, explicitly drew parallels between Irish and American history. Many saw themselves carrying on an Irish tradition of halting centralized government in local affairs. This is not to deny, of course, that white supremacy played a role in motivating the southern Irish. In a May 1861 letter to the editor of the New York *Irish News*, entitled "A Voice from the South," "L" in Macon, Georgia, stated a belief that the "kindness of [wealthy] Southern men to the laboring white men, eating at his table and treated as his equal," was something worth saving. "L" trusted that "the Irishman on this soil fighting for his honor, will meet no Irishman in the ranks of an army invading them." Yet many Irish believed that the South's campaign to unravel the United States reflected the Irish struggle to repeal the Act of Union. In an open letter to Meagher, a Thomas McMahon of Charleston wondered if the Young Ireland hero was "blind to the singular inconsistency" that he, "an Irish refugee, who in the sacred cause of Ireland's injured rights, rebelled against England's tyranny and oppression on the motherland . . . now buckles on the armor of Exeter Hall's fanaticism to strike down the liberties of a people contending only for the inalienable privileges of self-government." Southern secession was yet another struggle to safeguard homes from "foreign" invasion. Similarly, a letter to the editor of the *Charleston Catholic Miscellany* by an Irishman named "E. G." regretted to see "the Irish Catholics of the North side by side with the black-hearted Puritan, the enemy of their race and creed."[22]

Symbols of Irish ethnic and racial discourse played an important role in Confederate Irish martial culture. The war cry "Faugh a Ballagh," popularized by Charles Gavan Duffy in a pre-1848 poem published in the Dublin *Nation*, was used by several units. Military companies also routinely named themselves after heroes of Irish and Irish American history, while the Thirteenth Louisiana Regiment included an Irish company called the Southern Celts. Sometimes, split loyalties necessitated name changes. The South Carolina Meagher Guards and the New York Mitchel Light Guards did so when the war broke out. As in the North, flags were also emblazoned with symbols of both Confederate and Irish nationalism. In Charleston, South Carolina, Bishop Patrick Lynch had renamed the *United States Catholic Miscellany* the *Charleston Catholic Miscellany*. On September 17, 1861, he led the city's Irish community in a flag presentation ceremony in front of the Catholic cathedral. On one side, according to a contemporary report, "was the harp of old Ireland, encircled in a wreath of shamrock. . . . The reverse bore the palmetto—that noble tree, which stand[s] the faithful sentinel of our shores." Invoking God's blessing on the local Irish volunteers and their flags, Lynch told the men that they were "of a race that has ever made brave and valiant and chivalrous soldiers; that has won imperishable laurels of military glory on many a well-fought field." In his acceptance speech, Captain Magrath urged his Irish soldiers to remember that they came from a land "which had furnished heroes and orators and statesmen for the world—a land, whose valor had been illustrated in every land, upon every battle-field."[23]

Whether aligned with the Union or the Confederacy, Irish immigrants responded to the Civil War with variants of the same global nationalism. "As we write, the Celtic element is on fire throughout the city," declared the New York *Irish News* in the days after Fort Sumter. "No wonder that a proverbial race of soldiers, a race that has left its charging footprints on a thousand battle-fields and borne its own and other flags in fierce whirlwinds over the wide world should, at this very moment be vehemently stirred." This transnational ethnic solidarity worked for Irishmen on both sides of the Mason-Dixon Line as they decorated their battle flags with symbols of Irish Celtic racial identity such as harps, shamrocks, and wolfhounds. Ethnic solidarity transcended time and space, but so too did the ideological issues at stake in the war. Both sides believed that the Civil War was being fought over universal issues of freedom and democracy that their political activity in Ireland had prepared them for. It is ironic, therefore, that many, including the Fenians, portrayed the war as a training ground for the liberation of Ireland. In many ways, Ireland had prepared them for America. All of this undermined the anti–Irish Catholic nativism that had pockmarked antebellum society, North and South. As Americans of various backgrounds united under arms, a broader, more pluralist vision of American nationality emerged, which the Irish played a central role in formulating. Thus the pride with which Meagher noted "the mottoes and insignia of the various nationalities that diversified the character of the national army." This inclusive vision of the American nation, however, did not always include people of color.[24]

Slavery and Emancipation

When war broke out in April 1861, President Abraham Lincoln's main goal was to restore the Union, not to end slavery. Indeed, he explicitly reiterated his pledge to accept slavery in the states where it existed. Several factors encouraged the administration to maintain this cautious policy in the early days of the war. It helped to retain the loyalty of the border states while dodging legal questions over the president's authority to free the slaves. Racist attitudes among some northerners, who feared an influx of freed blacks, were also a factor. As the fighting progressed, however, runaway blacks forced the issue by crossing Union lines and providing the federals with valuable information and labor. The sheer number of these "contraband" fugitives soon made it clear that some form of emancipation was going to have to be enacted. Horace Greeley's *New York Tribune* poked at the president's temerity. "On the face of this wide earth, Mr. President, there is not one disinterested, determined, intelligent champion of the Union cause," wrote Greeley, "who does not feel . . . that the rebellion, if crushed tomorrow, would be renewed within a year if slavery were left in full vigor." By the autumn of 1862, the Lincoln administration had decided that complete emancipation, justified under the president's war powers, was now integral to the restoration of the Union. In the wake of the federal victory at Antietam in September, Lincoln issued a preliminary promise, which was followed on January 1, 1863, by the final Emancipation Proclamation. All slaves were "thenceforward and forever free," while free blacks were eligible to join the Union's armed forces.[25]

As we have seen, however, the spring and early summer of 1863 was a time of deep disillusionment for the Irish in the North. In three battles between June and December 1862 (Seven Pines, Antietam, and Fredericksburg), the Irish had lost staggering numbers of dead and wounded. "If the Brigade were not so markedly and distinctively *Irish*," complained the *Irish-American* in March 1863, "they would not have been treated with the positive injustice and neglect to which they have been exposed." This anger was enflamed by the government's new policy on slavery. Though some, such as the Pittsburgh *Catholic* and the Cincinnati *Telegraph*, supported the decision, the majority of Irish American Catholic leaders opposed abolition as a war aim. When President Lincoln issued his preliminary Emancipation Proclamation in September 1862, just days after the Irish Brigade's bloody losses at Antietam, the disillusionment deepened. The Boston *Pilot* complained that after nearly two years of loyalty to the Union, the Irish found themselves fighting "in an abolition war," while the *Irish-American* reminded its readers of "the irredeemable malignity of the Abolition hatred of [the Irish] race." Resentment continued to build in March 1863 when Congress passed the Conscription Act. Its substitution clause (offering exemption to those who could either pay a $300 fee or find someone to take their place) convinced many Irish that it was the poor who were going to finish fighting the war. Even though enforcement of the act was to be handled by Colonel Robert Nugent, a hero of the New York Sixty-Ninth, the local Irish were deeply opposed to the draft. "When the President called upon [the Irish] to go and carry on a war for the nigger," declared the New York *Freeman's Journal*, "he would be d——d if he believed they would go." Failure to resist the draft would constitute "an apathy that denotes an enervated, emasculated and slavish people."[26]

Irish Americans on both sides of the sectional divide were also largely opposed to the suggestion of offering southern blacks emancipation in exchange for military service. Archbishop J. J. Hughes never liked the idea. In a May 1861 editorial in the New York *Metropolitan Record*, Hughes urged both sides to conduct "a war that will be open and manly" and will secure "justice and equal rights to all." He derided the suggestion that captured southern plantations be divided among Union soldiers, noting that such a "wholesale system of spoliation" mirrored the English policy in Ireland. Yet Hughes was even more vehement in his attack on the proposal to incite insurrection among southern blacks, which, he warned, would unleash "all the horrors of a servile war." A black revolution would "re-enact on our own soil the fiendish brutalities" of the San Domingo revolution, "rouse the savage nature of the negro against our brothers in race and blood," and witness the "excesses and cruelties, which characterize all negro insurrections." Urging decision makers not to forget their Christian duties, Hughes feared the war would devolve into "a brutal and sanguinary struggle that will spread woe and desolation over nearly one half of the land."[27]

Peter Welsh, a private in the Irish Brigade, had more complicated views on the arming of blacks. Welsh was not an abolitionist and derided the "fanatical nigger worshippers" in the Lincoln administration. Echoing Mitchel, he held that abolitionism had been introduced through the "intriguing of that accursed harlot of nations, England," which sought "to divide this country and thereby destroy her power and greatness." Still, if slavery stood in the way of the unity of the United States, "then I say away with both slaves and slavery." When he saw "by late papers" that the governor of Massachusetts had been authorized to "raise nigger regiments,"

Welsh assured his wife that "whether they have the grit to go into battle or not, if they are placed in front [with] any brigade of this army behind them, they will have to go in or they will meet as hot a reception in their retreat as in their advance." Welsh noted that there was strong feeling against blacks among white soldiers who blamed them for the war. This sentiment, he wrote, "is especially strong in the Irish regiments." The idea of blacks serving in the military was given impetus when some began to argue that the policy might actually be advantageous to whites. The Irish-born poet and journalist Charles G. Halpine, who briefly served in the New York Sixty-Ninth, regularly sent popular poems and articles to the New York press under the pseudonym Private Miles O'Reilly. O'Reilly's ribald satire purportedly reflected the opinions of the average Irish soldier fighting in the Union army. One of his most famous songs, "Sambo's Right to Be Kilt," addressed the question of black military service:

> Some tell us 'tis a burnin' shame
> To make the naygurs fight;
> And that the thrade of bein' kilt
> Belongs but to the white:
> But as for me, upon my sowl!
> So liberal are we here,
> I'll let Sambo be murthered instead of myself,
> On every day in the year.

As one scholar has noted, the poem "could persuade whites to accept blacks as soldiers without in the least disturbing their fundamental prejudices against Negroes."[28]

By 1864, southerners were also wrestling with whether or not to employ black troops. The issue laid bare a paradox at the heart of the slaveholding republic: saving the Confederacy might require using blacks as soldiers, but doing so would undermine the notion that they were suitable only for slavery. Nevertheless, some were willing to countenance the idea. One was the Irish-born Protestant Patrick R. Cleburne, one of only two foreign-born Confederates to reach the rank of major general and undoubtedly the most famous Irish person to fight for the South. Born in County Cork in 1828, Cleburne spent a short stint in the British army before migrating to New Orleans in 1849 and eventually becoming a lawyer in Helena, Arkansas. In the spring of 1861, he raised the Yell (County) Rifles and soon rose through the ranks, eventually becoming major general of the Army of the Tennessee, where he earned the nickname Stonewall Jackson of the West. Alarmed by the South's draining manpower in January 1864, Cleburne caused a stir when he proposed offering emancipation to any black slave willing to enlist in the Confederate forces. "Between the loss of independence and the loss of slavery," he figured, "we assume that every patriot will freely give up the latter—give up the negro slave rather than be a slave himself." Jefferson Davis officially suppressed the idea, and many have subsequently suggested that the proposal prohibited any further promotion for Cleburne, although his lack of a West Point education, foreign nativity, and death later in the year certainly played roles too.[29]

By late 1864, however, as the war became less about saving slavery and more about maintaining national independence, the Confederate leadership began warming to the idea. With manpower at dangerously low levels, Jefferson Davis and his advisers were now willing to consider emancipating some slaves to fight. Blacks possessed all "the physical qualifications," reasoned Robert E. Lee, while their "habits of obedience and subordination . . . furnish an excellent foundation for that discipline which is the best guarantee of military efficiency." Many southerners, including lowly Irish laborers whose modicum of social elevation relied on the existence of slavery, remained vehemently opposed to the idea. John Mitchel feared that exchanging emancipation for military service would undermine one of the key foundations of Confederate identity: that slavery was a benevolent, paternalistic system that ultimately benefited the slaves. He later diarized what he felt at the time. If "freedom be a good thing for negroes," he reasoned, "why then it is and always was a grievous wrong and crime to hold them in slavery at all. If it be true that the state of slavery keeps these people depressed below the condition to which they could develop their nature, their intelligence and their capacity for enjoyment, and what we call 'progress,'" continued Mitchel, "then every hour of their bondage for generations is a black stain upon the white race." Unwilling to admit to any of this, he assured himself that Lee was an emancipist "of the Virginia School of gradual emancipation under State laws" and "a better and more conscientious abolitionist than Abraham Lincoln."[30]

The most famous, and certainly most violent, expression of Irish white supremacy during the Civil War occurred during the New York draft riots of July 1863. To a community already disillusioned by the heavy casualties suffered by the Irish Brigade, the draft denoted bias against the Irish poor and heavy-handed federal government involvement in their local affairs. It also magnified their racial fears from both above (abolitionist Anglo Saxons) and below (emancipated blacks). When Colonel Nugent began the draft on the morning of Saturday, July 11, 1863, he sparked a five-day series of riots that the weekly *Irish-American* was embarrassed to describe as a "saturnalia of pillage and violence." The demonstration steadily devolved from resistance to the draft, to attacks on the Republican administration, to an ugly and deadly race riot. The brutal murders of black men and women by mobs of Irish laborers, often involving sexual mutilation, occurred on the third day of the affray. When black sailor William Williams was murdered by an Irish mob on the Upper West Side, "there were several cheers given and something said . . . about vengeance on every nigger in New York." Iver Bernstein has pointed out, however, that the riots should not be regarded as "a simple one-dimensional episode of Irish Catholic ethnic hatred, white lower-class racism, Confederate or Copperhead sympathy, or resentment of the poor toward the inequities of the Conscription Act." Instead, it was a complicated combination of them all, which vented itself on a variety of victims, including the offices of the *New York Tribune* and local brothels. Even symbols of Irish nationalism were subjected to attack. When the mob invaded Colonel Nugent's house, portraits of Nugent and Meagher were slashed. When Colonel Henry O'Brien led a small military force to challenge the crowd, he was captured, beaten, shot, and lynched from a lamppost. The arrival of military and police units in the city finally restored peace to the streets of New York on July 17, 1863.[31]

Many native-born American responses to the draft riots emphasized the savagery of the Irish race. Such sentiments had a long pedigree. In his 1852 book *Comparative Physiognomy*, the noted American physician James W. Redfield likened the proverbial eloquence of the Irish to the barking of dogs. "Compare the Irishman and the dog in respect to barking, snarling, howling, begging, fawning, flattering, backbiting, quarrelling, blustering, scenting, seizing, hanging on, teasing, rollicking," argued Redfield, "and you will be convinced that there is a wonderful resemblance." Such attitudes provided the basis for anti-Irish responses to the riots. George Templeton Strong complained that "the atrocities these Celtic devils perpetrated can hardly be paralleled in the history of human cruelty." The Irish were a race of cowards. "No wonder St. Patrick drove all the venomous vermin out of Ireland!" he exclaimed. "Its biped mammalia supply that island its full average share of creatures that crawl and eat dirt and poison every community they infest." In a letter to the editor of the *New York Times* written under the pseudonym Carl Benson, Charles Astor Bristed believed that while "Copperhead editors and politicians" instigated the riots, the main perpetrators were Irish immigrants. Their violence upset Bristed's middle-class notions of gender. The "fiendishness of the women and children among the rioters," he exclaimed, "is a characteristic . . . of all mobs in which the Celtic element predominates." The *New York Evangelist* questioned Irish suitability for citizenship. The "Irish who thus attack a part of our population, are all *foreigners*," it editorialized, "while the negroes whom they hunt like fiends, are natives of the soil—Americans by birth, that have a far better right here than this scum of a foreign population."[32]

Not all native-born Americans blamed the riots on the Irish race's propensity for violence. Many historians have used Thomas Nast's cartoons in *Harper's Weekly*, which often depicted the Irish as a low-grade mix of human and ape, to illustrate the racial antipathy many native-born Americans felt toward the Irish. Yet the complexity of *Harper's* attitude toward the Irish was reflected in a lead editorial in the paper soon after the riots ended. "Some newspapers dwell upon the fact that the rioters were uniformly Irish," announced *Harper's*, "and hence argue that our trouble arises from the perversity of the Irish race." But such newspapers failed to take into account that similar riots had recently occurred in a diverse collection of cities across Europe. It ought also be remembered, continued the editorial, that Irish overrepresentation in the laboring classes and the "impulsiveness of the Celt" combined to place the Irish "foremost in every outburst, whether for good or for an evil purpose." Their limited education at home made them more susceptible, upon arrival in America, to being "misled by knaves" than "Germans or men of other races." *Harper's* continued by reminding its readers that "in many wards of the city the Irish were during the late riot staunch friends of law and order; that Irishmen helped to rescue the colored orphans in the asylum from the hands of the rioters; that a large proportion of the police, who behaved throughout the riot with the most exemplary gallantry, are Irishmen; that the Roman Catholic priesthood to a man used their influence on the side of the law; and that perhaps the most scathing rebuke administered to the riot was written by an Irishman—James T. Brady." Instead of reviving "Know-Nothing prejudices," concluded *Harper's*, Americans must remember that "riots are the natural and inevitable diseases of great cities, epidemics, like small-pox and cholera, which must be treated scientifically, upon logical principles."[33]

Many historians comfortably assume that the draft rioters spoke for the Irish American community at large, but the truth is that many Irish were deeply embarrassed by the blue-collar, thuggish violence. The *Irish-American* abhorred its edge of white supremacy. "The assaults on unfortunate negroes and the burning of their houses and their Orphan Asylum cannot be condemned in language too severe," it lamented. "These poor people were innocent of any complicity in bringing about our present troubles and . . . should not be made to suffer for the sins of others." It also accused the city's "abolition papers" and the Republican administration of exacerbating sectarian tensions for their own gain. Citizens "from every nationality . . . giving their lives for the defence of the Republic" were being manipulated by "men utterly devoid of principle and integrity, vampires who thrive and fatten on the disorders of the social system." In an open letter to the *Daily Cleveland Herald*, a Patrick O'Brien was similarly embarrassed by the racist violence of his fellow Irish Catholics. "The burning of the Colored Orphan Asylum in New York was the most inhuman act known to modern history," wrote O'Brien. "Is not the black man a human being, and therefore entitled to the same rights and privileges as the white man?" Those who participated in the riots were "undeserving the name of Irishmen." In camp with the Irish Brigade, Private Peter Welsh was sorry to read "in yesterday's newspaper" of the "disgraceful riots in New York." Fully aware that "the Irish men of New York took so large a part," he hoped the authorities would "use canister freely" to disperse the crowds and hang the ringleaders "like dogs."[34]

Irish American attitudes toward slavery and emancipation were as complicated during the Civil War as they were in the years leading up to the conflict. Blacks, both slave and free, were often a whipping post for Irish Catholics eager to vent their frustrations. Communal grief over the Irish Brigade's heavy casualties was another major accelerant. So too was the shift in the Lincoln administration's war aims, from restoration of the Union to the abolition of slavery. For a community whose job security was threatened by black emancipation, the thought of Irishmen being slaughtered in the countryside on behalf of slaves was too much to bear. Many also opposed the idea of arming freed slaves. For Mitchel and many Irish in the South, the suggestion undermined the truism that slavery was a beneficial institution for all involved. At the same time, Archbishop J. J. Hughes in the North feared that the black proclivity for blind violence rendered arming them a sin against society, although Charles G. Halpine was willing to defend "Sambo's right to be kilt."

At the same time, it is important to note that the Irish American community was not a monolith of white supremacy. The New York draft riots, for example, were not merely an orgy of antiblack murder. Racism obviously played a role, but the Conscription Act laid bare other sore spots, including class inequality and Copperhead sympathy. White representatives of the government were subjected to violence, and an Irish man was lynched by the mob. Loud voices in the Irish American community decried the cruelty meted out to innocent African Americans, and Irish personnel were at the forefront of suppressing the mob. Some, including those fighting in the field, like Private Peter Welsh, were willing to countenance the abolition of slavery if it meant saving the Union, while others supported African Americans' right to earn their freedom through sacrifice at war. Finally, some Irish simply stood for equality and human dignity. "There were one thousand orphan children rendered homeless [during the New York draft riots] to gratify the passions of an ignorant people," lamented Patrick O'Brien in his open letter to the Irish American Catholic community. "Will God or the world ever forgive them for committing such an act of inhumanity?"[35]

The Wartime Irish Popular Press

As a public sphere where politicians, soldiers, and noncombatants alike could find and disseminate news and opinion, the popular press was an important part of life during the Civil War. Editorials often enflamed popular tempers, and newspaper offices were intermittently attacked by mobs of angry soldiers. In the field, journalists were held accountable for the editorial positions of their employers. There is evidence to suggest, for example, that *New York Tribune* correspondents received unfavorable treatment in southern prisons, while the reporter Sylvanus Cadwallader reputedly talked his way out of a Confederate jail by convincing his captors that he worked for the *New York Herald*. Given the cost of sending a correspondent into the field ($1,000 to $5,000 a year), only the biggest newspapers could afford to do so. Embedded in armies on the march, these reporters sent home a heady mixture of official government documents and independent analysis. While reporters tended to get along with the rank and file, many officers treated them with deep suspicion. As a result, correspondents often went to great lengths to ingratiate themselves with their host commanders. "Early news is expensive news, Mr. Greeley," explained one *New York Tribune* reporter. "If I have the watermelons and whiskey ready when the officers come along from the fight, I get the news without asking questions." Those newspapers that could not afford to hire a reporter regularly reprinted information from regional and national newspapers, while readers themselves contributed as well. As we have seen, Irish soldiers sent open letters to the press, and family members sometimes shared personal correspondence they had received from the front.[36]

When he took command of the Irish Brigade in February 1862, Meagher warned his soldiers to be "blind to every newspaper, whatever it may teach." His warning hints at the weekly rag's ubiquity in camp. Like the political exiles in Australia, Irish soldiers had almost constant access to newspapers, often stocked with news and opinions originally published in Irish newspapers at home and abroad. In 1863, Meagher sent an open letter to James Roche, editor of the Dublin *Citizen*, thanking him for having "sent me your paper constantly" during the war. Camp life made it hard to stay in touch with society, let alone Ireland. "Strange to say, however, the Dublin *Citizen* used to make its way to me across the ocean, down to Washington, over the Potomac, into the heart of Virginia," wrote Meagher. "Many a pleasant hour it brought me, in the midst of the cares, worryings, hardships, and hard knocks of a campaign." Though welcome as sources of information, newspapers could also bring bad news. Margaret, the wife of Private Peter Welsh, was literally worried sick about him. "You must not pay so much regard to what you read in the newspapers," he told her, "for they do not know much about matters here." Given the sheer quantity of details, it is no surprise that misinformation was often published. While lying wounded in a hospital after Fredericksburg, Irish soldier William McCarter chanced upon a copy of the *Philadelphia Sunday Dispatch* that included lists of the dead and wounded. "Much to my surprise and horror," McCarter diarized years later, "I found my own name among the killed. I need hardly say that my letter to my home quickly dispelled the gloom and sadness which the announcement by the Sunday newspaper had cast over it."[37]

Newspapers reached soldiers fighting in the Irish Brigade through a variety of channels. Peter Welsh regularly thanked his wife for sending him copies of weekly periodicals. "I received the [Boston] *Pilot* with your last letter," he wrote her from Falmouth in January 1863; "it was a great treat as I had not got one for so long before." She was not his only source of newspapers. "Newsmen bring daily papers here," he told her, "but they charge ten cents for a New York *Herald* and five cents for a Philadelphia paper." Irish Brigade chaplain William Corby later described how newsboys operated in camp. Stationed about twelve miles from the supply depot at City Point on the James River, Corby told how an "enterprising boy" would wait until the steamer arrived with the latest newspapers. He would then grab a "*quantum* of several hundreds" and go "galloping out to the camp, crying out at the top of his voice: 'New York *Herald*!'" The deliverer would charge twenty-five cents per copy, "but even at that price we were delighted to get the news," explained Corby, "and he sold his papers like hot cakes." This

Newspaper vendor and cart in camp, Virginia, 1863. Printed news was part of life for Irish soldiers fighting in the Civil War, keeping them in touch with facts and opinions from around the world. Here, a vendor sells newspapers in camp. Courtesy of the Library of Congress, LC-DIG-cwpb-01140.

enterprising spirit, often associated with Saxon commercialism, was not always lauded among the Irish troops. Staff officer David Power Conyngham derided New England soldiers who, "true to their instincts of making 'the almighty dollar,' hawked and traded about camp, realizing large profits out of small sales." When he came across an Irish soldier "well laden with 'Yankee notions,' newspapers, and the like" for sale, he disparaged the trooper. "Hell blow you!" cried Conyngham, "can't you leave the peddling to the Yankees—an Irish soldier disgracing himself peddling like any Yank!"[38]

Newspapers threatened more than morale. They could also furnish the enemy with intelligence. Perhaps the greatest information leak during the war occurred when the *New York Herald* smuggled and then published the Confederate Army's full roster in September 1863. Given the value of news during the war, it is no surprise that copies of newspapers crisscrossed enemy lines daily. Noncombatants constantly smuggled them back and forth, and periodicals were often included in prisoner exchanges. Pickets were small units of soldiers operating forward of camps and marches in order to warn of enemy advances and positions. Operating outside direct control of their commanding officers, enemy pickets sometimes met in the middle of nowhere, offering the opportunity for soldiers on opposite sides of the conflict to fraternize with each other. Conyngham cited examples of Union and Confederate soldiers of Irish birth meeting between the lines and enquiring about mutual friends. "The canteen would be emptied, old times and friends discussed," wrote Conyngham, "as the little party seated themselves under the shelter of some clump of trees between both lines." Evidently, pickets sometimes shared newspapers, to the detriment of their own side's security. Peter Welsh informed his wife that "the rebels got considerable information by getting newspapers from our pickets." As a result, "all communication with the enemy pickets is prohibited now." Newspapers were, therefore, an important element of military life during the Civil War, and people energetically acquired copies of them whenever possible. They allowed immigrant combatants to stay in touch with the outside Irish world.[39]

John Mitchel's wartime experiences in Richmond offer a southern perspective on the matter. When he sailed from Paris to New York in September 1862 with the intention of joining the Confederacy, Mitchel brought his eighteen-year-old son Willie with him. From New York, they moved on to Baltimore, where, Mitchel later grumbled, slaves could "quit their masters when they please, sure of what they imagine to be freedom on going off to Washington, only a few miles." After surreptitiously crossing through federal lines into Virginia, Mitchel and his son went directly to Richmond, where the elder was soon employed as editor of Jefferson Davis's Richmond *Enquirer*. Emulating his two older brothers, who were each serving in different units of the Confederate Army, Willie joined the First Virginia Infantry Regiment. All three of Mitchel's sons were now serving in the Confederate military. Mitchel's position at the *Enquirer* put him at the heart of the Confederate war of secession, and the popular spirit of the capital city impressed him. "No doubt there are people whose hearts quake within them as they hear the roll of artillery," he diarized, "but public opinion requires an outward cheerfulness and courage." He was delighted by "the spectacle of a people roused in this way to a full display of all its manhood . . . without a friend in the world," but independent, proud, and firm. If he was impressed with the Confederate spirit, Mitchel was less heartened with Davis's prosecution of the war. In late 1863 he resigned from the *Enquirer* to serve as lead writer of John M. Daniel's Richmond *Examiner,* the organ of opposition within the Confederacy. Mitchel held the post from the fall of 1863 until the end of the war.[40]

Prohibited by his nearsightedness from military duty, Mitchel coupled his role as newspaper editor with service in Richmond's Ambulance Committee, an armed guard assigned to carrying the wounded from the battlefields to the capital city. The experience exposed him to the horrors of war. "Surgeons are assigned to duty with us to perform operations," Mitchel diarized, "and sometimes around our quarters are seen severed fragments of limbs." Mitchel's role at the *Enquirer* kept him busy reading any and all newspapers that made their way to Richmond. Occasionally, a paper would come "from some remote country town, printed upon the back of a square of wall-paper; forlorn-looking columns upon the gray surface at one side, and a pattern of scarlet and gold or flowers of all hues at the other." Later, he would wish he had kept "a complete collection of Confederate publications of all species. It would have furnished material for a strange chapter in a bibliography." But newspapers from Ireland also found their way through the federal blockade. The news was not always good. One day, he was working at the *Enquirer* office when a nervous army officer came in, Mitchel later wrote in his diary, "placed in my hand a newspaper closely folded up, shook hands with me, and went quickly out without another word. I found it to be a Dublin *Freeman's Journal*; and I soon found the paragraph which had induced my visitor to give me the paper, but which he would not stay to see me read. It was to announce the death of my daughter Henrietta at her convent school in Paris." Even in a blockaded city, news from home was a part of immigrant life.[41]

The popular press rendered the Civil War an international event open to debate around the world. As a rising star in Canadian politics, Young Ireland exile Thomas D'Arcy McGee used the conflict to shore up his image of nascent Canadian nationalism. In 1857, after giving up his interest in the *American Celt*, McGee moved to Montreal, where he established a weekly newspaper entitled the *New Era* and got elected to the legislative assembly as a member for Montreal West. By the early 1860s he was a cabinet member in the Eighth Parliament of the Province of Canada, and played a critical role in the creation of a self-governing Dominion of Canada in 1867. In a speech entitled "Canada's Interest in the American Civil War," which he delivered before several assemblies during the autumn of 1861, McGee decried the Confederate desire to found a society on slavery. Having turned his back on his Irish revolutionary past, McGee saw the Civil War as a fight for the liberal values that Canada and the British Empire were founded on. "We prefer our own institutions to theirs," he declared, "[but] as between negro emancipation and a revival of the slave trade; as between the Golden Rule and the cotton crop of 1861; as between the revealed unity of the human race and the heartless heresy of African bestiality; as between the North and South in this deplorable consequence, I rest firmly in the belief that all that is most liberal, most intelligent, and most magnanimous in Canada and the Empire, are for continental peace, for constitutional arbitrament, for universal, if gradual emancipation, for free intercourse, for justice, mercy, civilization, and the North." While McGee's support for the Union ingratiated him with many Irish Americans, his coziness with the British Empire made him mortal enemies among other Irish, including the Fenian Brotherhood.[42]

Despite their great distance from the affair, the Irish in Australia were constantly bombarded with updates on the progress of the Civil War and the Irish fighting in it. News articles, opinion pieces, and open letters, often relating to Meagher's Irish Brigade, were clipped from Irish, British, and American newspapers and reprinted every week. Overall, the Sydney *Freeman's Journal* supported antislavery but preferred peace to a bloody northern victory. The "sympathies of every Christian are enlisted on the side of the poor son of Africa," it editorialized in December 1862; "very few indeed would not desire . . . his liberation from that terrible bondage under which he has so long been labouring and groaning." But it was also suspicious of the Lincoln administration's motives. "As we have insisted over and over again," it explained in November 1863, "it is not the extinction of slavery that is calling forth all the power of the people of the North, to force the secessionists into submission, but the desire of monopolizing all the trade, commerce, and manufactures of the Union to themselves." In the wake of the Emancipation Proclamation, the *Freeman's Journal* described Lincoln's claim that the North was fighting to end slavery as "one of the most dishonest shams ever invented." When some Confederates suggested that black slaves be offered emancipation for military service, the paper noted ironically that the "slave-holders themselves have introduced the thin edge of the wedge" by which "the bonds of the slaves will be struck off for ever."[43]

Mirroring the language of Irish American leaders and editors, whose printed words were constantly reaching Australian shores, the *Freeman's*

Journal's analysis of the Irish performance in the Civil War described their military service in terms of a storied reputation transcending time and space. Thanks to the "recklessness of danger and death" that was "proverbial in Irishmen," it claimed in November 1863, "the wide world knows how Irishmen fight, 'fast, fiery and true,' for there is scarce a battle field from the North Pole to the South which Irish blood has not crimsoned, scarce a victory which Irish valour has not contributed to gain." Hence, in America, "men of Celtic blood are to be found fighting on both sides" of the conflict. Britain's unwillingness to interfere in the Civil War was rooted in the "well-founded apprehension . . . of a general uprising of the Irish race throughout the world to shake off the detested foreign yoke that during seven centuries of tyranny and persecution has debased and enslaved that people." To "the hands of her sons, scattered far and wide over the nations of the earth . . . has been committed the privilege of being the vanguard of the movement that must result in restoring to Ireland her ancient independence." Britain feared, therefore, that "the elements of hatred to the English name and nation that pervade the whole population of the American nation, and the Irish race and their descendants more especially, should be directed against that vulnerable heel of the British empire, her Canadian colonies." Unbeknownst to the *Freeman's Journal*, the Fenians would attempt to carry out that very goal a few short years later.[44]

Back in Ireland, the Civil War dominated the editorial columns of the popular press between 1861 and 1865. There were several reasons for its popularity. A decade and a half of mass migration had fomented a network of close interpersonal relations. "For every parish in Ireland, there is at the other side of the Atlantic an almost corresponding colony of people bound by ties of affection and blood," lamented the *Cork Examiner* in June 1861. The high levels of Irish participation in the opposing armies and the steady stream of information and opinion from Irish American emigrants also played a role. Open letters from leaders like Meagher and Mitchel, clipped and reprinted in countless weeklies, inundated the Irish population with insights from contending sides of the divide. Moreover, the Union and Confederate administrations both sent influential Irish American clergymen to Ireland on propaganda tours. Archbishop J. J. Hughes did a tour of Europe in 1861 that included a stint in Dublin, where he delivered pro-Union speeches. The Confederacy responded by sending the "Fighting Chaplain," Father John Bannon, to Ireland in the autumn of 1863. With the help of John Martin, Bannon wrote articles for the Dublin *Nation* and printed thousands of handbills, which he disseminated to parish priests and seaport boarding houses, in the hopes of dissuading prospective emigrants from enlisting in the Union army. Thanks in part to Bannon's efforts, Irish nationalist opinion tended to see parallels between the southern and Irish struggles for independence. By the midpoint of the war, the New York *Irish-American* recognized that "the foremost men of our race [in Ireland] are gradually taking sides in opposition to [the Union cause]. . . . It is worse than absurd."[45]

Many Irish Unionists, who wished to see Ireland remain within Great Britain, saw the bitterness over the sacrifices of the Irish in Lincoln's armies as an opportunity to undermine nationalism. In a series of articles entitled "The Grave of the Celts," the *Dublin Evening Mail* broadcast the harsh realities that had met Catholics fleeing the Famine. The United States had selfishly manipulated Irish immigrants by sending them to the slaughter and then tossing them aside when dead or wounded. "America, the refuge of the Celt," it claimed, "has become his grave." In the future, concluded the *Evening Mail*, "the reasonable conviction may steal into the minds of the survivors, that those who live under the benign shelter of the British flag had best 'let well alone.'" Other Irish Unionists, fearing that the growing influence of embittered Irish Catholic nationalist opinion was poisoning Anglo-American relations, blamed Irish Americans for the *Trent* affair, in which the federal navy intercepted a British mail ship with Confederate diplomats on board. The *Dublin University Magazine* charged that while they despised "the cock-a-doodle-doo of Meagher, Mitchel, and the other stage rebels," it was this "leaven of Celtism . . . which keeps up the estrangement and suspicion between the two branches of the Anglo-Saxon race." History was to blame. "Two operations in British husbandry have been carried on side by side, and often by the same agency," complained the magazine. "We have planted America, and at the same time weeded the old country. We sent out the choice of our citizens—the adventurers who planted Virginia, Maryland, Carolina and Georgia, but we also shipped off the famine-stricken remains of the Celtic population of the west and south of Ireland." The result was a Celto-Saxon hybrid population that left the United States "of two minds on all international questions with this country."[46]

The majority of Irish nationalists in Ireland supported the Confederacy on the grounds that its struggle to secede from the Union paralleled the Irish fight to separate from the United Kingdom. Despite his support for antislavery, for example, Smith O'Brien defended the southern cause. To militarily enforce reunion, he told Richard O'Gorman in a letter published in 1862, "would only produce disasters greater than those which would result from breaking up the Union." In November 1863, he explicitly denigrated

Meagher's participation in the war. It was "a spectacle painful and humiliating to all lovers of freedom," complained Smith O'Brien, "to find one of the representative men of the Irish race—himself an exile and a Catholic—vindicating a course of policy similar to that which expelled the natives of Ireland from their possessions and from their homes." John Martin also drew historical parallels between Ireland and the Civil War. "Glancing over Northern American papers that are sent to me," he wrote to a friend in 1865, "I am sometimes struck with the resemblance between those new English, the present Yankee rulers of America, and the old English of our 'sister country' that have been confiscating, robbing, and slandering the Irish these centuries past." Martin rued Irish participation in both the federal and British armies. "God help us, unhappy Irish!" he lamented in an open letter to P. J. Smyth of the Dublin *Irishman*. "Are the martial qualities of our people never to have a nobler development than in butchering Hindoos and Chinese at the bidding of English greed, or butchering the heroic Confederates at the bidding of Yankee hate?"[47]

As the war progressed, the steady circulation of newspapers from overseas meant that even regular soldiers in the Irish Brigade acknowledged that nationalists at home were largely supportive of the Confederacy. One private was disappointed to see, for example, that the *Cork Examiner* seemed "desperately biased in favor of the South." Realizing in the autumn of 1863 that pro-southern opinion emanating from Ireland was weakening the already-flagging spirits of the Irish in the North, Meagher began to answer the critics of the Union cause through open letters to the editors of newspapers in Ireland. He denied, for example, that there was a similarity between southern secession and recent European revolutions for liberty. "Not independence, but domination" had inspired "the rebellion of the Slave Lords" in the South, "where the slavery of the black man constituted the basis of wealth, of social consequence, and political power." He also defended Irish American participation in the war. He and his "noble little Brigade" had stood "on many a fiercely fire-swept field" to defend the United States government from treason and dishonor. "Thank God!" he continued, "that disgrace has been averted from our race by the splendid conduct of the thousands of Irish soldiers" who had fought for the Union. Nevertheless, Meagher refused to deride those who had fought for the South. Their martial ardor and "warm natures" had driven the Irish race to fulfill their duties on either side of the Mason-Dixon Line.[48]

Not all nationalists in Ireland supported the South. P. J. Smyth of the Dublin weekly *Irishman* supported the North in the Fenian hope that a strong United States would help realize Irish hopes for independence. A Union victory, argued Smyth, would see "America preserved, England humiliated, and Ireland freed!" Southern success in the war would not lead to lasting peace. "The evil would spread," warned Smyth in an open letter to John Martin, "and the one great nation of men, who speak the same language, are of the same mixed race, and formed naturally to live and grow under the shadow of the one flag, would be broken into fragments. It would be the ruin of America, and the extinguishment of the last hope of Ireland." A Confederate defeat, on the other hand, would leave the United States with a massive army and a world-class navy administered by a government heavily influenced by men devoted to Irish independence. Smyth also countered the claim that the war was not about slavery. "The South fights to establish a Confederacy . . . based on the great truth that the negro is not the equal of the white man, that slavery is his historical and normal condition," he wrote to Smith O'Brien. While willing to admit "my hatred of slavery is not as great as yours," he did consider it a "curious coincidence nevertheless, that while I occupy the position of a practical opponent of slavery, you occupy that of its defender and perpetuator." The debate in Ireland mirrored transnational discourses of race and nationality that had been developing since the 1840s.[49]

The international Irish community debated the American Civil War in the columns of their weekly popular press. It was through this international print culture that Irish people shaped each other's opinions of the sectional crisis. Whether in a bivouac along the Rappahannock River, an editorial office in Australia, or a drawing room in Dublin, Irish people had regular access to individual copies of weekly newspapers. The letters and diaries of foot soldiers in the Irish Brigade testify that copies of the weekly rag trickled among the rank and file. Leaders like Meagher, Mitchel, and Smith O'Brien argued through ongoing series of open letters. A close reading of this chapter's endnotes demonstrates the prevalence with which influential articles, editorials, and letters were reprinted in Irish newspapers abroad. There was also more to the debate than the opinions of these few leaders. Regular soldiers and their families shaped the discussion through open letters of their own. Thanks in part to the international nature of this medium, the Irish approached the Civil War from a transnational perspective. In Australia, the *Freeman's Journal* proudly claimed that there was "scarce a battle field from the North Pole to the South which Irish blood has not crimsoned," while in Ireland, nationalists were divided between those who felt common cause with the Confederacy and others who hoped that a triumphant Union would enable the eventual independence of Ireland. By facilitating this international discussion of the Civil War, the popular press perpetuated a transnational sense of community among the world-scattered Irish.

Conclusion

On February 28, 1863, the Dublin *Nation*, which had been edited by A. M. Sullivan since Duffy left Ireland in 1855, declared that a new column would now grace its pages. Entitled "The Irish Abroad," the goal was to use foreign newspapers to systematically gather and publish information on Irish communities around the world. "We have but to look over the letters and papers which we receive by every mail, we have but to speak to a member of any Irish family in this country," Sullivan editorialized, "and we are reminded how large, how faithful, how attached a portion of the Irish race are now sojourners beyond the blue waves of the Atlantic and Pacific." While newspapers in the United States, Canada, Australia, and beyond regularly copied news from Irish periodicals, Sullivan charged, journals in Ireland did not do so to a large enough degree. The *Nation* would rectify this shortcoming. "In every possible way we shall make those columns a medium of communication between our countrymen at home and in foreign lands," Sullivan promised, "and we shall feel happy if, by so doing, we assist in keeping fresh and active those noble sympathies which are so great an honour to our world-scattered race." Yet Sullivan's new initiative was simply formalizing a process of exchange and reciprocation that had been active for decades. During the Civil War, the steady transmission of printed words, clipped and republished in newspapers around the English-speaking world, played a critical role in the continued development of an international imagined community of Irish Celts.[50]

Irish American wartime racial discourse had important transnational dimensions. While white supremacy indubitably constituted part of how many Irish self-identified, this by no means monopolized how they thought about nations and nationalism. Instead, a Celtic identity, imported from Ireland but refashioned to fit the vagaries of life abroad, governed Irish racial discourse. Rather than seek to assimilate into a hegemonic, white core, Irish immigrants strove to expand the boundaries of their host society. They did so by tenaciously clinging to their identity as members of a race of Celtic soldiers whose martial ardor had, in the words of the New York *Irish News*, "left its charging footprints on a thousand battle-fields and borne its own and other flags in fierce whirlwinds over the wide world." The Celts were as transnational as the values for which they were fighting. Whether laboring to break or restore the Union, Irish immigrants portrayed themselves as agents in the universal human struggle for freedom and democracy. This transnational dimension imbued both the ethnic solidarity and civic republicanism that constituted the two sides of the coin of global nationalism among Irish Americans. By demanding the right, bought with their blood, to pledge simultaneous loyalty to their new and old homes, Irish Americans broadened the meaning of American citizenship. At a Fourth of July celebration in 1862, Irish American jurist Charles P. Daly drove the point home. "Our [American] nationality is like this bouquet of flowers, which the chairman has put into my hand," he explained. "It is a gathering together of things different in themselves. A mixture of many nationalities bound like this bouquet in confident union." Noting, to loud cheers, that the bouquet in question was "largely interspersed with green," Daly concluded that "the Irish race do not simply adorn [the American Union], but are one of the constituent parts of its unity, its strength, and its power." Each race had its place in the nation.[51]

BY THE TIME Lee surrendered on April 9, 1865, the surviving Young Irelanders were scattered overseas. Charles Gavan Duffy was a politician in Australia. John Blake Dillon, who had fled to the United States in 1848, had returned to Ireland, where he died in 1866. Tasmanian exile John Martin was also in Ireland, engaged in several unsuccessful attempts throughout the 1860s to achieve Irish legislative independence. His former fellow prisoner, Smith O'Brien, had died of a heart attack in 1864. Three leading exiles remained in North America. Thomas D'Arcy McGee was an influential statesman working to define sovereignty for Canada within the British Empire. John Mitchel moved to New York in 1865 but was soon imprisoned in Fortress Monroe with his ex-employer, Jefferson Davis. Thomas Francis Meagher went west to take up a post as de facto governor of the territory of Montana. In the wake of the war, they and their fellow Irish immigrants looked to Reconstruction with a mix of hope and fear. Would the Celts consolidate the gains they had purchased at such great cost on the battlefield? Or would the Anglo-Saxons seek to roll back their claim to equal citizenship?

CHAPTER FIVE

"American by Nationality
yet Irish by Race"

Citizenship in the Wake of the
Civil War, 1865–1880

The Young Ireland exiles found themselves at loose ends after Appomattox. Thomas Francis Meagher successfully petitioned the Republican administration for a government position and, in the summer of 1865, headed out West to serve as secretary of the Montana Territory. Tragedy struck two years later, however, when he suddenly drowned in the Missouri River. At the requiem mass held for him at the Church of Saint Francis Xavier in Manhattan a month later, the veterans of the Irish Brigade wore sprigs of boxwood in memory of Fredericksburg. Later that evening, fellow exile Richard O'Gorman delivered a eulogy before a packed crowd in the Cooper Union. After reminiscing about Meagher's days as a revolutionary in Ireland and an exile in Australia, O'Gorman lauded his old friend's leadership during the Civil War, when "the great mass of the people of the Irish race on this Continent" had sided with the Union. Wherever he had gone, Meagher had found an Irish spirit of generosity. "For, let me tell you, all over the earth, North and South, East and West, wherever you may wander," concluded O'Gorman, "you shall scarcely find a spot so remote or desolate that an Irishman who loves Ireland, and whom Ireland loves, will not find there a welcome and a friend." By contrast, John Mitchel was imprisoned in Fortress Monroe after the war. He later reflected on the fact that the British and American governments had both seen fit to incarcerate him. "The Anglo-Saxon race and the nineteenth century seem to have no use for me," he wrote glumly, "except to chain me up."[1]

This final chapter examines the development of global nationalism among Irish Americans in the wake of the Civil War. The postbellum years were a period of fluidity in American social relations as notions of nationality and citizenship, turned upside down by war, were redefined. There were several factors at play. Recently emancipated African Americans were demanding that their new constitutional rights be enshrined in law and practice. Immigrant groups such as Irish Catholics, whose numbers were being continually augmented by a steady stream of newcomers, sought to use their military service as a lever to establish equality between native-born and naturalized citizens. They also used the Democratic Party to strengthen their voice, nurturing powerful municipal machines in cities such as New York. Nativism, though weakened by the war, remained a part of life in the postwar years, as Radical Republicans feared that immigrants were corrupting the body politic. Irish American Catholics responded to these pressures in a number of ways. Some turned inward, adopting the white supremacist language of their patrons in the Democratic Party and opposing the rights of blacks, Amerindians, and Chinese immigrant laborers. Yet others, including some of the leading Irish American editors of the day, reacted differently, by pressing an agenda that sought to break down, rather than build up, walls around the American polity. By insisting that humans were entitled to multiple loyalties, these immigrants helped reshape modern notions of citizenship and belonging.

Redefining Citizenship in the Wake of the Civil War

Irish migrants continued to flood out of Ireland for decades after the Famine. Following a peak of 989,834 during the 1850s, another 690,845 migrated to the United States during the 1860s, with 449,549 to follow between 1871 and 1880. The United States was the preferred but not the only destination for those leaving Ireland. Between 1860 and 1880, 144,863 headed to Australia and New Zealand, another 65,862 went to British North America (Canada), while 10,166 moved to other overseas locales, including southern Africa and South America. Together, these cohorts comprised a worldwide exodus of over four and a half million people between 1840 and 1880. Although the Irish represented a decreasing share of the immigrating population overall, service in the Civil War gave the Irish in America an advantage over the "new" immigrants coming from eastern and southern Europe. Their high concentration in urban centers spawned ethnic societies such as the Irish Catholic Benevolent Union (1859), Catholic Total Abstinence Union (1872), and Knights of Columbus (1881), which doubled as mutual aid societies for the sick, widowed, and destitute. Irish Americans also controlled several of the political machines that ran many city governments. Building on their decades-old affiliation with the Democratic Party, Irish politicians used corruption, violence, and meticulous planning to wrest control of administrations such as New York City's Tammany Hall, of which "Honest John" Kelly became the first Irish boss in 1871. These power brokers used municipal machines to consolidate the electoral power that decades of Irish immigration had built.[2]

While immigrant military service during the Civil War undermined nativism, the political power of postbellum Irish American Catholics stoked fears among those who still felt that foreigners, especially Irish Celts, were eroding Anglo-Saxon democracy. Anti-Irish sentiment still abounded, and there were many who shared Edward A. Freeman's belief that "this would be a grand land if only every Irishman would kill a negro, and be hanged for it." For the wealthy Protestant merchants who dominated the Union League Clubs, Reconstruction and city reform had replaced war as the most urgent issues at hand. Success required curtailing the power of the uncivilized, immoral foreigners and their political cronies in the Democratic Party who had hijacked municipal politics. It was in this spirit that Reconstruction era Republicans passed federal legislation aimed at both protecting the rights of African Americans in the South and undermining the Irish and their allies in the North. The Enforcement Act (1870), which sought to protect black voters from violence and intimidation, simultaneously attacked false registration and repeat voting. Machine bosses had also gotten in the habit of trading citizenship certificates for votes. The Naturalization Act (1870) took aim at this practice by tightening federal control over the process. While these laws were clearly devised by middle-class reformers bent on defending emancipated slaves' constitutional rights and rooting out corruption, they also served to weaken the Irish immigrant community's electoral power.[3]

When this animosity toward Irish Catholics spilled out onto the streets, Irish Protestants were often involved. Indeed, the postwar years were a time of great growth for Irish Protestant immigrant organizations in the United States. Following the formal establishment of the Loyal Orange Institution in New York in 1867, the organization rapidly expanded to 100 lodges and 10,000 members by 1873 and to 364 lodges and 30,000 members in 1914. Modeled on the Orange Order, which was founded near Loughgall, County Armagh, in 1795, these American Orange lodges allowed Irish Protestants, Anglican and Presbyterian alike, to distinguish themselves from their Catholic fellow immigrants while simultaneously pledging loyalty to American democracy. Distinctive by virtue of class, religion, and a sense of themselves as proud members of the Anglo-Saxon race, these Irish Protestants viewed Catholics as, in the words of Michael Gordon, "debased papal agents . . . [who] threatened republican institutions." Having comfortably integrated into American society during the eighteenth and early nineteenth centuries, many Irish Protestants feared being associated with the waves of impoverished Catholics landing in the United States after 1845. More recent arrivals also brought sectarian animosities and a pan-Protestant consciousness, which were strengthened in the crucible of American religion and politics. In the wake of the Civil War, this sectarian animosity culminated in New York City's "Orange and Green" riots of 1870 and 1871, which killed almost seventy people. Irish Catholics still faced determined opposition.[4]

Using their military service as a lever, these Catholics joined other European immigrants in claiming that the naturalized and the native-born must now enjoy equal status as American citizens. Their active participation in the "Lost Cause," for example, enabled the Irish to claim full membership in the Solid South. The argument was part of a broader trend, elucidated by David Blight, whereby "sectional partisanship dissolved into celebration of the ethnic diversity of the fallen." While African Americans sought to have their rights as citizens legally defined as clearly as possible, the Irish were more concerned with erasing any stigma associated with naturalization. Their control of municipal machines gave Irish Catholics weight in local and state governments, while Democrats courted them at the national level. In many ways, native-born reactions to the revolutionary Fenian Brotherhood, a transatlantic organization dedicated to the violent overthrow of British power in Ireland, embodied Irish Americans' new status. Rather than feel frightened of their dual loyalty to the United States and Ireland, many Americans embraced the Fenians as political and ideological members of the same struggle against monarchism. "American political leaders now publicly embraced the idea," writes Christian Samito, "that Irish Americans acted as global leaders furthering a transnational republican movement with the United States located at its apex." Eager to downplay their virulent criticism of Lincoln during the war, which some native-born Americans had equated with disloyalty and ingratitude, the postwar Irish set out to paint a broadly inclusive portrait of the United States as a pluralist mosaic of hardy nationalities.[5]

Meagher's outspoken advocacy of the Irish race's contribution to American unity reflected a global nationalist identity that combined ethnic solidarity with civic republicanism. Returning to a theme he had repeatedly emphasized throughout the Civil War, Meagher portrayed Irish service as part of a timeless tradition witnessed "the world over," which had endeared Irish soldiers to their commanding officers and "flung a redeeming splendor over the baffled fortunes . . . [and] intractable destiny of the Irish race at home." Irish glory on foreign battlefields stoked the pride of those still living in Ireland, but it strengthened the Irish hand in America as well. Their heroic performance during the sectional crisis had planted an irrefutable rejoinder in the annals of American history against those who might, in the future, seek to disparage the Irish race. "Out upon the bastard Americanism that spews this imputation in the face of the gallant race," he cried, "whose blood, shed in torrents for its inviolability and its glory, has imparted a brighter crimson to the Stripes and made the Stars of that triumphant flag irradiate with a keener radiance." Meagher's message to future generations proved prophetic when, in 1894, the American Protective Association sought to undermine the Irish war record. While framing the history of the Civil War in terms of the sacrifices made by a specific ethnic group, Meagher was simultaneously confirming that community's fidelity to American republican ideals. In 1866, he urged both sections to reunite and pledge themselves to "the vindication of the Republic against the malevolence of faction, [and of] nationality over sectionalism."[6]

Irish American nationalist and Civil War veteran David Power Conyngham went one step further by writing a book on Irish service in the war. Published in New York in 1867 and later reprinted in Boston and in Britain, *The Irish Brigade and Its Campaigns* was the first systematic attempt to create a usable past of Irish service during the war. The book was "a history of the gallant exploits of that noble little band," which aimed to "illustrate the elastic vitality of the [Celtic] race." Published just two years after the cessation of hostilities, Conyngham's account expressed, at times, bitterness toward "the aristocratic doctrines of monarchism" that had threatened the United States. For the most part, however, his book told a story that downplayed sectional differences. He recounted, for example, a meeting between a northern doctor and a wounded Confederate soldier. When they learned that they shared the last name Dougherty, Conyngham explained, "the pride of Irish ancestry" erased all sectional hostility. While ignoring blacks' contributions, the book painted a picture of the American army, and by extension American society, as one big, happy family of various European nationalities. "On they marched," he said of an advance by George B. McClellan's army, "dark Puritans from the New England States; stalwart Yankees, of bone and muscle; men from the West and Northwest; exiles of Erin, from

Munster's sunny plains, from Connaught's heights, and Leinster's vales; peasants from the Rhine; all march along through the glorious woods, through forest paths, as if of one race and nation." For folks like Conyngham and Meagher, Irish service in defense of the Union had purchased the right to maintain dual loyalty to their home and host communities.[7]

The years following the Civil War were, therefore, a period of flux during which various groups struggled to consolidate their respective positions within the American polity. Successive constitutional amendments and acts of federal legislation in the immediate aftermath of the war enshrined these rights in law, and the Department of Justice was created to enforce them. Yet many obstacles remained, not the least of which was an enduring belief in the right of individual states to define the limits of citizenship. For a country whose constitutionalism stood on the notion of popular sovereignty, the question became subject to wide-ranging, heated debate. Groups like Irish Catholic immigrants and African Americans used their military service during the war as an instrument for amplifying their demands. The armed forces had raised the political consciousness of countless citizens, drawn them closer to the federal government, and given them firsthand experience working and living with people from various backgrounds. Although they often failed to see their plights as part of the same struggle, marginalized groups were emboldened by wartime service to demand a more pluralist definition of American citizenship. This was especially true of Irish immigrants, who described the question as part of a worldwide struggle for freedom from tyranny. In the mid-1870s, ex-soldier William McCarter reflected on his motivations for joining the Irish Brigade during the war. "I owed my life to my whole adopted country," he wrote, and to "its noble, generous, intelligent, brave people, [who were] ever ready to welcome and to extend the hand of friendship to the down-trodden and oppressed of every clime and people."[8]

An International Irish Press

The decades following the Civil War were a period of great growth for the American popular press. The number of dailies and weeklies in operation almost trebled in twenty years, from over 4,000 in 1860 to about 11,300 in 1880. This expansion of print culture was closely linked to the concomitant spread of railroads and telegraphs. Before the war, railroads were more or less limited to the eastern and midwestern states, but in 1869 the first transcontinental line was established, and by 1880 there were four such lines in operation. Telegraph lines branched out from these railroads to connect small towns with cities. The tone of the press also became more varied during this period. Whereas political partisanship had dominated the news before and during the Civil War, the postbellum period witnessed the rise of independent publishers unwilling to side with one political party or the other. This is not to suggest, of course, that all political allegiances were dead. In the fiery context of Reconstruction, many editors remained staunchly committed to one political party or another. This kind of group loyalty was reflected in the Irish American press as well, whose boat was lifted by the rising tide of American journalism. Several of the major weeklies enjoyed national circulations, which enabled them to transcend the ecclesiastical control of clerics such as Archbishop J. J. Hughes. By the early 1870s, the Boston *Pilot* could boast a staggering circulation of 103,000, while New York City alone supported four popular Irish weeklies.[9]

The press also played a role in the success of the Fenian Brotherhood, the main voice of Irish separatism in the 1860s and early 1870s. The Fenians were a transnational organization founded in 1858 with the objective of using violence to create an independent Irish republic. In the United States, Irish American participation in the Civil War had given Fenian recruits the kind of military experience, discipline, and organization their co-conspirators in Ireland could only dream of. Successful national conventions in Chicago (1863) and Cincinnati (1865) galvanized the membership. Across the Atlantic, Fenians in Ireland exploited the transatlantic press for propaganda purposes. In the autumn of 1861, the remains of Young Ireland exile Terence Bellew McManus, who had died in obscurity earlier in the year, were disinterred in San Francisco and shipped to Dublin for an extravagant funeral procession presided over by the Fenians. Their leader, James Stephens, exploited the event's propaganda value by sending batches of Dublin newspapers in which the funeral was reported to colleagues in the United States. "Astounding as the Newspaper accounts of the Funeral must appear to every Irishman in the States," he wrote to Fenian cofounder John O'Mahony, "the most favorable [estimate of procession participation] is far below the reality." John Martin, who had accompanied McManus to Van Diemen's Land, was suspicious of the funerary spectacle. "When I first saw stated in newspapers that [McManus's] remains were to be disinterred and sent from California to Ireland, I hoped it was only one of the projects suggested by indiscreet zeal and unpractical spirits," Martin told a friend living in Michigan. "However, newspaper-talk grew into serious intentions of the people in America. I think the Irish there got persuaded by the newspapers that there was really a pervading sentiment in Ireland in favour of the scheme." Delighted by the power of the press, Stephens founded the Dublin weekly *Irish People* in 1863.[10]

The new weekly quickly spread the Fenian message beyond Ireland. In a letter to O'Mahony in New York, Stephens explained that Irish American fund-raising had not generated as much money as he had hoped for, "& to the paper alone could we now look for these essential funds." On balance, the journal ended up losing more money than it made, but there was always more to the *Irish People* than financial profit. Its goal was to propagate the notion that, in the words of one of its first editorials, "national independence never was and never will be anywhere achieved, save by the sword." Britain, which held Ireland in "the fetters of alien rule," must be defeated militarily. Irish priests, comfortable farmers, and constitutional separatists were revolutionary nationalism's natural enemies. Echoing the Chartist message of earlier decades, the Fenians also deplored the deprivation experienced by many Irish workers at home and abroad, and the new weekly organ did well among the Irish artisans and laborers who had fled to Britain during the 1840s and 1850s. In reading rooms established by the National Brotherhood of St. Patrick, Irish emigrants could read (or hear read) articles and editorials from Irish weeklies such as the *Irish People*. In later years, Fenian member Thomas Clarke Luby claimed that the *Irish People* had single-handedly introduced Fenianism to much of mainland Britain. Even A. M. Sullivan, editor of the rival Dublin *Nation*, admitted that the Fenian weekly "swept all before it amongst the Irish in England and Scotland, almost annihilating the circulation of the *Nation* in many places north and south of the Tweed."[11]

Unnerved by the success and revolutionary rhetoric of the *Irish People*, the police raided its office, which doubled as the Fenian headquarters, in September 1865. Staff were detained, documents seized, and the journal itself suppressed. While the London *Times* praised the government's "act of political vigour," the maneuver failed to stem the tide of Fenian propaganda. By March 1866, the New York Fenians were advertising the advent of a new weekly periodical named after its Dublin predecessor. Its goal was "to unite and organize the now widely scattered branches of the Irish Race in a harmonious bond of national brotherhood" and to achieve "THE LIBERATION OF IRELAND." It also shared the anticlerical, working-class sensibility of its Irish progenitor, imploring its readers to fund charities at home before wasting "one cent in rearing aristocratic steeples over the roofless cabins and graves of the famine-slain." Back in Ireland, the government and its supporters were deeply troubled by the tenacity of transatlantic Fenianism. The conservative *Irish Times*, in particular, was annoyed to see that the *Irish People* had been revived in America. Following its appearance in New York, "large numbers of copies [of the new periodical] were transmitted by every mail steamer to Ireland . . . in parcels as goods to agents" who surreptitiously circulated them to be "read out by members of the Fenian Confederacy and others, wherever a crowd could be collected." The irrepressibility of the Fenian message irked the editor. "It was of little use to have suppressed the *Irish People* in Dublin," it concluded, "if the New York Press could deluge the country with publications whose treason certainly was not diluted."[12]

The misadventures of John Sarsfield Casey demonstrate that Fenian newspaper activity transcended the Atlantic Basin. Writing under the pen name "The Galtee Boy," Casey was a popular member of the Dublin *Irish People* staff and was arrested in September 1865 when manuscript letters matching his handwriting were found in the Fenian headquarters during the government raid. Convicted of treason felony, which had first been used almost twenty years earlier against his childhood hero, John Mitchel, Casey was sentenced to five years' penal servitude. After short stints in Irish and English prisons, he was transported to Western Australia in October 1867. Coincidentally, the *Hougoumont*, which carried Casey and his fellow Fenians away, was the last convict ship Britain ever sent to the Antipodes. Casey's diary, written soon after returning to Ireland in 1871, illustrates that newspapers kept the prisoners in touch with the outside Irish world. While awaiting trial in Cork, the Fenians were entitled to receive food and clothing from friends and family. Oftentimes sympathizers would remove the soft middle of a loaf of bread, stuff it with tobacco "and a scrap or two of the most interesting items in the papers," and carefully replace the crust before slathering it over with butter. At other times, friendly guards, workers, and even the daughters of the deputy governor would surreptitiously pass newspapers to the prisoners. Keeping alert, especially when being transported from one place to another, worked as well. While traveling on trains in England, for example, Casey found that "standing on the platform we had an opportunity of learning scraps of news, by reading the contents sheet of the Saxon papers, which were pushed all round." When a priest came to say mass soon after they arrived in Portland prison, he brought two candles "wrapped in a piece of the *Universal News*," an English weekly devoted to Irish Catholic immigrants. After the service, the priest discarded the newspaper, but the prisoners secreted it and took turns reading it that night in the common water closet at the end of the prison block.[13]

During their voyage to Western Australia, Casey and his fellow Fenian prisoners produced several issues of an onboard newsletter entitled the *Wild Goose* composed of "purely literary" articles, excerpts of which were later reprinted in the Dublin press. Nine months after his arrival in Australia, Casey accepted a ticket-of-leave, and the following May he and others received an amnesty from the British government. In September 1869 they returned to Ireland on board the *Suffolk*. During their time in the Antipodes, the Fenians maintained two-way communication with the international Irish press. On the one hand, friends and family sent newspapers to the prisoners. "I was glad to learn, from the [Dublin] *Irishman*," Casey told his parents, "that the people of Ireland are exerting themselves to procure the release of the gallant men still detained in bondage." On the other hand, Casey and his friends did their part to keep their plight in the public eye. The prisoners regularly sent letters for publication in nationalist weeklies such as the Dublin *Irishman* and the New York *Irish People*. These letters were sometimes subsequently clipped and reprinted in the Australian press. "I have seen my last letter in a Melbourne paper," Casey gleefully reported to his parents in August 1869; "how the prison authorities are dancing with madness here now." Indeed, Fenian letters to the outside world were so common that Casey complained that his friend Patrick Dunne "has ambitions to see his name in Print—others are always writing to the American papers." The activity of these Fenian prisoners shows that the worldwide network of communication and exchange that had kept the Young Irelanders in touch with the outside Irish world during the early 1850s was still alive and well twenty years later.[14]

Twelve thousand miles away in New York City, one of those Young Ireland exiles, John Mitchel, was hard at work editing his latest weekly journal, the *Irish Citizen*. Following his release from Fortress Monroe in October 1865, Mitchel shared the Fenian hope that postbellum tensions between England and the United States would erupt into open conflict, which Irish revolutionaries could capitalize on. He went to Paris as a financial agent for the Fenian Brotherhood but resigned and returned to New York a year later when he realized the dream's hopelessness. In February 1867, four months after returning to the United States, he was offered the position of chief executive officer in the American Fenian movement. He refused, which further increased tensions between himself and an organization from which he had always withheld his undivided loyalty. Later that same year, he issued the first number of the New York *Irish Citizen* with his one remaining son, James, employed in the business office. Mitchel dedicated the new paper "mainly to the well-being, social, industrial and otherwise, of the great masses of the Irish race in the United States." In the columns of the new paper, he berated Fenianism, which had split into two factions. Irish American nationalism could one day be revitalized, he wrote, "but it will never, never more rise upon the 'wings' of Fenianism." Later, his criticism was even more damning. "False pretences have been the main machinery of [Fenianism] from the first," he editorialized in February 1868. Irish sympathizers on both sides of the ocean had been misled by fictitious descriptions, propagated in the press, of the organization's real potential for revolution.[15]

As ever, John Mitchel's newspaper relied on a base of support among Irish Americans, but his pro-Confederate and anti-Fenian policies hurt him. In 1869, his *Irish Citizen* had a circulation of only 6,300, a small number compared to the Boston *Pilot*'s 45,000, the *Irish-American*'s 35,000, and the Fenian *Irish People*'s 9,200. Using an agent named P. O. Aherne, Mitchel attempted to expand the paper's circulation to California. Aherne soon began issuing circulars and free copies of the paper to potential subagents and subscribers up and down the West Coast. He told prospective customers that the paper's "intrinsic merits alone . . . aside from the duty which every good Irishman owes to Mr. Mitchel, whose genius has done so much to elevate the Irish race," would compensate subscribers "for the small price charged for it." The response was less than enthusiastic. In Sacramento, John S. Barrett told Aherne that while he disagreed with Mitchel "on American politics," he did respect "his constant advocacy of Irish Freedom." Nevertheless, a bad experience acting as newspaper agent for the *Irish People* a few years earlier led Barrett to refuse Aherne's offer of a subagency. Mitchel's Confederate activity during the Civil War caused James A. Duffy, also in Sacramento, to refuse to canvass the local Irish on his behalf. Fenian sympathizers also declined to support Mitchel's paper. Matt Sarpy of Watsonville complained that Mitchel "affects to know better how to redress the grievances of Ireland than the combined wisdom of the Irish race assembled in council for that purpose." Mitchel was, Sarpy concluded, "utopian and impracticable, and although a flaming writer, a very sorry statesman." Despite these challenges, the newspaper enjoyed a transatlantic circulation. "I would write to you more at length," Mitchel wrote to a friend in Dublin, "but I say all I know about these matters once a week—if you ever happen to see the I. C. [*Irish Citizen*]."[16]

In the years following the Civil War, the Irish American community remained ensconced in a transcontinental media network that connected the global Irish reading public. John Mitchel often reminded his readers to be suspicious of the "cable canards" sent from England to the United States. "The chief use of our Atlantic cable," he warned them in October 1870, "is in the very rapid transmission of Lies." Yet this steady advance of communication technology also nurtured the international Irish imagined community. Larger circulations meant increased revenue, which led to the proliferation of semiprofessional "foreign correspondents." These people, often friends or family of the editors themselves, sent information and opinion from faraway places. By the mid-1870s, every major Irish paper had at least one such correspondent sending detailed reports on a semiregular basis. With so many Irish papers sending each other material through exchange and subscription agreements, the most interesting letters were subsequently clipped and reprinted in other newspapers, thus multiplying each piece's audience. Even prisoners entombed in a Victorian panopticon on the far side of the globe managed to maintain two-way communication with the outside Irish world through print material. The Fenians in Australia, who regularly received contraband copies of weekly periodicals, were particularly successful at making their voices heard in the international press. Indeed, John Sarsfield Casey suspected that some of his fellow prisoners were merely eager to see their names in print. The popular press enabled Irish migrants to define themselves to their home and host communities. Their complicated relationship to people of color was part of that process.[17]

Indigeneity and Color in the United States and Australia

One often hears it said that the North won the Civil War but lost the peace. The Compromise of 1877 signaled the final collapse of reformist Republican power in southern state governments and the end of a difficult twelve-year process during which racial equality ebbed and flowed. The Thirteenth, Fourteenth, and Fifteenth Amendments to the Constitution prohibited slavery and established black equality in matters of citizenship and voting, but these mandates proved very difficult to enforce. While historians debate the nature of Reconstruction, most agree that it saw a massive increase in the power and scope of the federal government. Kick-started by the war effort, its income, bureaucracy, and responsibilities ballooned through the mid- and late 1860s. The federal budget increased from $63 million to over $1 billion between 1860 and 1865. Its 53,000 nonmilitary employees made it the nation's largest employer. Radical Republicans saw this strengthened federal government as a new "custodian of freedom" for all citizens, regardless of their skin color or place of birth. Many believed they were witnessing the inauguration of a new nation of equals. The real story was far more complicated than that. As David Blight has demonstrated, Reconstruction featured a great debate among Americans over how to define the new nation's relationship to healing and justice. The result, argues Blight, was an imbalanced compromise in which sectional reunion was achieved through the resubjugation of American blacks. "In the half century after the war, as the sections reconciled," Blight concludes, "by and large, the races divided." Some Irish immigrants were agents of this racist restructuring.[18]

Black emancipation hit the Irish in the South hard. As freed slaves moved to the towns and cities in search of work, the black population of New Orleans doubled between 1860 and 1870, from 6,000 to 13,000, while the Irish population dropped from 20,000 to 15,000. Soon, these blacks, not the Irish, began to dominate the port city's labor force. To add insult to injury, "Radical Reconstruction" rolled back much of the municipal and state government control previously granted by Andrew Johnson's "Presidential Reconstruction." A centralized authority, backed up by an occupying army, reminded many Irish southerners of the British occupation of Ireland, driving them further into the arms of the Democratic Party. Irish opposition to black emancipation helped them prove for a second time their loyalty to the white South, writes David Gleeson, while simultaneously encouraging native southerners to finally accept the Irish "as fellow, if still somewhat distinct, members of southern society." In the spring of 1866, a series of riots in Memphis, Tennessee, revealed the depths of Irish racism. On May 1, a group of black soldiers, encountering some Irish policemen in the street, raised three cheers for "Old Abe Lincoln, the Great Emancipator." Insults were exchanged, a crowd gathered, and shots were fired. Over the next two days, an Irish mob ran rampant through the city, attacking black churches, homes, and schools while killing and raping blacks and their white sympathizers along the way. The Irish in the South were using white supremacy to cement their socioeconomic status, although a Radical Republican congressional inquiry blamed the riot on "the natural hostility between the Irish and Negroes."[19]

Some Irish in the North, whose antebellum loyalty to the Democratic Party still had currency during Reconstruction, also used white supremacy to strengthen their position. Young Ireland exile Richard O'Gorman, by now a distinguished jurist and orator in New York, made this clear in a speech at the Cooper Union in October 1867. With whites in the South more or less disenfranchised by Radical Reconstruction, he warned his audience, all southern senators would henceforth be black men. Representing the interests of their colored constituencies, these senators would enjoy a disproportionate amount of influence over federal legislation by holding the balance of power in Congress. "Do you wish, fellow-citizens, to be governed by black men?" he demanded. "No! No!" replied the audience. He urged his listeners to save the nation by defeating Radical Reconstruction. "I care not from what race you sprung," he told them, whether Irishmen or Germans "whose memories are of the bright Rhine." All must unite to save the United States from the ruin and degradation that black equality would usher in. O'Gorman's attitude toward African Americans was more patronizing than hateful. They were, he argued, merely the victims of Radical Republicans who had "infused into the minds of these simple-minded, unintelligent, half-barbarous people, the poison of their own theories." The following year, O'Gorman drew a harder line. The Radical Republicans' pet theory of the innate equality of blacks and whites had indeed been carried out, he told the Young Men's General Committee of Tammany Hall, "but only by degrading them both to the level of one common ruin."[20]

In the columns of his weekly *Irish Citizen*, John Mitchel, who had shocked the Irish world a decade earlier by openly yearning for a slave plantation in Alabama, compared Radical Reconstruction to the British oppression of Ireland. There were, he argued, striking similarities between how the Republican and British governments controlled the southern states and Ireland, respectively. By passing emergency legislation, suspending habeas corpus, and conducting regular searches for arms, both governments had constructed identical systems that were "exclusively and intensely Anglo-Saxon." Beneath Mitchel's opposition to centralized authority and occupying armies, however, was a layer of white supremacy. Even the Penal Laws of eighteenth-century Ireland, Mitchel admitted, had "lacked the darkest feature" of Reconstruction in the South, "for there was in Ireland no mass of black barbarism to be set over the superior race." As abominable as the Penal Laws were, at least they were devised by fellow Caucasians. Reconstruction had outmatched those horrors by rendering white men the political subjects of their former slaves, "the wildest and most brutal of all savages." Mitchel's comments interwove several strands of mid-nineteenth-century Irish racial discourse. The Radical Republican and British governments were two branches of the same transnational Anglo-Saxon race that had been oppressing the Irish since time immemorial. Yet in the context of postbellum American society, the fear of black emancipation trumped Ireland's historical wrongs.[21]

At the same time, there were strong voices in the Irish American community who opposed white supremacy. Perhaps the loudest and most influential belonged to Boston *Pilot* editor John Boyle O'Reilly. An ex-Fenian prisoner who had been transported to Australia with John Sarsfield Casey, O'Reilly escaped to the United States in 1869. Having previously had years of newspaper experience, O'Reilly soon found work with the Boston *Pilot* and within a year had been promoted to editor. As lead writer (and later co-proprietor) of Irish America's most popular periodical, O'Reilly used the *Pilot*'s columns to argue that the "African soul" was "as precious in God's sight as that of the European." Convinced that slavery had temporarily retarded African Americans' civic abilities, O'Reilly believed it would take some time before they were ready to realize their full potential. Yet this was not, he stipulated, due to inherent shortcomings. Blacks were an intelligent, cheerful, faithful people and, though he opposed the immediate integration of white and black schools, O'Reilly nevertheless maintained that the "child with black skin is as good as the child with white skin in the sight of God and just men." As the years progressed, O'Reilly's consistently antiracist agenda won him many friends in the African American community, and he was often invited to lecture before black civic assemblies. At one such meeting in 1885, O'Reilly argued that racial distinctions were designed to "help us to see God's beauty in the world in various ways." O'Reilly's influential editorials represent that segment of the postbellum Irish American population which envisioned the American republic as a steadily expanding, pluralist polity capable of transcending white supremacy.[22]

African Americans were not the only people of color struggling against white hegemony in the decades after the Civil War. West of the Mississippi, Amerindians were making their last stand against territorial dispossession. While the term "manifest destiny" had been coined only as recently as 1845, the notion that the American continent was a *terra nullius* given by God as a massive experiment in liberty and democracy had justified white settlement since the seventeenth century. Settlers had uprooted natives from the eastern states, while the Mexican-American War of the late 1840s gave the United States control over large swaths of northern Mexico. In the 1860s, 1870s, and 1880s, white settlers consolidated these gains by spreading further west, to the detriment of Amerindian society. The native Indian response was varied. Some resorted to military force, some attempted to integrate with the newcomers, while others simply turned and fled toward ever-shrinking unclaimed lands. In spite of President Grant's stated intent to institute a new "peace policy," warfare continued to pockmark the western plains.

Experienced generals such as Philip H. Sheridan, a second-generation Irish American, often prosecuted these military campaigns by replicating methods employed against the Confederacy, including the razing of villages and fields. Native Indians scored some symbolic victories, most notably at the Battle of Little Bighorn in June 1876, but by the late 1880s they were reduced to harmless objects of curiosity. The Dawes Act of 1887 fatally undermined tribal lands, while the massacre at Wounded Knee three years later symbolized the final collapse of native resistance.[23]

Thomas Francis Meagher attempted to participate in this campaign to violently remove Amerindians from the West. In the end, however, his personal campaign against what he called the "savages on our borders" devolved into little more than a tragicomic farce ending in his death. In the wake of Appomattox, Meagher's petitions for a position in the government were rewarded when President Andrew Johnson made him secretary of the territory of Montana in August 1865. One month later, Meagher arrived in Bannack, where Governor Sidney Edgerton, glad to be relieved of responsibility for the troublesome place, promptly departed for the East, leaving the Irishman as de facto governor. Meagher traveled to Virginia City the following day with, legend has it, all the territory's documents in one pocket. He relied on newspapers to stay in touch with developments back East. Soon after arriving, he wrote to his friend, fellow veteran, journalist, and future biographer, Captain W. F. Lyons. "The enclosed slips from our local paper— the 'Montana Post'—will inform you of my arrival at my destination at last," wrote Meagher. "I want you, like a good fellow, to have this announced in the [New York] 'Herald.'" As a long-time Democrat enjoying the patronage of a Republican administration, Meagher soon found himself squeezed by partisan struggle. Within six months he was openly identifying with the Montana Democratic Party's largely Irish "Turbulent Men." The "less Federal officialism, and the more of popular activity and government they had," he told an assembly of citizens in Diamond City in August 1866, "the better would it be for the Territory."[24]

The Bozeman Trail, which connected Montana to the Oregon Trail, was at that time the focal point of repeated Sioux offensives led by Red Cloud. As de facto governor, Meagher fantasized about crushing the Sioux raids with direct military action. While Meagher lauded the Irish peasant for his attachment to the natural environment, he refused to extol the same virtues in Aboriginal Americans. Montana, he told an assembly of whites in 1866, stood as a "temple, which, rising by [his audience's] industry and adventurous manhood," usurped "the domain of the savage and his kindred herd of the plain and forest" to bear witness to "the triumph of civilization over nature, and the irresistible advance of American heroism and American Democracy." After months of hounding the federal government to allow him to raise a militia, during which he complained of having command "not of an invincible, but invisible, force," Meagher was finally given permission to do so in the spring of 1867. A ragtag mob of about 200 unemployed young men signed up. Over the next two months, they caused more harm than good without actually engaging the enemy at all. One Montana Indian agent later described Meagher's alleged campaign against the Sioux as "the biggest humbug of the age, got up to advance his political interest, and to enable a lot of bummers who surround and hang onto him to make a big raid on the United States treasury." Unaware of the situation, and probably tired of Meagher's repeated demands, General Sherman finally agreed to send 2,500 rifles up from St. Louis in June 1867. After riding six days to receive the weapons in Fort Benton, however, Meagher slipped on the deck of the houseboat he was staying on and fell into the fast-moving waters. It was July 1, 1867. Though his New York socialite wife combed the banks of the Missouri River for months afterward, Meagher's body was never found.[25]

While some Irish, like Meagher, were eager to participate in the systematic extermination of Amerindians west of the Mississippi, others were vocally opposed to the project. The obdurate editor of the New York *Freeman's Journal*, James A. McMaster, was one such protester. Throughout the late 1860s and 1870s, his editorials castigated the federal government's violent and mendacious treatment of the aboriginal population. In steady correspondence with missionaries and laypeople operating on the western frontier, McMaster was outraged by the stories of broken promises that trickled back to him. In the columns of his weekly journal, he campaigned against the "seething corruptions" of crooked agents working for the Office of Indian Affairs who divested gullible, confused, and frightened Amerindians of their lands before selling them to greedy white settlers. He was also angered by the brutal violence employed against the Plains Indians and often cited General Sherman's famous December 1866 suggestion to President Ulysses S. Grant, which encouraged the government to "act with vindictive earnestness against the Sioux, even to their extermination, men, women, and children." Ten years later, McMaster rued the many "treaties made between the United States Government and the Indians . . . broken by the white people while kept by the Indians." Beyond the desire to uphold human decency, McMaster's concern was part of an ongoing turf war between

Protestants and Catholics for unclaimed souls, and the *Freeman's Journal* raised funds for Catholic missionaries working on the western frontier. Mc-Master's editorial position on what he called "Indian wrongs" demonstrates that not all Irish American voices supported the removal and extermination of Amerindians.[26]

Irish Americans also had mixed opinions of imported Chinese "coolie" workers. Much has been written on the pivotal role that Irish immigrants such as Denis Kearney and Frank Roney played in developing the racist ideologies of labor organizations like the Workingmen's Party of California. Certain Irish American editors back East shared these sentiments. John Mitchel recoiled at the thought of American society "deluged with vast multitudes of these most obscene [Chinese] Pagans, who would starve out both the white laborers and artisans, and speedily ruin the very foundations of human society." Eager to come, quick to learn, and willing to work for a pittance, imported Chinese laborers would swamp the labor market. Within a few years, warned Mitchel, "our white artisans and their families will have to eat dead dogs." Yet Irish American opinion was far from unanimous on the matter. In Charleston, South Carolina, where the Irish population was already experiencing increased job competition from emancipated black workers, the weekly *Southern Celt* opposed the coolie trade on moral grounds. The importation of such laborers was, wrote the editor in February 1873, "a fraudulent trade in human flesh, at once ruthless and contemptible . . . [and] a deep disgrace to our civilization." While willing to admit that African and Chinese workers were physiologically better suited to working in certain climates, the editor insisted that they be free to sell their labor on the open market. By attracting free workers to the Americas, vast tracts of underdeveloped land might be brought into production "while the condition of millions of men, now starving in China, would be hopefully and firmly advanced in the scale of civilization."[27]

Perhaps due to the fact that their plights had less direct impact on events in Europe and North America, Irish attitudes toward Aboriginal Australians and New Zealanders in the 1860s and 1870s were often sympathetic. In private, the demeaning view of them as uncouth savages remained a favorite trope, as when Fenian prisoners awaiting trial in Ireland joked about their future lives in Australia. John Kenealy would, one predicted, "skidaddle, join the blacks, and marry a chief's daughter, whose beauty consisted of a flat nose, thick lips, frizzled hair, and a shining black skin." In the popular press, by contrast, Irish writers tended to treat Aboriginal Australians more kindly. After returning to Ireland from imprisonment in the Antipodes,

John Sarsfield Casey decried the violence meted out to natives in an open letter published in the Dublin *Irishman*. When the white settlers grow tired of killing each other, wrote Casey, "they organize hunting parties, and ruthlessly pursue the unfortunate Aborigines whom they . . . shoot down in dozens with impunity." Casey admitted that the natives often painted themselves with ocher and grease but urged his readers to pause before passing judgment. "Don't be shocked at this," he wrote; "don't many ladies of Europe spend hours before a looking glass daubing their faces with horrid Rose pink, etc.?" In Ireland, the Fenian *Irish People* drew parallels between the Irish and Maori struggles for independence. The native New Zealanders had, like the Irish, continually resisted the encroachment of "Anglo-Saxon strangers" on their "native isles."[28]

While white supremacy indubitably played a role in Irish American identity during the postbellum period, it is also clear that vocal elements within that population refused to countenance this racism. On the one hand, many Irish laborers in the South used violence to protect their slightly elevated social status over freed slaves. In the North, comfortable jurists and newspaper editors such as Richard O'Gorman and John Mitchel portrayed emancipation as a political problem of black elected officials holding the balance of power in Congress. Out West, Meagher and others helped to forcibly remove the "savages on our borders," while men like Denis Kearney decried Chinese immigration. Yet these many and varied examples of Irish racism only tell part of the story. Influential voices, including John Boyle O'Reilly and James A. McMaster, explicitly used the columns of their weekly periodicals to castigate the ill treatment of blacks and Amerindians, while the *Southern Celt* offered an interpretation of coolie labor that defended the Chinese worker on both moral and economic grounds. Two decades after William Smith O'Brien drew parallels between indigenous struggles for freedom around the world, Irish newspaper editorials at home and abroad were still doing so. It is true that sticking up for the Maori carried few political liabilities for people living thousands of miles away. What is important, however, is what that posture suggested about their self-image. The Irish situated their Celtic identity in a transnational context.

Irish American Identity in the Postbellum Era

In the years following the Civil War, Anglo-Saxonist discourse continued to steadily develop along that racialist trajectory, which culminated in 1916 with Madison Grant's *The Passing of the Great Race*. The trend derived intellectual legitimacy from the works of what are nowadays called Social Darwinists, such as Herbert Spencer, who applied aspects of Charles Darwin's theories on evolutionary biology to contemporary social issues. Ideas such as natural selection and the "survival of the fittest," a term coined by Spencer in 1864, attracted Anglo-Saxonists for obvious reasons. The works of English and American historians such as John Mitchell Kemble, Edward A. Freeman, and, later, Herbert Baxter Adams and James K. Hosmer further legitimated these beliefs. Postbellum American Anglo-Saxonists believed that the United States' democratic institutions were latter-day versions of the ancient folkmotes carried by their ancestors from the German Black Forest to Britain and hence to America over the course of several centuries. These ideas were popular in the press. A December 1867 editorial in the *New York Times* warned that Radical Reconstruction would give political power to "that [negro] race which more than any other on earth is repugnant to Anglo-Saxon sentiment and prejudice." A year later, "A Veteran Observer" explained why the immigrant Irish could never dominate American society. "With few exceptions . . . the Celt (Irish) does little to elevate himself," he wrote, while "the Saxon (German) generally gets land, if he can, and cultivates it. He sets up a newspaper and establishes a school at once." These allegedly ineffaceable facts proved that American success and prosperity "depend on preserving the original Anglo-Saxon thought and spirit."[29]

Returning to a posture adopted before the Civil War, Irish American editors counterattacked this Anglo-Saxon myth. In an 1869 lecture before the Celtic Association of Philadelphia, John Mitchel portrayed the battle between Celts and Saxons as a timeless transnational struggle between freedom and oppression. Echoing the words of the late John McElheran, Mitchel argued that transnational Anglo-Saxonism was an insidious English invention. In Ireland, various races had settled, traded, intermarried, and become "successively not only nationally Irish, but strictly and physiologically Celts." To justify their oppression of Ireland, however, the English had invented the Anglo-Saxon legend, which claimed that "Teutons are born to rule and to be aggressive, Celts to be ruled or exterminated, and that the English are Teutons and the Irish Celts." The following year, Mitchel laid bare the transatlantic connection. The Anglo-Saxon myth had been "transmitted, like all other British cant, to America," where it offered "a comfortable sense of superiority over the Teagues and Bridgets, and the satisfaction one has in being of kin to a rich and dominant people; for nobody loves poor relations." Some, such as the English biologist Thomas Henry Huxley, had recently suggested that the theory of indelible differences between the

Celts and Saxons was no longer tenable. Mitchel saw ulterior motives in Huxley's words. The condescension was a ruse, he warned, to remove "that disturbing, distracting idea of Celts and Teutons not being fitted for the same political institutions" and thereby undermine the Irish demand for sovereignty at home and abroad.[30]

Throughout the postbellum period, many Irish Americans continued to emphasize the timeless ethnic solidarity that bound them together as Celts. The Fenians' September 1867 *Declaration of Principles* claimed that Providence had wedged "distinctions marked by differences of national character" between the English and Irish peoples, which inscribed "on imperishable record the claims of our country to independent national existence." Meagher also liked to reiterate one of his favorite idioms from the pre-1848 days by emphasizing the connection between the Irish people and the natural environment of their native land. In a December 1866 lecture on fellow Forty-Eighter Michael Doheny, who had died four years earlier, Meagher described his old comrade as a "true Irish Celt." Doheny's heart, voice, spirit, mind, and looks, Meagher explained, "were as Irish as the skies that spanned his modest but hospitable home," while his physical and intellectual powers were as inexhaustible "as the granite of his native cliffs." Born at the foot of the Rock of Cashel in County Tipperary, Doheny had been raised in a landscape dotted with ancient ruins, which bore witness to stately powers of ancient Ireland. At a Saint Patrick's Day celebration in Virginia City, Meagher suggested that this tie to the Irish natural environment was transferrable abroad. The national holiday allowed Irish men and women, wherever they were, to go home for a day. "Why, every one of you, boys and girls, (great cheering and applause) are at home with me today," he insisted. "There's not one of you in Montana. There's not one of you has seen the Rocky Mountains this morning. You have seen the Galtees, or the gray mountains of dark Donegal, or Knock-mel-down." Their ethnic identity as scattered Celts was transferrable to any natural environment.[31]

At the same time, civic pluralism, couched in the rhetoric of American republicanism, continued to characterize how Irish Americans talked about their role in the United States. The Fenians often paraphrased key tropes of American democracy. "We believe and declare that freedom—the right to 'life, liberty, and the pursuit of happiness'—is inherent in every creature made in the image and likeness of God," asserted their 1867 *Declaration of Principles*. The fight for Irish freedom was part of a wider "effort of enslaved humanity to emancipate itself from the thralldom and debasement of feudal tyranny." John Mitchel claimed that republican democracy reached back through the annals of Irish history. "It runs, we believe, in the Celtic blood." The Irish had proved the fact by fighting on behalf of their respective states during the Civil War. In his lectures to audiences in Manhattan, Richard O'Gorman also portrayed the United States as a welcoming environment uniting various European nationalities. "We see here men of all races, of all nations under the sun, Celt, Saxon and Teuton, live together, work together, bound together by ties of friendship and sympathy," he told an audience gathered to greet exiled Fenians in February 1871. "Why should there be quarrel amongst men where none are privileged and all are free?" For his part, Fenian escapee and Boston *Pilot* editor John Boyle O'Reilly thought that immigrant dual identity served the host community well. "I am indeed intensely fond of my native country—I love the queer varieties of her character," he told a friend after a decade in exile. "I am all the more truly American because of this old love—all Irishmen are."[32]

In Canada, Thomas D'Arcy McGee's form of Irish Canadian nationalism was even more explicitly based on a civic pluralism beneath a benevolent British constitution. He sought, writes David Wilson, "to balance core values with minority rights . . . [while insisting] that immigrants and ethnic groups should not inject old hatreds into their new environment." By the summer of 1867, McGee was part of the coterie of politicians responsible for the British North America Act, which created the independent Dominion of Canada within the British Commonwealth on July 1, 1867. There was room in Canada "for one great, free people," he declared, "but there is not room enough, under the same flag, and the same laws, for two or three angry, suspicious, obstructive 'nationalities.'" If Canadians did not embrace diversity, they would return to a Hobbesian state of nature where brutish ethnic groups were perpetually at each other's throats. "Analyze our aggregate population," he insisted; "we have more Saxons than Alfred [the Great] when he founded the English realm; we have more Celts than Brien [Boru] had when he put his heel on the neck of Odin; we have more Normans than William [the Conqueror] had when he marshaled his invading host along the strand of Falaise." Not all Irish immigrants were enamored of McGee's vision of British integration. In particular, many Fenians, whom McGee regularly castigated for their dedication to "the construction of imaginary Republics beyond the seas," saw him as a threat to Irish freedom. On April 7, 1868, while walking home from a parliamentary sitting in Ottawa, McGee was shot in the head and killed instantly. A speedy trial, stoked by public revulsion, convicted a Fenian named P. J. Whelan for the murder, and he was hanged soon after.[33]

Throughout the 1860s and 1870s, the portrait of themselves as a global nation continued to serve the needs of Irish people caught between the desire to maintain premigration bonds of ethnic solidarity and the need to prove their suitability for new world communities based on civic pluralism. The Fenians demanded Irish independence "in the name of every man of Irish blood throughout the whole earth" and hoped to harness "the power which fifteen millions of the Irish people, scattered between the old world and the new, must necessarily exercise." As Irish migrants diffused "the spirit of independence throughout the world, wherever her scattered children are to be found," they would confer a benefit upon all nations. Though unwilling to join forces with the Fenians, John Mitchel agreed that the global dimensions of the Irish race made them an instrument in the universal struggle against tyranny. After centuries of oppression, the "Irish race has been not only preserved miraculously in two hemispheres to bear a hand in the righteous work of retribution," Mitchel opined, "but also providentially *educated* . . . in order that it may execute the judgment with good will and with all its heart." The Irish Celts' duty as transnational agents of liberty came with liabilities as well. Failure to achieve independence for their homeland would undermine their reputation. The Fenian leader Thomas Sweeny touched on this in a speech soon after the Civil War. To fail in its pledge to free Ireland would stigmatize the Irish race "in the eyes of the World." Just think, he implored his audience, "how the Saxon will laugh in his pride and insolence at the weakness and cowardice of the Celt!"[34]

Global nationalism also served the ends of nationalist politicians in Ireland. Following the collapse of Fenianism, the Home Rule movement became the main voice of Irish separatism throughout the 1870s. In 1871, former Young Irelander John Martin was elected to the British Parliament as a Home Rule candidate. During the 1870s, Martin regularly encouraged the worldwide Irish to work together. There was, he claimed, a "general feeling among the Irish in Ireland, and all around the globe, in favor of national independence and a more general disposition to act in concert" toward that goal, but the sheer distances between them rendered it hard to unite behind a single campaign. The problem was that each Irish community was operating in a unique political context. Those living in Ireland and in British colonies such as Canada and Australia were subject to the laws of London, while the Irish in the United States, though free of English influence, still owed allegiance to their adopted republic. Martin recognized the difficulty of uniting these various communities and urged the Irish in faraway lands to work with each other. The "Irish in each division must recognize and respect the situations of the other," he argued, "else the Irish in one quarter might be thwarting the action of the Irish in another." His firsthand experience with the Irish in Ireland, Australia, and the United States (which he visited during the winter of 1869–70) had convinced Martin that "the Irish in each country are proper judges of the policy best suited to their circumstances." Global nationalism was not a one-dimensional monolith but a kaleidoscope of local shapes and colors.[35]

Thousands of miles away, global nationalism served the Irish in Australia as well. Success hinged, in part, on the idea that Irish immigrants shook off distasteful national characteristics when freed from English oppression. In a speech entitled "Why Is Ireland Poor and Discontented?" which he delivered at the Polytechnic Hall in Melbourne on February 10, 1870, Charles Gavan Duffy charged that Ireland had been "habitually misgoverned" by successive British Parliaments whose centuries of bad laws had a deleterious effect on "that sensitive and plastic race." Upon migrating to the Antipodes, however, the Irish became upright, happy citizens. "We [Australians] have all observed," Duffy said, "how soon the drill and the jacket transform an Irish peasant into a sub-constable, with as military a carriage and as expert an eye and hand as a veteran soldier." Two years later, a new Irish Australian weekly entitled the *Irish Citizen* was founded in Sydney. By forwarding free issues to its namesake in New York, the newcomer immediately entered the international network of circulating Irish weeklies. It addressed the issue of dual loyalty in its first lead editorial. Migrants who had left their homes could not be expected to erase the memories of their native race. At the same time, immigrants must take care not to disturb the harmony of their new communities. The new *Irish Citizen* was pledged to find a middle ground. "In making Australia our home, we intend to remain Irishmen to the heart's core," it explained, "while we are at the same time peaceful and upright citizens of Australia."[36]

Transnational Anglo-Saxonism was also enjoying renewed energy in books like Charles Wentworth Dilke's *Greater Britain* (1869), which was based on a trip he had taken along "the Anglo-Saxon highway round the globe" in 1866–67. "Our citizenship of the greater Saxondom which includes all that is best and wisest in the world," Dilke explained, transcended the provincialism of England itself. Dilke visited the Antipodes, Asia, and Europe, but was particularly impressed by the United States, which "offers the English race the moral directorship of the globe, by ruling mankind through Saxon institutions and the English tongue." Similarly, Dilke's fellow English contemporary, James Anthony Froude, embarked on a lecture tour of the

United States in the autumn of 1872 in which he argued that the intractability of the Irish nature, not British misgovernment, was to blame for Ireland's woes. The United States "is the supreme Court of Appeal in the Irish imagination," he declared, "and if ever the hatchet is to be buried, if ever Celtic and Saxon are to end their quarrel in a general conciliation, it will be when this country has pronounced that Ireland ought to be satisfied and has no longer a grievance which legislation can remove." Irish Americans shouted Froude down with nasty editorials and vociferous speeches, many of which were subsequently reprinted in foreign Irish weeklies. Plagued by angry crowds, vituperative editorials, and rumors that he was a British spy, the historian cut his trip short and returned to England. "Froude is really a man to be congratulated, or almost envied," sneered John Mitchel, for having "stirred up hosts of vindictive enemies on both sides of the Atlantic."[37]

In the wake of the Civil War, the revived ambitions of transnational Anglo-Saxonism, along with the continued migration of the 1860s and 1870s, encouraged Irish people in the United States, Ireland, and beyond to continue to portray themselves as an international community of Irish Celts. United by ethnic solidarity but capable of embracing various kinds of civic pluralism, whether American democratic republicanism or Australian settler colonialism, the Irish were model citizens in any host community. In the years during and immediately after the Great Famine, many had seen the worldwide dispersal of Irish people as a disaster. By the mid-1870s, some writers, such as the Irish American priest James O'Leary, perceived it in a positive light:

> We blush not, for we feel the effluence of a national Irish spirit, wider than the boundaries of Ireland, which is building up, on a world-wide scale, a grander, nobler, and more magnificent Ireland. One by one the instruments of annihilation have been destroyed by the Irish race. Was Ireland divided, vanquished, decimated, pulverized by wars? To-day we have three Irelands—one in the British Islands, one in America, one in Australia. Was Ireland confiscated? To-day the Irish race holds title-deeds of land ten times the area of old Ireland. Was Ireland oppressed by legislation? To-day the Irish race can control the destinies of the two greatest governments on the globe. Did laws degrade the Irish intellect, corrupt Irish morals, and trample the Irish conscience? To-day Irish intellect is a password to power, preferment, and emolument the world over.

This was the kind of stridency that accosted Froude on his tour of the United States, causing him to return to England earlier than planned. In New York, a relative newcomer to the Irish American press was glad to see the historian go. With "the deceptive varnish of modern culture washed off, James Anthony Froude is to-day, in instinct and in essence," he declared, "the same treacherous, untaught barbarian as was his cannibal Saxon progenitor some dozen centuries ago." The author was Patrick Ford. His newspaper was the *Irish World*.[38]

Patrick Ford and the Idea of an *Irish World*

In many ways, Patrick Ford's New York weekly *Irish World* offers a core sample of Irish American global nationalism during the postbellum era. Born in Galway in 1837, Ford escaped the Famine along with his family and landed in Boston in 1845. After a primary education at Saint Mary's Catholic School, the teenager left to work as a printer's assistant at William Lloyd Garrison's antislavery *Liberator*. His time there endowed Ford with practice running a periodical, a keen sense of the power of the popular press, and an abiding belief in the equality of mankind. After several years of working for Garrison, Ford began editing his own abolitionist paper, the *Boston Tribune*, in 1861, but it folded after only a few issues when the Civil War broke out. Ford soon joined the Ninth Massachusetts Regiment and participated in the bloody charge of Marye's Heights at Fredericksburg in December 1862. Following the war, he returned to journalism and briefly edited the Charleston *South Carolina Leader*, which was dedicated to protecting free blacks, and then the Irish Catholic *Charleston Gazette* between 1866 and 1870. Selling his share in the latter, he moved to New York City, where the size and intensity of the Irish population convinced him of the feasibility of founding a new paper. As a youth looking for work in Boston in the 1850s, Ford would later recount, he had often experienced prejudice on account of his Irish birth. "I would see a notice," he remembered, "'Boy Wanted; no Irish need apply.'" These experiences galvanized his desire to use the popular press to champion the rights of Irish immigrants. On September 10, 1870, he sold the first issue of the *Irish World*.[39]

Billing itself as a "religious and national" weekly newspaper dedicated to "the Irish Race throughout the World," Ford's publication steadily grew over the course of the next three decades to become Irish America's leading journal. Definite circulation numbers are very difficult to ascertain, but between annual subscriptions and newsstand sales, Ford's weekly circulation seems to have reached 35,000 in 1876 and 50,000 in 1878. By 1884, Edwin Alden's *American Newspaper Catalogue* was estimating the paper's circulation at 100,000, and by the early twentieth century, it was being listed at 125,000. By contrast, the Boston *Pilot's* circulation dropped during the same period, from 103,000 in the early 1870s to 69,000 in the early 1880s. Other New York competitors, such as the *Irish-American* and the *Irish Nation*, lagged far behind, with circulation estimates of 35,000 and 10,000, respectively, in 1882. To achieve this long-term success, Ford had to overcome financial difficulties early on. Short on capital following his foray in South Carolina, and unable to acquire considerable advertising accounts in New York City, Ford was often short on cash during the first decade of the *Irish World's* existence. Although traditionally associated in modern historiography with labor radicalism, the new weekly initially held class struggle at a distance. The prospectus stated that the paper's primary goals were "to work for the achievement of Self-Government for Ireland, to bear aloft the standard of Truth and Religion, to hold the State true to the Declaration of Independence, [and] to confront the pretensions of Anglo-Saxon ascendancy, [which were] set up in derogation of the equal rights of others."[40]

Indeed, contradicting "the usual Anglo-Saxon slang" was somewhat of an obsession for Ford's new newspaper. For the first few years, practically every week featured at least one article, editorial, or speech attacking the Anglo-Saxon myth. Between March 1871 and January 1872, Ford also ran a weekly series entitled "The Celt and the Saxon, or Celtic Civilization Versus Anglo-Saxon Civilization" by the perennially popular late ethnologist John McElheran, who had been such an important pseudo-scientific auxiliary in the antebellum Irish struggle against Anglo-Saxon "cant." For Ford, as it had for his predecessors in the Irish American press, Saxon perfidy transcended time and space. "For fourteen centuries—from the day that Saint Patrick lit the sacred fires in our Western Island down to this day, when the tempest, set loose by the Saxon invader, has striven to quench those fires," Ford reminded his readers, "the God of our fathers has gone before us, and with his right hand has conducted us through the ages." Anglo-Saxonism remained a transnational phenomenon perpetuated in the columns of the popular press. "Our enemy the Saxon—on the stage, in the pulpit, and through the press—has persistently libeled us," warned Ford. "*Harper's Weekly*, the pictorial organ of Anglo-Saxon American 'civilization,' has specially signalized itself by its vile caricatures on the Irish," he added, "while beyond the sea, the London *Times*, the leading organ of British Anglo-Saxondom, derides the sufferings . . . and savagely gloats over the poor emigrant's departure." After the economic downturn of 1873, the plight of the laboring classes began to garner increased editorial attention, but anti-Anglo-Saxonism was always part of the *Irish World*'s message.[41]

Ford balanced this ethnic solidarity with a heady dose of civic pluralism based on American republicanism. In Ford's mind, all members of the American population, regardless of race or country of birth, were entitled to full equality as citizens. "Who and what are the American People?" asked a June 1871 editorial. "This people are not one. In blood, in religion, in traditions, in social and domestic habits, they are many. Leaving out the aborigines, the veritable Americans (but who are now falsely called Indians), there are the Anglo-Americans, the Franco-Americans, the Irish-Americans, the Spanish-Americans, the German-Americans, and the African-Americans." There were those who argued that the United States was an Anglo-Saxon nation and that all other races must adopt English customs and language before being considered full Americans. This desire to Anglicize the United States was precisely what the *Irish World* fought against. As democrats, they were opposed to any class ascendancy, but as "Irish-Americans we are opposed to any race ascendancy." The United States was a confederation of unique races, all on a footing of political equality. To crush the individuality of any race was a step toward centralized oligarchy, Ford argued, and "a blow at the *natural* constitution of each race, as well as the *written* constitution of the whole." In the context of postbellum politics, it comes as no surprise that the *Irish World* made repeated references to Irish military service during the American War of Independence and the Civil War. These conflicts had proved that Irish American loyalty to their host community did not preclude love and pride of home. It was a dual loyalty that Irish Americans had earned and were determined to defend. "Though American by nationality," Ford insisted, "we are yet Irish by race."[42]

With the onset of economic depression in 1873, the *Irish World* began to sympathize with the plight of the American laboring classes, but the paper never embraced white supremacy. Ford supported the workers' right to organize and strike, advocated land reform along lines elucidated by Henry George in *Progress and Poverty* (1879), and defended the Molly Maguires, who, he claimed, had been driven to violence by the "grinding tyranny of the coal ring!" In December 1878 he broadened his periodical's title to the *Irish World and American Industrial Liberator*. Despite the historical, and historiographical, connection between Gilded Age Irish American labor and antiblack racism, the columns of the *Irish World* reflected a pluralist vision of American citizenship that included freed black slaves. "We sympathize with the people of the South—black and white—in their trials," he wrote, and "feel assured that nothing good can result from violent measures." It was the local people, not adventurers from the North, who could best govern the southern states. "But when we say the 'people,'" cautioned Ford, "we mean the *whole* people, acting through their chosen representatives, without regard to race or color, and not any particular faction or class of the people." White supremacy actually perpetuated the South's problems. In "defending the rights of the Negro," Ford concluded, society protected "the rights of the white man too."[43]

The *Irish World* also supported Amerindians, in part because their story mirrored that of the native Irish Celt. Ford rejected the "cant of the day," which claimed that Amerindians had melted away in the face of civilization. It was truer to say, he claimed, that they had been pushed aside by Protestantism, that "sycophantic agent of materialism." Any Amerindian duplicity was an understandable response to a government whose policies had been, from the very beginning, "a series of treacheries." Even the Chinese laborer, that much-maligned threat to white working labor during this period, was treated with respect by Ford. A few months after adding "American Industrial Liberator" to the title of his newspaper, Ford published an editorial entitled "The Irish and the Chinese" in which he opposed the importation of Chinese laborers. His grounds for exclusion were not, however, the same as those of West Coast racists such as Denis Kearney and Frank Roney. Hostility to Chinese laborers on the grounds of racial animosity, Ford asserted, "is unchristian, undemocratic, and uncivilized." The *Irish World* opposed the introduction of Chinese immigrants "not because of the color of the Chinaman's skin, nor because of his language, or his religion; but because that people are brought hither *en masse* virtually as bond slaves by speculating combinations, at the desire of a villainous class which seeks to put the stamp of servility upon every honest but humble avocation." Deriding the "bugaboo stories" that claimed that the Chinese would damage American religion and civilization, Ford assured his readers that his paper's position on Chinese exclusion was "not a question of race . . . [but] altogether one of Industrial Rights."[44]

Like so many of its predecessors, Ford's weekly paper boasted an international circulation. "Wherever men of the Irish race are to be found—and where are they not?" declared a September 1877 editorial, "there the *Irish World* is read." It created this international readership by employing strategies that Irish editors had been using for decades. Subscription and exchange agreements with other newspapers around the world ensured a steady stream of news and opinion from near and far. Agents were hired to sell it in foreign countries. "Go to India—go to Australia—go to New Zealand," exhorted Ford—even there one would find copies of his paper. While other periodicals had impressive local and national circulations, "not a journal among them all—*not one*—has the world-wide circulation of the *Irish World*." In the late 1870s, Ford forged an alliance with Michael Davitt's Land League in Ireland. As part of his work for that cause, Ford organized a Spread the Light campaign. Between 1879 and 1882, Ford sent almost half a million free copies of the *Irish World* to Ireland, where Land League volunteers distributed them to reading rooms and individuals free of charge. Ford prodded his readers to participate too. Individual copies, wrapped and ready to mail abroad, could be purchased in the office. "Propagate the *Irish World*," encouraged one editorial. "Read it to your friends. Get your neighbor to subscribe for it. If your neighbor is too poor to subscribe, loan it to him. When both you and he are done with the paper, wrap it up, put a postage stamp on it, and send it to some friend in Ireland or America. [Should a specific editorial] particularly attract your attention, mark the article and send it to your Member of Congress, with a letter of recommendation from your self. Send marked articles to your local newspaper also. In this way, and in a score of other ways . . . you may advance the *Irish World* and [its cause]." Ford's weekly was part of the worldwide web of Irish print culture that had been growing for decades. Its sheer scale was reflected in a September 1873 cartoon entitled "The Empire of the Press," which symbolized the international Irish reading public and its popular press.[45]

The mass circulation of weekly papers like the *Irish World*, whose carefully chosen title explicitly expressed global nationalism, nurtured a sense of shared identity across the Irish international imagined community. Ford's columns professed to be "a weekly history of the Irish race over the round earth" and promised "the latest and [most] complete news" of the Irish in Ireland, the United States, "France, Rome, England, in Canada, in Australia." Its masthead had an image of the globe in its center topped by a crucifix, with a sunburst in the background. On the left was an old man playing a harp in rural Ireland, and on the right was a young woman holding a document, probably the Declaration of Independence or the U.S. Constitution, in an industrial United States. Together, the title and masthead portrayed the Irish as a global nation capable of dual loyalty to their home and host communities. A mission statement published every week for the first several years of the newspaper's existence defined the Irish race. "All Irishmen, and all Irishmen's sons, the world over, are parts of one mighty

"The Empire of the Press." In this cartoon, the New York *Irish World* is depicted as part of a global network of communication and exchange embodied in the weekly press. By connecting the Irish at home and abroad, these newspapers laid the intellectual basis for an international imagined community. *Irish World* (New York), September 13, 1873. Courtesy of American Antiquarian Society.

whole," it explained. "Perhaps there is no other people on the face of the earth whose identity is more clearly marked and defined. There are forces of attraction, ever at work, which draw the members of our race instinctively together, and knit them into an integral body. And if ever there was A Providential People on the face of the earth, ours is one." Ford's "Mission of the Irish Race" reflected a blend of ethnic solidarity and civic pluralism. While dedicated to self-government for Ireland, Irish immigrants also pledged loyalty to the U.S. Constitution. Beyond this dedication to freedom and democracy, Ford held, the Irish race was also "an apostolic people" pledged to "carry the light of the [Catholic] faith." There was something for everyone in the *Irish World*.[46]

Saint Patrick's Day offered an annual opportunity to reassert the global dimensions of Irish identity. "The green flag waves and the shamrock is worn in every clime and country," Ford boasted, "whether the Southern Cross, or the Great Bear, shines over the lands where the festivities are held." Even along "the banks of the Ganges, in the country of the Hindoos . . . everywhere the same. The sun in his circling course ushers in the day in all lands; and in every land, and among every people that have 'a habitation and a name,' Erin's banner of emerald and gold salutes his rays." Capitalizing on the increased affordability of publishing images, Ford often used pictures to portray the worldwide reach of the Irish nation. A March 1872 cartoon featured Saint Patrick with his arms outstretched over the earth. Snapshots of parades around the world, from Rome, Montreal, San Francisco, Buenos Aires, Calcutta, Sydney, and elsewhere, dotted the border of the portrait. Along the bottom ran a quote from Virgil's *Aeneid* in which Aeneas asked Achates, "What region throughout all the world that is not full of our labors?" Images like this reinforced Ford's central message: that the Irish were a global nation, possessing a flexibility and power that transcended the day-to-day travails facing them in their individual countries. He lauded the ovation that Saint Patrick's followers tendered him "on every returning anniversary, over the globe." This annual effusion of love infected those around them, fostering feelings of jealousy and guilt in those who demeaned the Irish the rest of the year. "A change seems to come over the dream even of the vainglorious Anglo-Saxon," exhorted Ford. "*The whole world has turned Irish.*"[47]

Conclusion

The years following the Civil War witnessed a great debate over how to define the parameters of American citizenship. Constitutional amendments and robust legislation had created a legal framework that recognized the right to full citizenship of both African Americans and naturalized newcomers. To consolidate these newfound rights, blacks and immigrants loudly recalled the sacrifices they had made during the late war. When Froude visited the United States in 1872, for example, Father Graham, a Catholic priest, exploited Anglo-American tensions to show how fighting had rendered the Irish a constitutive element of the American body politic. "Where were you, sir . . . your countrymen and backers, when Irishmen swept up the fearful heights of Fredericksburg, even when they knew that certain death awaited them at the summit?" demanded Graham. "While

Americans from New England and Irish-Americans were mingling their blood upon a thousand battlefields, shaking hands before they fell, and sobbing their last sighs upon each other's shoulders, where were you then O 'eminent historian!'" Despite the commonality between the postwar plights of African Americans and European immigrants, sectional reconciliation was built, in part, on the simultaneous division of whites and blacks. Still wedded to the Democratic Party, which had brokered their participation in the antebellum polity, many Irish Catholics embraced this racism. Those in the South fought to ensure that the best-paying jobs be strictly designated as "white" work, while many in the North sought to undermine the new black electorate's power in Congress. White supremacy was a big part of postwar Irish American identity.[48]

Using the lens of global nationalism, however, we see that there was much more to Irish identity than this blue-collar racism. Influential voices in the Irish American press such as James A. McMaster, John Boyle O'Reilly, and Patrick Ford refused to countenance the dehumanization of Amerindians, freed blacks, and Chinese coolies. Moreover, their rights and responsibilities as American citizens was only one part of how Irish immigrants thought of themselves. It is true that the Irish went out of their way to prove their suitability as defenders of American republicanism. The Fenians were pledged to defend everyone's right to life, liberty, and the pursuit of happiness, while John Mitchel claimed that republicanism came naturally to Irish immigrants. At the same time, this civic pluralism, molded to fit the contours of contemporary American political discourse, went hand in hand with an ethnic solidarity that portrayed the Irish as members of a worldwide Celtic race. Decades of despoliation and dispersal had created "a grander, nobler, and more magnificent Ireland," which transcended international borders. In the postbellum United States, this portrait came to full fruition in Patrick Ford's *Irish World*. Unlike previous Irish American weeklies, which had either copied titles from Ireland to emphasize connections with the homeland (for example, *Freeman's Journal* and *Pilot*) or defined Irish American identity in landlocked terms (for example, the *Nation* and *Citizen*), the *Irish World* wholeheartedly embraced the sheer scale of the phenomenon. The idea of the Irish as a global nation authenticated their efforts to reformulate power and community in the wake of the Civil War. Yet it also illustrated an awareness that such struggles transcended time, space, and the nation-state.

BY 1880, MOST OF THE original members of the Young Ireland movement were dead. In 1874, after twenty-six years in exile, the recalcitrant John

Mitchel returned to Ireland to stand as a Home Rule candidate in County Tipperary. Having completed a full circumnavigation of the globe, he died in his childhood home, Dromalane House, in Newry, County Down, on March 20, 1875. His childhood friend and housemate in Van Diemen's Land, John Martin, caught bronchitis at Mitchel's funeral and died a few days later. Following the deaths of Michael Doheny in 1863 and John O'Mahony in 1877, Richard O'Gorman was the last remaining Young Ireland leader in the United States after Reconstruction. An accomplished orator and a leading New York jurist who sat as judge on the superior court from 1883 to 1890, O'Gorman died in Manhattan in 1895. That left only Charles Gavan Duffy, last of the three original founding members of the Dublin *Nation*. After a reasonably successful political career in Australia between 1855 and 1880, during which he founded a weekly newspaper entitled the *Advocate*, Duffy moved to the European continent, where he spent the next twenty years writing contentious firsthand accounts of Irish history. He died in Nice in 1903. By then, the transnational networks of newspapers and identities that the Young Irelanders had helped pioneer were stock pieces of modern life.

Conclusion

When the Irish Race Convention met in Paris in January 1922, its organizers ultimately hoped to create an Irish International capable of coordinating the social, economic, and political policies of Irish communities at home and abroad. In South Africa, an Irish immigrant newspaper lauded the plan. "It is not the Ireland of four millions that we are thinking of now, nor merely the potential Ireland of ten or fifteen millions," editorialized the *Republic*. "We are thinking also of the Greater Ireland, the Magna Hibernia across the seas, the millions of Irish people throughout the world. Though these Irish are now citizens of their adopted lands, they must not be, and they are not, wholly lost to Ireland. They also are to share in the great destiny of their motherland." To describe Irish nationalism in these terms eighty years earlier would have probably elicited a mix of skepticism and bemusement. Writing in April 1847, Charles Gavan Duffy was convinced that each nationality had its own unique "abiding place" in the natural environment. "Separate Irish Nationality from Ireland, and it must perish," he explained. "As well might you make a bird live and sing in the depths of the sea, or a fish live on the solid earth." The sheer shock of several million people leaving Ireland over the course of the next forty years, however, fundamentally recast how the Irish and their hosts thought about races and nations. The motif of migration, which lay at the heart of the origin myths of both Celts and Saxons, was a hot topic in the debate over the nature of nationality then raging in the Western world. By demanding the right to remain, in the words of Patrick Ford, "American by nationality . . . yet Irish by race," migrants ensured that civic pluralism became encoded in the DNA of modern nationalism.[1]

While consistently portrayed as a coherent ideology, Irish global nationalism was actually an endlessly multivalent discourse. Though constantly shifting to fit different times and places, it everywhere featured a paradoxical blend of ethnic solidarity and civic pluralism. As they adapted to Carlyle's

Handwritten margin notes (top): combined old + new / reality of new / love of old necessity with

Handwritten margin notes (left): existing / surviving

"strange new Today," its employers simultaneously yearned for a lost home while integrating into a new one. In the years preceding the exodus of the late 1840s, the idea that the Celtic spirit and Saxon laws were inherently incompatible attracted many Catholics while simultaneously alienating Protestants. After endlessly underlining the irreconcilable differences between the races, Thomas Davis's words rang hollow when he claimed, "We employ the word [Saxon] in the popular Irish idiom, not as accurately descriptive of race, nor as a word of offence." The mass migration that accompanied the rapid development of global capitalism in the 1850s, 1860s, and 1870s tore asunder extant bonds of community and power. Reconstituting these relationships, while proving suitable for citizenship in new societies, required that migrants imaginatively weave strands of both ethnic solidarity and civic pluralism. The shape and tone depended on their host community. In Australia in the 1850s, the Irish portrayed themselves as an amicable race of hearty Celts capable of productively contributing to settler colonies throughout the British Empire. In the United States, by contrast, where their fealty to the Constitution was constantly under question, the Celts became republicans dedicated since time immemorial to political ideals that their fellow migrants in Australia and British North America shied away from.[2]

As a sweeping rhetorical device that ignored underlying tensions, global nationalism was riddled with ambivalence, ambiguity, and, at times, outright contradiction. Was popular knowledge and understanding of the Celts based on the scientific findings of learned men or on an incontrovertible folk memory buried deep in the hearts of the people? Was the Celt/Saxon dichotomy a useful category for understanding how societies operated or a sad but surmountable hangover of ancient history? Were races the slaves of physiology, or could they master their own destinies? Could the Celtic *esprit* and Saxon *lois* ever adapt to each other, or were the two forever at odds? Had God, as Saint Paul claimed in Acts 17:26, "made of one blood all nations of men," or were the races derived from different species? All agreed that the Celts were changeless across time. Yet was their nature immutable across space? If restricted to the island of Ireland, how could Celts survive abroad? If they did endure in foreign climes, what happened to the offspring of sexual unions between Celts and non-Celts? Was the global scattering of the Irish race a gift from God or a calculated act of national extermination? Irish global nationalists constantly disagreed on points like these. Instead of openly bickering, however, most simply ignored them as best they could. In this way, they inadvertently followed John Martin's advice to those desirous of coordinating the world-scattered Irish toward self-government for Ireland. Nationalists "must recognize and respect the situations" of their compatriots abroad, he wrote in 1870, lest "the Irish in one quarter [thwart] the action of the Irish in another."[3]

This transnational perspective also sheds new light on how the Irish understood their relationship to people of color. To accuse politicians of molding their racial attitudes to fit the expectations of their constituencies is nothing new. Whether denouncing antislavery or cheering anti-imperialism, Irish nationalists always had their own interests in mind. What this book has shown, however, is the degree to which they situated those interests in transnational contexts. Unwilling to espouse blacks' inherent inferiority, Irish nationalists in the 1840s opposed antislavery on constitutional grounds mirroring their own struggle with Britain. Southern slave owners were fellow members of a universal drive for self-government, while freedom fighters in Afghanistan were brethren in an international struggle against British imperialism. Irish nationalists claimed common cause with people of color as long as useful parallels could be drawn between their campaigns. Contradictions abounded in eastern Australia as well, where some Irish Catholics, though participants in the sprawl of white settlement, saw parallels between the land expropriations suffered by Aboriginal Australians and Irish Celts. The paradoxical nature of Irish attitudes to blacks was heightened in the crucible of midcentury American politics. Job competition combined with loyalty to the Democratic Party to ensure that white supremacy remained an element of mainstream Irish American identity. Yet the outcry over Mitchel's Alabama Article reminds us that there was more to the story than blue-collar racism. Whether in Ireland, Australia, or the United States, Irish people thought and talked about race and nation in transnational terms.

The popular press did more than simply articulate Irish global nationalism. It laid its intellectual basis by facilitating the growth of a borderless Irish reading public, which, through the constant exchange of news and opinion, imagined itself into being over the course of the mid-nineteenth century. Looking through Irish papers sent in from foreign countries, the Dublin *Nation* was impressed by their ability to keep readers abreast of news from home. "It would seem from some of them as if they were, by purchase or exchange, in receipt of all the papers of our thirty-two counties," it editorialized in February 1863. As a medium of communication between compatriots at home and abroad, the weekly periodical kept far-flung communities of Irish people in contact with each other. Open for sale and exchange between anyone in the world, the newspaper created a transnational public sphere, which constantly evolved with its readership. As David Gerber has written of the immigrant letter, the popular press "lifted people out of conventional time-space and rendered the national and natural boundaries that separated them insignificant . . . [by leaving] physical and political borders powerless to create impediments for sustaining mutually desired relationships." Newspaper exchange also maintained personal bonds disrupted by migration. This was true even if it was just, as John Martin wrote to an old friend in America, "the hasty tying up of a newspaper and dispatch of it, addressed in my hand, as a message that I was living and remembering you."[4]

In 1873, historian R. R. Madden hoped that the Irish abroad "should never abandon the idea of coming back to [Ireland]." In comparison to later groups such as Italian "birds of passage," however, the Irish rate of return was remarkably low. As the decades wore on, and Britain replaced the United States as the preferred destination, Irish society became imbued with a migration mind-set. As the novelist Joseph O'Connor explained in 1994, "Growing up in Dublin, you just expect emigration to happen to you, like puberty." With tens of millions of people around the world claiming Irish heritage, the diaspora's sheer size has rendered its relationship to the homeland increasingly complicated. The Irish Race Convention of 1922 failed due to the dissonant expectations of the newly founded Irish Free State government and the various diasporic delegates. In the 1970s, Irish American support for the Provisional Irish Republican Army put groups such as Noraid at odds with the home government. Despite these inherent difficulties, the Irish government has maintained at least a rhetorical commitment to the diaspora. When Mary Robinson became president of Ireland in 1990, she emphasized the need to "cherish" the diaspora and placed a candle in the window of her official residence, Áras an Uachtaráin, to remember them by. Her successors Mary McAleese and Michael D. Higgins have continued to popularize the notion of the diaspora as a "fifth province." In the early twenty-first century, successive finance ministers aggressively pursued the Irish abroad to invest in the Celtic Tiger economy, which collapsed in 2008, thanks in part to its reliance on highly mobile international capital. Given the earlier role of print culture, it should come as no surprise that, beyond these government initiatives and tourism, the Internet is currently the primary location for the perpetuation of an international Irish imagined community.[5]

The story of the rise of Irish global nationalism has important implications for our understanding of modern history. It undermines, for example, the exceptionalism that often characterizes studies of individual nation-states. As this book has illustrated, the steady transmission of printed words ensured that the reading publics of various countries were constantly exposed to, and subtly influenced by, news and opinion originally generated elsewhere around the world. This story also offers a forceful argument for the centrality of migration to our understanding of modern nationalism. The processes of nation building and mass migration that characterized the nineteenth century were not awkward bedfellows but reciprocal dynamics in each other's development. As the shifting needs of global capitalism and imperialism transferred humans overseas, state builders adjusted accordingly. Host nations such as the United States and Australia, which needed migrant laborers and managers, redefined citizenship until the naturalized and native-born were equal before the law. In Ireland, where membership in the United Kingdom rendered state building a moot point before 1921, the lack of national boundaries actually made transnational solidarity easier to achieve.

These complicated processes shed light on the world we live in today, where one's passport, last name, country of birth, skin color, and place of residence often fail to fit into neat categories of belonging and identity. If, as Anthony Giddens has suggested, social dislocation lies at the heart of modern society, the nineteenth-century popular press (and its twenty-first-century successor, the Internet) can be seen as part of humanity's response to that condition. Finally, and perhaps most importantly, by laying bare their mutability across time and space, this book reminds us that races and nations are social constructs designed to express and legitimate power relations. Our ultimate goal should not be to teach our children that there is a white race too. It is to *remind* them that we are all born without race.[6]

NOTES

Abbreviations

BLCU   Butler Library, Columbia University (New York City)
BPL   Boston Public Library (Boston)
CGD   Charles Gavan Duffy papers
JVM   Jane Verner Mitchel papers
KOD   Kevin Izod O'Doherty papers
MCIH   Maloney Collection of Irish Historical Papers
NLI   National Library of Ireland (Dublin)
NYPL   New York Public Library (New York City)
RIA   Royal Irish Academy (Dublin)
TCD   Trinity College Dublin Archives (Dublin)
WSOB   William Smith O'Brien papers

Introduction

1. *Irish World* (New York), January 28, 1871; June 24, 1871; December 27, 1873.

2. "Diaspora" is a notoriously loose, sometimes useful, often over-used term, which I have avoided employing in this book to save lengthy digressions and qualifications.

3. Guglielmo, *White on Arrival*; Kenny, "Diaspora and Comparison," 135; Habermas, *Structural Transformation*; Anderson, *Imagined Communities*. Anderson defined a nation as "an imagined political community . . . inherently limited and sovereign" (6) because he was interested nation-*states*. I reconfigure Anderson's definition to describe a nation that was inherently limited though not politically sovereign.

4. Knox, *Races of Men*, 39.

5. *Freeman's Journal* (Sydney), November 26, 1853; *Irish-American* (New York), January 28, 1854. For more on the development of racial ideologies in the United States and the British Empire, see Cha-Jua, "Changing Same," and Koditschek, "Capitalism, Race."

6. Kevin Williams, *Read All*, 75–76. The boozy English laborer is cited in Barker, *Newspapers, Politics*, 58. For an excellent examination of the mid-nineteenth-century Irish press in England, see McNicholas, *Politics, Religion*. For more on newspaper history, see Raymond Williams, *Long Revolution*; Anthony Smith, *The Newspaper*; O'Malley and Soley, *Regulating the Press*; Boyce and Wingate, *Newspaper History*. In this study, the term "popular press" refers to all newspapers and periodicals published for a mass audience. Hence, although the Australian *Sydney Gazette* was originally a government organ designed to disseminate official notices, it is considered a member of the popular press because its audience was the colonial population at large.

7. Handlin, *Boston's Immigrants*; Thomas Brown, *Irish-American Nationalism*, 34; Miller, *Emigrants and Exiles*; Diner, *Erin's Daughters*; Wilson, *United Irishmen*; Kenny, *Making Sense*; Fitzgerald and Lambkin, *Migration*; Murphy, *American Slavery*; Gleeson, *Irish in the Atlantic*; Timothy Meagher, *Inventing Irish America*; Akenson, *Irish in Ontario* and *If the Irish*; O'Farrell, *Irish in Australia* and *Vanished Kingdoms*; Fitzpatrick, *Oceans of Consolation*; Campbell, *Ireland's New Worlds*. Some historians continue to emphasize either the host or home's impact on immigrant identity. For the former, see Doorley, *Irish-American Diaspora*, while for the latter, see Kelly, *Shamrock and the Lily*. For a geographer's perspective, see Mulligan, "Forgotten 'Greater Ireland.'" For recent studies of Irish transnationalism, see Whelehan, *Dynamiters* and *Transnational Perspectives*.

8. Roediger, *Wages of Whiteness*; Ignatiev, *How the Irish*; Jacobson, *Whiteness of a Different Color*. Famous critiques of the early whiteness literature include Arnesen, "Whiteness"; Fields, "Whiteness, Racism, and Identity"; Kolchin, "Whiteness Studies." Recent whiteness works of note include Guglielmo, *White on Arrival*; Kazal, *Becoming Old Stock*; Goldstein, *Price of Whiteness*. For a discussion of how the scholarly debate over whiteness can inform current affairs, see McMahon, "Pages of Whiteness." Transnational diasporic identities are analyzed in Gabaccia, *Italy's Many Diasporas*; Azuma, *Between Two Empires*; Choate, *Emigrant Nation*; and Gerber, "Forming a Transnational Narrative."

9. Young Ireland's dual loyalties, narrowly nationalist as well as broadly universal, were shared by other republicans such as Young Italy, but the connections between these groups remain understudied by historians. See Nowlan, *Ireland*; Costigan, "Romantic Nationalism"; Belchem, "Nationalism, Republicanism"; Barr, "Giuseppe Mazzini"; and Huggins, "The *Nation*."

10. Griffin, *People with No Name*; Miller, *Ireland and Irish America*, 233. See also chapters 6 and 7 in Miller, *Ireland and Irish America*. Other useful works include Doyle, *Ireland, Irishmen*; Leyburn, *The Scotch-Irish*; Dickson, *Ulster Emigration*; Peter Gilmore, "Rebels and Revivals"; Wilson and Spencer, *Ulster Presbyterians*; Miller, Schrier, Boling, and Doyle, *Irish Immigrants*. For females and Irish diasporic nationalism, see Brundage, "Matilda Tone"; Janis, "Nationalism, Gender" and "Petticoat Revolutionaries"; Kibler, "Stage Irishwoman"; Moloney, "Land League Activism."

11. Barr, "'Imperium in Imperio,'" 612, 650. See also Gilley, "Roman Catholic Church"; Rafferty, "Catholic Church"; Carey, *God's Empire*, esp. 114–47 and 287–304.

12. Murphy, *American Slavery*; Nelson, *Irish Nationalists*. Nelson's book is an important contribution to the literature, although his overreliance on the black/white conceptual framework understates the equally important Celt/Saxon dichotomy.

13. Fitzgerald and Lambkin, *Migration*, 173; Miller, *Emigrants and Exiles*, 569; Campbell, *Ireland's New Worlds*, 46. Limits on the scope of this project prohibited a full examination of how global nationalism played out among the Irish in Great Britain.

14. Kenny, *American Irish*, 90.

15. *Nation* (Dublin), September 23, 1843; *Irish News* (New York), January 10, 1857; June 27, 1857. Declan Kiberd connects migration and national identity in *Inventing Ireland*.

Chapter One

1. Duffy, *Young Ireland*, 24; *Nation* (Dublin), October 15, 1842. For the Phoenix Park meeting and "Young Ireland" nickname, see Duffy, *Young Ireland*, 17–18, 107.

2. McKeown, "Global Migration"; Baum, *Rise and Fall*, 122–23; Miller, *Emigrants and Exiles*, 35, 41, 29. Localism also played an enduring role in nineteenth-century Irish political culture. See Hoppen, *Elections, Politics*.

3. Young, *Idea of English*, 96, 43; Stocking, *Victorian Anthropology*, 62–63; Young, *Idea of English*, 18; Baum, *Rise and Fall*, 38; *Times* (London), December 2, 1848; Young, *Idea of English*, 88.

4. MacPherson, *Fragments of Ancient Poetry*, iii; James, *Atlantic Celts*, 43–59; Snyder, *Celtic Revival*, 1–7; Chapman, *The Celts*, 120–45; Curley, *Samuel Johnson*, 123–55; Hobsbawm and Ranger, *Invention of Tradition*.

5. Young, *Idea of English*, 41–42; MacDougall, *Racial Myth*, 2–3; Curtis, *Anglo-Saxons and Celts*, 1–16, 36–48.

6. This summary of the United Irishmen is based on Whelan, *Tree of Liberty*, 59–132; Curtin, *United Irishmen*; Wilson, *United Irishmen*, 12–35; Boyce, *Nationalism in Ireland*, 123–53. This portrait of O'Connellism is based on Boyce, *Nationalism in Ireland*; MacDonagh, *The Emancipist*; MacIntyre, *The Liberator*; Nowlan, "O'Connell."

7. Theobald Wolfe Tone, "Declaration and Resolutions of the Society of United Irishmen in Belfast," in Killen, *Decade of the United Irishmen*, 21; Whelan, *Tree of Liberty*, 3–4, 129; Curtin, *United Irishmen*, 4, 10–11; Boyce, *Nationalism in Ireland*, 134, 145; Whelan, *Tree of Liberty*, 130; Boyce, *Nationalism in Ireland*, 134; O'Connell, *A Memoir*. For competing analyses of the sectarianism of the 1790s, see Whelan, *Tree of Liberty*; Curtin, *United Irishmen*; Elliott, "Origins and Transformation."

8. Bartlett, *Ireland*, 206, 210; Curtin, *United Irishmen*, 175; Whelan, *Tree of Liberty*, 95; Wilson, *United Irishmen*, 25, 31.

9. Davis, *Young Ireland Movement*, 25, 56; MacGrath, "Writers," 218; Dwan, *Great Community*, 141–68.

10. Cited in Duffy, *Young Ireland*, 23, 24; J. B. Dillon to C. G. Duffy, n.d. [1843] (CGD, MS 5756, NLI); cited in Duffy, *Young Ireland*, 70.

11. Miller, *Emigrants and Exiles*, 70–71; Boyce, *Nineteenth Century Ireland*, 275; Ó Ciosáin, *Print and Popular Culture*, 31–39, 186–91; Duffy, *Young Ireland*, 62; James Fintan Lalor to C. G. Duffy, January 11, 1847 (Gavan Duffy Bequest Box 1, MS 12/P/15/6, RIA); Duffy, *Young Ireland*, 145. As an exile in New York City in 1850, Thomas D'Arcy McGee estimated the circulation at "some twenty thousand every Saturday" (*American Celt* [Boston], August 31, 1850). In 1972, Malcolm Brown claimed that with "a circulation of twenty-five thousand and an estimated ten readers for each copy," the *Nation*

"had a regular audience of a quarter of a million persons." See Brown, *Politics of Irish Literature*, 67. Neither McGee nor Brown offer hard data to support their estimates, but numbers do exist. Each newspaper bore a penny stamp as it traveled through the mail system, and the Custom House published quarterly returns of stamps issued. Examination of this data may allow future historians to calculate how many copies of the leading weeklies were mailed each week. On occasion, these Stamp Returns were published in the Dublin *Nation*. On March 30, 1844, numbers printed in the *Nation* indicated that the *Nation*'s average weekly circulation sat at 10,730—impressive compared to its weekly Dublin competitors, the *Freeman's Journal* (7,230) and *Pilot* (1,146). For more on the interaction of literacy and orality as an aspect of Young Ireland nationalism, see Huston Gilmore, "Shouts of Vanished Crowds."

12. Joyce, *Editors and Ethnicity*, 52–54, 69. There was much overlap between "Catholic" and "Irish American" newspapers. See the *Boston Pilot*, December 3, 1842.

13. *Vindicator* (Belfast), October 1, 1842; Pappin, *Metaphysics of Edmund Burke*, 81; *Nation* (Dublin), January 25, 1845; January 28, 1843; September 23, 1843; February 18, 1843; Duffy, *Voice of the Nation*, iii; *Nation* (Dublin), October 15, 1842; April 22, 1843. Given Burke's preference for patriotic institutions over excitable populations, it is ironic that Young Ireland liked to quote him. See Mandler, *English National Character*, 25.

14. *Nation* (Dublin), October 22, 1842; Thomas Davis to John Windele, November 22, 1843 (John Windele papers, MS 4/B/2/156, RIA); Dwan, *Great Community*, 52; *Nation* (Dublin), April 15, 1843; May 6, 1843; November 4, 1843; September 16, 1843; December 10, 1842.

15. Duffy, *My Life*, 2:125–30.

16. Dillon, *Life of John Mitchel*, 1:48, 51, 54, 45; Davis, *Young Ireland Movement*, 56; *Nation* (Dublin), November 22, 1845.

17. Wilson, *Thomas D'Arcy McGee*, 1:107, 109; Duffy, *Four Years*, 20.

18. Duffy, *Young Ireland*, 107.

19. Townend, *Father Mathew*.

20. Davis, *Young Ireland Movement*, 38–44; *Nation* (Dublin), September 23, 1843. Gary Owens has written on the monster meetings in some detail. See his "Nationalism without Words," "Hedge Schools of Politics," and "Constructing the Repeal Spectacle." While modern historians and contemporary newspapers alike disagree over the numbers of attendees at these monster meetings, Owens concludes that these assemblies constituted "an unparalleled achievement in political mobilisation in the British Isles" ("Nationalism without Words," 244).

21. *Nation* (Dublin), December 17, 1842.

22. Ibid., October 22, 1842; Duffy, *Voice of the Nation*, iv; *Nation* (Dublin), November 26, 1842.

23. Duffy, *Young Ireland*, 107; *Nation* (Dublin), April 15, 1843; December 30, 1843; J. Martin to C. G. Duffy, August 22, 1845 (CGD, MS 5756, NLI); *Nation* (Dublin), October 28, 1843; October 7, 1843. Davis originally published his "unpeopled and inexplicable" article before he joined the *Nation*, probably in the *Dublin Monthly Magazine*. It was republished in the *Nation* (Dublin), November 13, 1847.

24. *Nation* (Dublin), October 14, 1843; Thomas Davis papers (MS 14056, n.d., NLI); *Nation* (Dublin), April 1, 1843; December 30, 1843; April 29, 1843; September 23, 1843; Smiles, *History of Ireland*, v; *Nation* (Dublin), May 18, 1844; November 4, 1843; December 9, 1843.

25. *Nation* (Dublin), May 13, 1843; August 5, 1843; May 27, 1843.

26. Ibid., March 25, 1843; MacGrath, "Writers," 217; *Nation* (Dublin), June 10, 1843.

27. *Nation* (Dublin), July 1, 1843.

28. Davis, *Young Ireland Movement*, 45.

29. Young, *Idea of English*, 95, 100; *Times* (London), August 28, 1845.

30. Carlyle, *Chartism*, 26; Knox, *Races of Men*, 27. For analyses of the *Times* commissioner's racial discourse, see Young, *Idea of English*, 29–30, 74, 100–101 and Lengel, *Irish through British Eyes*, 46–48. Koditschek, *Liberalism, Imperialism*, 325–34, examines how British politicians historicized their anti-Irish racism.

31. *Times* (London), October 7, 1845; *Nation* (Dublin), September 6, 1845; September 27, 1845. In 1846, Zachariah Wallace founded the *Anglo-Celt*, a Unionist, pro-landlord weekly sympathetic to the working poor. "We tell the *Times* Commissioner and the *Nation* that they are both—the former foolishly, the latter foolishly and wickedly, mistaken," editorialized Wallace. "There is hardly a pure Celt—not one pure Saxon in the island." "We are neither Saxons nor Celts," he concluded. "We are Anglo-Celts, every mother's son of us" (*Anglo-Celt* [Cavan], February 6, 1846).

32. *Nation* (Dublin), August 2, 1845; W. S. O'Brien to Thomas Davis, August 3, 1845 (Thomas Davis papers, MS 2644, NLI).

33. Thomas Davis to C. G. Duffy, n.d. [August 1845] (Gavan Duffy Bequest Box 2, MS 12/P/16/21, RIA); Duffy, *Young Ireland*, 273; Malcolm Brown, *Politics of Irish Literature*, 85.

34. Ó Gráda, *Black '47*, 13–46; Gray, *Famine, Land*, 337; *Times* (London), October 15, 1847. Nally, *Human Encumbrances*, offers a nuanced analysis, rooted in postcolonial studies and famine theory, of the British government's response to the Famine.

35. *Nation* (Dublin), September 9, 1843.

36. Ibid., November 26, 1842; March 25, 1843; Duffy, *Voice of the Nation*, 108–9. The Irish people's fraught relationship with the British Empire has spawned a lively field of study. A key text remains Howe, *Ireland and Empire*. Some have argued that Irish anti-imperialism could cross the color line. For examples, see Bayly, "Ireland, India"; Gibbons, *Transformations* (especially chapter 12, "Race against Time: Racial Discourse and Irish History," 149–64); Lynch, "'Live Ireland, Perish the Empire'" and "Defining Irish Nationalist"; McMahon, "Transnational Dimensions." Others see Irish anti-imperialism as largely opportunistic. See Townend, "Between Two Worlds"; Whelehan, "Skirmishing." Other important works include Nelson, *Irish Nationalists*, 121–77; Fitzpatrick, "Ireland and the Empire"; Akenson, *Irish Diaspora*.

37. Kohl, *Travels in Ireland*, 87, reviewed in *Nation* (Dublin), November 4, 1843; De Beaumont, *Ireland*, 130; *Nation* (Dublin), July 1, 1843, reprinted as "Orange Anniversaries" in Duffy, *Voice of the Nation*, 132–33.

38. *Nation* (Dublin), June 3, 1843; June 10, 1843; May 16, 1846.

39. A wealth of scholarship has traced the rise and fall of mid-nineteenth-century Irish antislavery. The most recent full-length work is Murphy, *American Slavery*. Previous works of note include Osofsky, "Abolitionists"; Riach, "Daniel O'Connell," "Ireland and the Campaign," "O'Connell and Slavery," and "Richard Davis Webb"; Rodgers, *Ireland, Slavery*. Riach, "Ireland and the Campaign," 162; *Nation* (Dublin), April 5, 1845; October 22, 1842; Riach, "Ireland and the Campaign," 219.

40. *Boston Pilot*, March 19, 1842; July 6, 1844; Murphy, "Abolition, Irish Freedom," 224–225, 123. See also Nelson, *Irish Nationalists*, 57–118.

41. *Nation* (Dublin), April 12, 1845; January 13, 1844; August 9, 1845.

42. James Haughton to Rev. Samuel May Jr., February 2, 1846 (Anti-Slavery Collection, MS B.1.6 vol. 3, no. 9, BPL); James Haughton to George Thompson, December 13, 1846 (Anti-Slavery Collection, MS A.1.2 vol. 16, p. 138, BPL).

43. Davis, *Young Ireland Movement*, 71; Thomas Meagher, *Meagher of the Sword*, 36; Duffy, *Four Years*, 145, 324. Many reading rooms grumbled about the ban on the *Nation*. Some complained that their decision to donate to the Repeal Rent had been predicated on the subscription. Others offered to subscribe to the *Nation* above and beyond their donation to Repeal. A few American Repealers sent money to help alleviate the cost of the lost subscriptions. Duffy thanked one such contributor from New Orleans, seeing in the donation a "clear and practical illustration, surely, of how completely the Irish race at home and abroad are outgrowing their chains—the chains of custom as well as the chains of England." See *Nation* (Dublin), November 14, 1846.

44. *Nation* (Dublin), January 16, 1847; January 30, 1847; April 10, 1847.

45. Ibid., January 9, 1847; January 16, 1847; April 17, 1847.

46. Cited in Davis, *Young Ireland Movement*, 103; Mitchel, *Life and Times*, viii, ix. The edition used here was published in 1868, but the excerpts cited were unchanged from the 1845 edition.

47. Thomas Meagher, *Meagher of the Sword*, 65–66; *Nation* (Dublin), January 16, 1847.

48. Cited in Davis, *Young Ireland Movement*, 131; Wilson, *Thomas D'Arcy McGee*, 1:182; Davis, *Young Ireland Movement*, 145. Years later, Duffy would claim that Mitchel "had tried my patience sorely by defending negro slavery, and denouncing the emancipation of the Jews as an unpardonable sin. I could not permit the *Nation* to be carried over to the side of oppression on any pretence, and I struck both these escapades out of the proofs" (Duffy, *Four Years*, 500–501). Mitchel never broached slavery in his *United Irishman*.

49. Duffy cited in Campbell, *Ireland's New Worlds*, 40; *Nation* (Dublin), April 1, 1848.

50. For a firsthand account of the rebellion, see Doheny, *Felon's Track*, 97–120.

51. Baum, *Rise and Fall*, 38.

52. Duffy, *Four Years* 6.

Chapter Two

1. Touhill, *William Smith O'Brien*, 20–21; John Martin papers [Diary 1848–1858], (Pos. 5788, NLI); O'Brien, *"To Solitude Consigned,"* 33–34; T. F. Meagher to C. G. Duffy, February 1850 (Alan Queale papers, MS 11,705 [Pos. 8429], NLI). This letter (dated Van Diemen's Land, December 1, 1849) is also reprinted in Thomas Meagher, *Meagher of the Sword*, 235–67. The quote cited above appears on 235. It was originally published in the *Nation* (Dublin), May 4, 1850, and reprinted in *Nation* (New York), May 25, 1850.

2. *Freeman's Journal* (Sydney), April 21, 1855.

3. Madgwick, *Immigration to Eastern Australia*, 1; MacIntyre, *Concise History*, 42–50; John Williams, *Ordered to the Island*, 2–3.

4. McLean, *Why Australia Prospered*, 11–12; MacIntyre, *Concise History*, 85; Atkinson, *The Europeans*, 304; Roberts, *Squatting Age*; McMichael, *Settlers*.

5. MacIntyre, *Concise History*, 87. See also Blainey, *Rush That Never*; Goodman, *Goldseeking*; Serle, *Golden Age*.

6. MacIntyre, *Concise History*, 91–92. See also Cochrane, *Colonial Ambition*; Hirst, *Strange Birth*.

7. Campbell, *Ireland's New Worlds*, 4, 12–20, 30–36; Reece, "Irish Convicts," 448; John Williams, *Ordered to the Island*, 158.

8. Miller, *Emigrants and Exiles*, 569; Campbell, *Ireland's New Worlds*, 37–38, 59. For more on Irish identity in New Zealand, see McCarthy, *Scottishness and Irishness*.

9. Meagher's description of Cooper's cabin was published in the *Nation* (Dublin), July 27, 1850, and reprinted in the *Irish-American* (New York), August 17, 1850; T. F. Meagher to K. I. O'Doherty, January 10, 1850 (Thomas F. Madigan collection [Thomas F. Meagher letters, 1848–1867], NYPL).

10. Cullen, *Young Ireland in Exile*, 41; Mitchel, *Jail Journal*, 235; J. Mitchel to T. F. Meagher, n.d. [April 1850] (KOD, Pos. 1396, NLI).

11. Atkinson, *The Europeans*, 47.

12. Ibid., 246; *Sydney Morning Herald*, April 11, 1854; Campbell, *Ireland's New Worlds*, 43; J. Martin to Eva, June 6, 1850 (KOD, Pos. 1396, NLI).

13. *Australasian Chronicle* (Sydney), August 2, 1839. The biographical information on Father McEncroe is from Phillips, "McEncroe, John." See also Rigney, *An Account*; Birt, *Benedictine Pioneers*; Birchley, *John McEncroe*.

14. Dowd, *Rome in Australia*, 163–67. The standard work on Roman Catholicism in the Antipodes at this time remains O'Farrell, *Catholic Church and Community*.

15. *Freeman's Journal* (Sydney), June 27, 1850; August 29, 1850. For an analysis of newspaper connections between Ireland and New Zealand in the early twentieth century, see McNamara, *"New Zealand Tablet."*

16. Patrick O'Donohoe to K. I. O'Doherty, November 9, 1849 (KOD, Pos. 1396, NLI); *Irish Exile and Freedom's Advocate* (Hobart Town), January 26, 1850; February 23, 1850. The prospectus was reprinted in the *Nation* (Dublin), May 25, 1850, and noticed in the *Irish-American* (New York), June 9, 1850.

17. Mitchel, *Jail Journal*, 39, 55, 57, 9, 74.

18. W. S. O'Brien to K. I. O'Doherty, October 26, 1852 (KOD, Pos. 1396, NLI); C. G. Duffy to W. S. O'Brien, December 2, 1854 (WSOB, MS 445/2877, NLI); C. G. Duffy to T. F. Meagher, September 13, 1850 (KOD, Pos. 1396, NLI).

19. W. S. O'Brien to Lucy O'Brien, September 29, 1852 (WSOB, MS 8653 (28) [Pos. 8394/5], NLI); W. S. O'Brien to K. I. O'Doherty, September 29, 1852 (WSOB, MS 10,515 (3) [Pos. 8428], NLI); W. S. O'Brien to K. I. O'Doherty, July 21, 1853 (WSOB, MS 10,515 (3) [Pos. 8428], NLI); W. S. O'Brien to K. I. O'Doherty, April 29, 1854 (KOD, Pos. 1396, NLI); K. I. O'Doherty to W. S. O'Brien, n.d. [1852] (WSOB, MS 444/2799, NLI).

20. Fitzpatrick, *Oceans of Consolation*, 290, 291, 289.

21. Ibid., 290, 294, 287.

22. Cited in Touhill, *William Smith O'Brien*, 36. For a more detailed examination of Smith O'Brien's motivation to refuse parole, see ibid., 36–38; W. S. O'Brien to Lucy O'Brien, October 29, 1849 (WSOB, MS 8653 (25) [Pos.8394/5], NLI); cited in Touhill, *William Smith O'Brien*, 46.

23. *South Australian Register* (Adelaide), December 12, 1849; *Irish Exile and Freedom's Advocate* (Hobart), January 26, 1850; *Nation* (Dublin), April 21, 1850, reprinted in *Nation* (New York), May 11, 1850; *Nation* (Dublin), June 1, 1850, reprinted in *Mississippi Free Trader and Natchez Gazette* (Natchez), July 6, 1850; *Freeman's Journal and Daily Commercial Advertiser* (Dublin), July 9, 1850; *Boston Pilot*, July 6, 1850; *Freeman's Journal* (Sydney), October 31, 1850; C. G. Duffy to W. S. O'Brien, September 13, 1850 (WSOB, MS 444/2730, NLI). For narratives of the affair, see Touhill, *William Smith O'Brien*, 47–66, and Touhill, "*The Times.*"

24. C. G. Duffy to T. F. Meagher, September 13, 1850 (KOD, Pos. 1396, NLI). For an examination of New Zealand Catholic connections to the international Irish press in the early twentieth century, see McNamara, "*New Zealand Tablet.*"

25. Atkinson, *The Europeans*, 247; *Launceston Examiner*, February 7, 1846; *Melbourne Morning Herald* cited in *Launceston Examiner*, December 29, 1855; *Bathurst Free Press and Mining Journal*, December 13, 1851. Useful starting points on Australian collective identity include White, *Inventing Australia*; Feingold, "From Empire to Nation"; Inglis, *Australian Colonists*; Martin, "Australia's History"; McGregor, "Necessity of British-ness"; Meaney, "Britishness and Australian Identity"; Wolfe, *Settler Colonialism*.

26. West cited in *Courier* (Hobart), June 8, 1854; *Sydney Morning Herald*, June 2, 1854; *Empire* (Sydney), July 27, 1855.

27. *Freeman's Journal* (Sydney), October 10, 1850; October 3, 1850; May 8, 1851; January 20, 1855; February 27, 1851.

28. Ibid., June 27, 1850; July 4, 1850; July 11, 1850; January 23, 1851; July 14, 1855.

29. Ibid., July 25, 1850; February 5, 1852; October 10, 1850.

30. *Argus* (Melbourne), May 30, 1850.

31. Mitchel, *Jail Journal*, 238, 242, 246; J. Mitchel to W. S. O'Brien, October 21, 1850 (WSOB, MS 444/2754, NLI).

32. Mitchel, *Jail Journal*, 259; O'Conner, *Jenny Mitchel*, 120, 123; J. V. Mitchel to Mary Thompson, July 21, 1851 (JVM, 1851–1855, MS 64-358, NYPL); J. V. Mitchel to Mary Thompson, September 11, 1851 (JVM, 1851–1855, MS 64-358, NYPL). Jenny's luggage included back issues of the Dublin *Nation*, *United Irishman*, and *Irish Felon*.

33. *Nation* (Dublin), July 27, 1850, reprinted in *Irish-American* (New York), August 17, 1850; J. Martin to W. S. O'Brien, June 27, 1850 (WSOB, MS 444/2701, NLI).

34. *Irish Exile and Freedom's Advocate* (Hobart Town), February 22, 1851; Mitchel, *Jail Journal*, 253, 279, 253.

35. J. Martin to Mrs. Connell, August 9, 1851 (Connell family papers, MS 3224, NLI); Mitchel, *Jail Journal*, 271.

36. Knox, *Races of Men*, 10, 39, 21, 253–254. Knox had floated the idea that races were ill suited for foreign climates in his translation of Quetelet, *A Treatise on Man*, 122–26. For a fuller analysis of Knox's *Races of Men*, see Young, *Idea of English*, 71–87.

37. Ellis, *Irish Ethnology*, 5, 10.

38. *Times* (London), October 7, 1852. McElheran's letter was reprinted in the *Nation* (Dublin), October 2, 1852, the *Freeman's Journal and Daily Commercial Advertiser* (Dublin), October 8, 1852, the *Boston Pilot*, October 16, 1852, and the *Freeman's Journal* (Sydney), March 3, 1853. Young, *Idea of English*, 112–19, discusses Ellis's and McElheran's racial theories.

39. *Freeman's Journal* (Sydney), March 25, 1852; Anderson, *Imagined Communities*.

40. Andrew Markus, *Australian Race Relations*, 20–22; MacIntyre, *Concise History*, 61–65. These statistics on Aboriginal mortality point to rapid population decline but should be seen as indicative of general trends rather than a definitive body count. Over the past twenty years, historians have developed increasingly nuanced understandings of frontier violence. See Broome, "Aboriginal Victims and Voyagers" and *Aboriginal Australians*; Thorpe, "Frontiers of Discourse"; Mitchell, "'The galling yoke'"; Ryan, "Settler Massacres."

41. Andrew Markus, *Australian Race Relations*, 21–22; MacIntyre, *Concise History*, 65.

42. *Nation* (Dublin), January 4, 1845; Griffith, *Present State and Prospects*; MacDonagh, *The Emancipist*, 19–21; Davis, *Revolutionary Imperialist*, 142, 135, 168.

43. O'Brien, *"To Solitude Consigned,"* 90–92. For the population statistics, see 55. Between 1830 and 1834, the government rounded up the Tasmanian Aboriginal population and moved them to Flinders Island, which lies in Bass Strait, between Tasmania and the Australian mainland. Their numbers continued to decline until the remaining survivors were returned to a reserve on Van Diemen's Land in 1847.

44. O'Brien, *"To Solitude Consigned,"* 90, 244–45, 205.

45. Ibid., 182, 131, 301–5, 91–92. *Principles of Government* included a model constitution for an independent Tasmania, which Smith O'Brien had anonymously published in the *Launceston Examiner* on August 30, 1853.

46. *Irish Exile and Freedom's Advocate* (Hobart Town), January 26, 1850; *Nation* (Dublin), March 25, 1843, reprinted in *Irish Exile and Freedom's Advocate* (Hobart

Town), June 29, 1850; *Nation* (Dublin), April 1, 1843, reprinted in *Irish Exile and Freedom's Advocate* (Hobart Town), August 31, 1850.

47. *Irish Exile and Freedom's Advocate* (Hobart Town), September 28, 1850.

48. *Freeman's Journal* (Sydney), December 4, 1851; November 26, 1853. See also July 24, 1851; September 25, 1851; May 13, 1852.

49. Ibid., July 8, 1852; December 4, 1851; April 29, 1852; April 28, 1855. For more on Chinese and Indian immigration to Australia, see Price, *Great White Walls*.

50. For works that seek to complicate straightforward narratives of Irish-Aboriginal relations, see Morton and Wilson, *Irish and Scottish Encounters*, and McGrath, "Shamrock Aborigines."

51. Address by the "Residents of Victoria" to W. S. O'Brien, n.d. [July 1854] (WSOB, MS 9049 [Pos. 8397], NLI); Address by the Residents of Sydney (New South Wales) to W. S. O'Brien, n.d. [July 1854] (WSOB, MS 35,277, NLI); *Freeman's Journal* (Sydney), July 22, 1854.

52. Martin's and Smith O'Brien's speeches were reprinted in Australian, Irish, and American newspapers including the *Freeman's Journal* (Sydney), July 29, 1854, and August 19, 1854, *Nation* (Dublin), October 14, 1854, and October 28, 1854, *Citizen* (New York), November 4, 1854, and *Freeman's Journal and Catholic Register* (New York), November 4, 1854. Smith O'Brien's point about the international reach of the Irish popular press was accurate.

53. C. G. Duffy to W. S. O'Brien, November 30, 1854 (WSOB, MS 445/2876, NLI); C. G. Duffy to W. S. O'Brien, December 14, 1854 (WSOB, MS 445/2878, NLI); W. S. O'Brien to C. G. Duffy, December 1854 (CGD, MS 2642, NLI); W. S. O'Brien to C. G. Duffy, September 11, 1855 (WSOB, MS 15,742 [Pos. 8434], NLI); *Nation* (Dublin), August 18, 1855.

54. Mitchel, *Jail Journal*, 357–58.

Chapter Three

1. R. O'Gorman to W. S. O'Brien, May 17, 1857 (WSOB, MS 445/2958, NLI).

2. Thomas Brown, *Irish-American Nationalism*; Foner, "Class, Ethnicity"; Roediger, *Wages of Whiteness*; Ignatiev, *How the Irish*; Jacobson, *Whiteness of a Different Color*. The "ceased to be Green" quote is from Ignatiev, *How the Irish*, 3. McGee's "world-wide race" quote is from the *Nation* (New York), October 28, 1848.

3. Kenny, *American Irish*, 54–61; Campbell, *Ireland's New Worlds*, 4–12; Doyle, "Irish in North America," 171–212; Ó Gráda, "Across the Briny Ocean"; Miller, *Emigrants and Exiles*, 193–279. The "productive powers of man" quote is from the *Belfast News-Letter*, October 25, 1839.

4. Miller, *Emigrants and Exiles*, 280, 569; Diner, "The Most Irish City," 88–92; Campbell, *Ireland's New Worlds*, 39–42; Daniels, *Coming to America*, 129, 136. See also Kenny, *American Irish*, 104–12, and Dolan, *Immigrant Church*. For the regional and religious divisions within the pre-Famine Irish American community, see Walsh,

"'A Fanatic Heart,'" and Way, *Common Labor*. The "hand of death" quote is from the *Freeman's Journal and Daily Commercial Advertiser* (Dublin), February 16, 1847.

5. Foner, *The Story*, 69–71, 74–79. See also Wiebe, *Self-Rule*, 86–112; Berlin, *Slaves without Masters*, 182–216; Litwack, *North of Slavery*, 30–63, 153–86.

6. Roediger, *Wages of Whiteness*, 14; Ignatiev, *How the Irish*, 1. For an earlier approach to anti-Irish stereotypes, see Knobel, *Paddy and the Republic*. For a recent, excellent overview of the nineteenth-century racialization of the Irish, see Nelson, *Irish Nationalists*, 30–54. Meanwhile, Irish employment discrimination may be overstated. See Jensen, "'No Irish Need Apply.'"

7. Foner, *The Story*, 79. Leading critiques of whiteness include Arnesen, "Whiteness"; Kolchin, "Whiteness Studies"; and Fields, "Whiteness, Racism, and Identity." Others argue that by overattributing agency to immigrants, the "whiteness" scholars underestimate the ways in which the subaltern status of Irish Americans affected their identity. See Miller, *Ireland and Irish America*, 380.

8. Higham, *Strangers in the Land*, 4, 57; Anbinder, *Nativism and Slavery*, ix.

9. *Nation* (New York), November 1, 1848.

10. Ibid., October 28, 1848; *Irish News* (New York), April 12, 1856; Mott, *American Journalism*, 312. The prospectus for McGee's new weekly journal was reprinted or noticed in American, Irish, and Australian newspapers such as the *Boston Pilot*, November 4, 1848, the *Anglo-Celt* (Cavan), November 24, 1848, and the *Launceston Examiner*, June 9, 1849.

11. Humphrey, *Press of the Young Republic*, xiii–xiv, 155–60; Huntzicker, *Popular Press*, 163–76; Lee, *History of American Journalism*, 100–284; Payne, *History of Journalism*, 240–68; Mott, *American Journalism*, 204. The "newsboys" quote is from Huntzicker, *Popular Press*, 19. Greeley's "neutrality" quote is from Payne, *History of Journalism*, 269. For a description of a newspaper-printing house in action, see the *New York Herald*, September 11, 1848.

12. Joyce, *Editors and Ethnicity*, 49–54, 68–69; Huntzicker, *Popular Press*, 11; Doyle, "Irish in North America," 195; McMahon, "Ireland and the Birth." See also Park, *Immigrant Press*; Foik, *Pioneer Catholic Journalism*; Willging and Hatzfeld, *Catholic Serials*; Baumgartner, *Catholic Journalism*. For early biographies of leading Irish American editors, see Frawley, *Patrick Donahoe*, and Kwitchen, *James Alphonsus McMaster*.

13. Wilson, *Thomas D'Arcy McGee*, 1:74–97; Skelton, *Life of Thomas D'Arcy McGee*, 22, 162; *Nation* (New York), October 28, 1848.

14. Skelton, *Life of Thomas D'Arcy McGee*, 163–66, 168; Wilson, *Thomas D'Arcy McGee*, 1:237–44. Patrick Lynch had emigrated from Ireland in 1847. After stints at the New York *Herald* and the *Boston Pilot*, he founded the *Irish-American* in New York in 1849. Suspicious of both McGee and Duffy, Lynch was particularly incensed by the New York *Nation's* insistence that the Irish in America must overcome poverty through self-education. He called an open letter by McGee published in Duffy's new Dublin *Nation* "the vilest, most calumnious, most lying, most insulting, document ever published

against the Irish race, in America" (cited in Wilson, *Thomas D'Arcy McGee*, 1:263–64). For more on Lynch, see Joyce, *Editors and Ethnicity*, 7, 62–67.

15. Duffy, *My Life*, 2:5; *American Celt* (Boston), August 31, 1850; R. O'Gorman to W. S. O'Brien, December 12, 1852 (WSOB, MS 445/2842, NLI).

16. John Blake Dillon scrapbook, n.d. [June 10, 1852] (J. B. Dillon papers, MS 6458, TCD). As with most of Meagher's speeches in America, this one was reprinted in Irish newspapers overseas including the *Irish-American* (New York), June 19, 1852, *Nation* (Dublin), June 26, 1852, and *Freeman's Journal* (Sydney), October 28, 1852. For Meagher's comments on McGee and the American Catholic press, see T. F. Meagher to C. G. Duffy, January 17, 1853 (CGD, MS 5757, NLI). Meagher and McGee had been feuding since the latter had publicly denounced Meagher's republicanism. For examples, see *American Celt and Catholic Citizen* (Buffalo), December 24, 1852; January 1, 1853; January 22, 1853; March 19, 1853.

17. *Freeman's Journal* (Sydney), May 20, 1854. H. Searson was advertised as the agent of the New York *Citizen* in the *Nation* (Dublin), March 11, 1854; *Freeman's Journal and Daily Commercial Advertiser* (Dublin), April 11, 1854; *Citizen* (New York), April 8, 1854; *Nation* (New York), June 1, 1850; *Citizen* (New York), September 2, 1854; February 11, 1854; April 8, 1854; September 2, 1854; May 27, 1854.

18. *Irish News* (New York), April 12, 1856; Rory Cornish, "Irish Republican Abroad," 144; *Irish News* (New York), June 28, 1856; June 7, 1856; June 21, 1856.

19. Only 15 percent of the American population lived in urban areas (defined as containing 2,500 or more people). The population statistics are cited in Legler, Sylla, and Wallis, "U.S. City Finances," 348. *American Celt* (Boston), November 16, 1850; *Irish News* (New York), July 12, 1856; February 21, 1857; May 9, 1857; May 30, 1857; *Nation* (New York), June 15, 1850; *Irish News* (New York), June 9, 1860.

20. J. V. Mitchel to Mary Thompson, April 20, 1854 (JVM, 1851–1855, MS 64-358, NYPL); *Citizen* (New York), April 15, 1854; *Nation* (New York), October 28, 1848; *Irish News* (New York), March 10, 1860.

21. Duffy's original letter to Mitchel was published in a special supplement of the *Nation* (Dublin) on April 15, 1854, and reprinted in whole or in part in various foreign newspapers including the *Times* (London), April 17, 1854, *Boston Pilot*, May 6, 1854, *United States Catholic Miscellany* (Charleston), May 13, 1854, and *Sydney Morning Herald*, July 22, 1854. For the impact on the Dublin *Nation*'s staff, see A. M. Sullivan to J. Martin, May 31, 1858 (A. M. Sullivan papers, MS 15,714, NLI). Letters in defense of Mitchel were published in the New York *Citizen* on May 6, May 20, July 1, September 2, September 9, and November 4, 1854. See also T. B. McManus to C. G. Duffy, June 3, 1854 (MS 27,609 (1), NLI).

22. *Nation* (New York), July 14, 1849; *American Celt and Adopted Citizen* (Boston), September 20, 1851; *Irish News* (New York), May 24, 1856; May 31, 1856; May 30, 1857; *Freeman's Journal* (Sydney), April 7, 1855; November 11, 1852. For more on the Young Irelanders' celebrity status, see McMahon, "International Celebrities."

23. For more on the Doheny/McGee scuffle, see *Nation* (New York), November 24, December 1, and December 8, 1849, and Wilson, *Thomas D'Arcy McGee*, 1:264–65. For the Meagher/McMasters fight, see *Citizen* (New York), July 29, 1854, *Freeman's Journal and Catholic Register* (New York), July 22, 1854, and Athearn, *Thomas Francis Meagher*, 47.

24. *Boston Pilot*, January 6, 1855; *Irish News* (New York), June 13, 1857; December 20, 1856.

25. Winthrop, *Addresses and Speeches*, 26; Baum, *Rise and Fall*, 124–25; Curtis, *Anglo-Saxons and Celts*, 90; Saunders and Thorpe, *Voice to America*, 89; *Times* (London), June 3, 1847; *Christian Intelligencer* cited in *Nation* (New York), April 21, 1849.

26. Painter, "Ralph Waldo," 980; Turner, *History of the Anglo-Saxons*; Painter, "Ralph Waldo," 982. For more on Emerson's Anglo-Saxonism, see Painter, *History of White People*, 151–89. For Anglo-Saxonism and slavery, see Knobel, "'Celtic Exodus,'" 79–93.

27. *Brownson's Quarterly Review* [3rd ser.] 2, no. 3 (July 1854): 328–54; Rt. Rev. [Michael] O'Connor, *Celts and Saxons*, 46–47, 68, 32–33; *Citizen* (New York), July 15, 1854.

28. *American Whig Review* 81 (September 1851): 192–93; *Nation* (New York), April 21, 1849; May 4, 1850; *American Celt* (Boston), August 31, 1850; *American Celt and Adopted Citizen* (Boston), May 17, 1851.

29. *Citizen* (New York), August 26, 1854; November 11, 1854; November 25, 1854; Kenny, *American Irish*, 115–16; Miller, *Emigrants and Exiles*, 323; *Irish News* (New York), June 27, 1857; January 10, 1857; July 11, 1857.

30. *Irish News* (New York), June 27, 1857; January 10, 1857; September 19, 1857; *Citizen* (New York), December 9, 1854; March 25, 1854.

31. *Irish News* (New York), November 1, 1856. McElheran's work was serialized in the *Boston Pilot* (April–July 1856) and the New York *Irish News* (October 1857–March 1858). See also McElheran, *Condition of Women*.

32. *Nation* (New York), October 28, 1848; January 6, 1849; *American Celt* (Boston), August 31, 1850; *Citizen* (New York), March 11, 1854.

33. *Nation* (New York), June 9, 1849; *Irish News* (New York), April 18, 1857; March 7, 1857.

34. *Irish News* (New York), March 23, 1861; *Nation* (New York), March 10, 1849; *American Celt and Adopted Citizen* (Boston), March 15, 1851.

35. *Nation* (Dublin), May 7, 1853, reprinted in *Irish-American* (New York), May 28, 1853, and in *Freeman's Journal* (Sydney), January 7, 1854; *Irish News* (New York), October 11, 1856; J. Martin to Miss Connell, December 15, 1858 (Connell family papers, MS 3224, NLI); C. G. Duffy to J. B. Dillon, April 13, 1858 (J. B. Dillon papers, MS 6455-7/333, TCD).

36. Duffy, *My Life*, 2:3; *Nation* (New York), April 14, 1849.

37. *Citizen* (New York), January 7, 1854, reprinted in whole or in part in *Freeman's Journal and Daily Commercial Advertiser* (Dublin), January 17, 1854, and in *Freeman's Journal* (Sydney), May 20, 1854. Kerby Miller uses Antonio Gramsci's concept of

"cultural hegemony" to analyze Irish American dual loyalty in "Class, Culture," as does McMahon in "International Celebrities."

38. *Sun* (Baltimore), March 29, 1853, reprinted in *Freeman's Journal and Daily Commercial Advertiser* (Dublin), May 3, 1853, and in *Freeman's Journal* (Sydney), September 17, 1853; *Citizen* (New York), March 25, 1854. As teenagers, Enoch Louis Lowe and Meagher were classmates at Clongowes Wood College in County Kildare, Ireland. See Magruder, *Year-Book*, 45.

39. *Nation* (Dublin), November 26, 1853; *Citizen* (New York), January 14, 1854; *Irish-American* (New York), January 28, 1854; *Citizen* (New York), December 30, 1854. If, as Mitchel claimed on January 14, 1854, the newspaper's circulation stood at 50,000 per week, the Alabama Article chopped 20 percent off his predominantly Irish readership. Several historians have discussed Mitchel's proslavery. The original, apologetic account appears in Dillon, *Life of John Mitchel*, vol. 2. For modern interpretations, see Knowlton, "Politics of John Mitchel"; Newsinger, "John Mitchel and Irish Nationalism"; Quinn, "John Mitchel"; Toomey, "Saving the South"; McGovern, *John Mitchel*, 119–54.

40. *Boston Pilot*, March 19, 1842; *American Celt and Adopted Citizen* (Boston), January 18, 1851; Mitchel, *Jail Journal*, 153–54.

41. *Nation* (New York), August 4, 1849; September 8, 1849; October 20, 1849; May 12, 1849. For more on O'Connell, antislavery, and Repeal, see Murphy, *American Slavery*.

42. *Citizen* (New York), June 3, 1854; *Richmond Dispatch* quoted in *Daily South Carolinian* (Columbia), May 31, 1854; Charleston *Courier* quoted in *Daily Morning News* (Savannah), January 19, 1854; *Citizen* (New York), April 15, 1854; *Liberator* (Boston), January 27, 1854; *Boston Investigator*, February 15, 1854. Beecher quoted in *Frederick Douglass' Paper* (Rochester), January 27, 1854; *Citizen* (New York), February 11, 1854; August 5, 1854.

43. *Irish Citizen* (New York), August 7, 1869; *Pittsburgh Catholic*, March 18, 1854; *Boston Pilot*, February 18, 1854; *Irish-American* (New York), January 21, 1854; *Citizen* (New York), August 19, 1854; July 1, 1854.

44. *Irish-American* (New York), January 28, 1854; *Irish News* (New York), October 11, 1856; November 15, 1856; M. Doheny to W. S. O'Brien, August 20, 1858 (WSOB, MS 446/3058, NLI). Duffy also noticed Irish immigrants being blamed for John Mitchel's proslavery. "Yesterday Mr. Cobden showed me an American newspaper containing an address signed by about fifty Dissenting Ministers assailing John Mitchel for his late longing for a plantation of fat niggers," he diarized in 1854, "and most unfairly holding the Irish people responsible for this offence." See Duffy, *My Life*, 2:88.

45. J. Mitchel to Mrs. Williams, February 16, 1858 (Fr. W. Hickey papers, MS 3226, NLI); *Citizen* (New York), May 20, 1854; *Belfast News-Letter*, February 27, 1854; *Nation* (Dublin), April 15, 1854; *Citizen* (New York), March 4, 1854; *Dublin Evening Mail*, February 10, 1854; *Anglo-Celt* (Cavan), April 20, 1854; *Citizen* (New York), May 6, 1854; *Freeman's Journal and Daily Commercial Advertiser* (Dublin), August 8, 1854. When Duffy met Gottfried Kinkel, the German revolutionary poet, at a dinner party in 1855,

he gleefully diarized of Kinkel's claim that "the European party of revolution" were "disgusted" by Mitchel's proslavery. See Duffy, *My Life*, 2:108.

46. J. Mitchel to Mary Thompson, April 24, 1854 (Autograph collection, MS 3/D/8/12(5), RIA); J. V. Mitchel to Mary Thompson, April 20, 1854 (JVM, 1851–1855, MS 64-358, NYPL).

47. *Freeman's Journal* (Sydney), November 3, 1855; October 22, 1853; October 22, 1853; May 27, 1852; November 3, 1855. For examples of news about fugitive slaves and antislavery, see March 25 and April 22, 1852; October 22, 1853; November 3, 1855.

48. *Southern Citizen* (Knoxville), January 21, 1858; *Southern Citizen* (Washington, D.C.), May 21, 1859; Toomey, "Saving the South,"123; Dillon, *Life of John Mitchel*, 2:104–6, 107, 130; Gleeson, "Securing the 'Interests.'" Mary Thompson continued to voice her opposition as well. See J. V. Mitchel to Mary Thompson, August 18, 1857 (Spec. MS Coll. Meloney-Mitchel, Box 1, BLCU).

49. John Martin papers [Diary 1848–1858], (Pos. 5788, NLI); *Citizen* (New York), December 30, 1854.

Chapter Four

1. Cavanagh, *Memoirs*, 368–69.

2. Conyngham, *Irish Brigade*, 382.

3. Susannah Bruce, *Harp and the Eagle*, 245; Samito, *Becoming American*, 103–33; Susannah Bruce, "Irish-Americans," 1036; Gleeson, *Irish in the South*, 164; Hernon, *Celts, Catholics*, 23; Spann, "Union Green," 193; Susannah Bruce, *Harp and the Eagle*, 2; Halpine, *Life and Adventures*, 159; Spann, "Union Green," 207.

4. Lonn, *Foreigners in the Union*, 643–62; Öfele, *True Sons*, xi–xiii, 86, 87; Burton, *Melting Pot Soldiers*, 48–58; Ural, "Introduction," 2–6; Dudley Cornish, *Sable Arm*, ix; John Smith, "Let Us All," 1–2; Ramold, *Slaves, Sailors, Citizens*, 4–5, 55, 182–83. W. M. Andrews is cited in Gleeson, "Irish Rebels, Southern Rebels," 142. G. E. Hystuns is cited in John Smith, "Introduction," xiii.

5. The fullest examination of the Irish in the Confederacy is Gleeson, *Green and the Gray*. Gleeson, "To Live and Die"; Gleeson, *Irish in the South*, 187; O'Grady, *Clear*, 248, 259; Gleeson, *Irish in the South*, 143; Lonn, *Foreigners in the Confederacy*, 481. Mitchel's claim of 40,000 was published in the *Nation* (Dublin), February 14, 1863, and reprinted in the *Irish-American* (New York), February 14, 1863, and the *Freeman's Journal* (Sydney), April 22, 1863. Gleeson, *Green and the Gray*, 7, 60.

6. Lonn, *Foreigners in the Confederacy*, 29, 33, 391; Öfele, *True Sons*, 22–23, 76–77; Gleeson, "Irish Rebels, Southern Rebels," 141.

7. Öfele, *True Sons*, 100–106; Burton, *Melting Pot Soldiers*, 12–13, 30–31, 230–31; *Irish-American* (New York), July 5, 1862; Carl Uterhard cited in Öfele, *True Sons*, 101.

8. Higham, *Strangers in the Land*, 13; Susannah Bruce, *Harp and the Eagle*, 3; Samito, *Becoming American*, 109; Öfele, *True Sons*, 106; Gleeson, *Irish in the South*, 144–45.

9. Athearn, *Thomas Francis Meagher*, 104; Fleche, *Revolution of 1861*.

10. Cavanagh, *Memoirs*, 374; Thomas Meagher, *Last Days*, 9. Meagher's fifteen-page pamphlet was originally published in serial form in the *Irish-American* (New York) and the *New York Daily Tribune* and reprinted in the *Nation* (Dublin) during August 1861. The "slaughtered like sheep" quote is from an open letter by Captain William J. Nagle, Eighty-Eighth New York Infantry, to his father, which was originally published in the *Irish-American* (New York), December 27, 1862, and is cited in McCarter, *My Life*, 229.

11. Conyngham, *Irish Brigade*, 56, 59–62. The book was originally published in 1867. Frawley, *Patrick Donahoe*, 187, 195.

12. Conyngham, *Irish Brigade*, 21; Rory Cornish, "Irish Republican Abroad," 147; *Irish News* (New York), July 20, 1861. For a Civil War era account of the Irish at Fontenoy, see the *Pilot* (Boston), October 19, 1861. Patrick Donahoe dropped the word "Boston" from his weekly's masthead in 1858.

13. Cavanagh, *Memoirs*, 438; *Irish News* (New York), July 13, 1861; Cavanagh, *Memoirs*, 412.

14. *Irish-American* (New York), August 2, 1862. An article in the *Nation* (Dublin), August 23, 1862, mentioned but did not reprint this speech. It did suggest, however, that other Irish newspapers, including the *Cork Reporter*, reprinted the speech in full.

15. *Irish-American* (New York), October 12, 1861. The speech was reprinted in the *Nation* (Dublin), October 26, 1861, and the *Freeman's Journal* (Sydney), January 1, 1862.

16. O'Grady, *Clear*, 102, 114, 250; Corby, *Memoirs*, 131–32; Cavanagh, *Memoirs*, 466, 470–71; Susannah Bruce, *Harp and the Eagle*, 132; Hernon, *Celts, Catholics*, 18; *Times* (London), January 13, 1863. The London *Times* article was reprinted in weekly journals across the Irish world including the *Nation* (Dublin), January 17, 1863, *Irish-American* (New York), February 7, 1863, and *Freeman's Journal* (Sydney), March 25, 1863. For more on the Irish at Fredericksburg, see *Irish-American* (New York), January 10, 1863, Welsh, *Irish Green*, 43, and Spann, "Union Green," 201. Gleeson, *Green and the Gray*, 104–5, debunks the myth that there was an entire Confederate regiment of Irish immigrants fighting behind the wall at Fredericksburg.

17. Reports of the requiem mass appeared in the *Irish-American* (New York), January 24, 1863. Savage's poem appears in Conyngham, *Irish Brigade*, 356. Meagher's formal letter of resignation was published in the *Irish-American* (New York), May 23, 1863, and reprinted in the *Nation* (Dublin), June 6, 1863.

18. Watson, *Normans and Saxons*, 43–46, 86–89; Moore, *Rebellion Record*, 67; *Southern Literary Messenger* 11/12 (November/December 1863), 677, 682. See also Knobel, "Celtic Exodus," 91–93. In the late twentieth and early twenty-first centuries, the idea that racial differences explained the sectional divide enjoyed a renaissance among a small group of scholars, including Cantrell, *How Celtic Culture*, McWhiney, *Cracker Culture*, and McWhiney and Jamieson, *Attack and Die*. Horowitz, *Confederates in the Attic*, labels these scholars "neo-Confederates." The most enduring critique of their work remains Berthoff, "Celtic Mist over the South."

19. Dillon, *Life of John Mitchel*, 2:54, 105–6; *Irish News* (New York), June 15, 1861.

20. *Irish News* (New York), March 6, 1858; *Nation* (Dublin), January 2, 1864, reprinted in *Irish-American* (New York), January 23, 1864, and *Freeman's Journal* (Sydney), March 30, 1864; McGovern, *John Mitchel*, 177.

21. *Nation* (Dublin), January 2, 1864, reprinted in *Irish-American* (New York), January 23, 1864, and *Freeman's Journal* (Sydney), March 30, 1864. The second letter, intended for the Dublin *Nation*, was intercepted by the Union government, published in the *New York Times*, January 25, 1863, and reprinted in the *Nation* (Dublin), February 14, 1863, the *Irish-American* (New York), February 14, 1863, and the *Freeman's Journal* (Sydney), April 22, 1863.

22. *Irish News* (New York), May 11, 1861; Gleeson, *Irish in the South*, 159; *Charleston Catholic Miscellany*, May 25, 1861. The author "L" was probably the Irish-born Protestant Osborne Lochrane for whom the Lochrane Guards were named. I am grateful to David T. Gleeson for making this connection.

23. O'Grady, *Clear*, iv, 233, 309, 24–25; Gleeson, *Irish in the South*, 143, 142, 140. For the flag ceremony, see the *Charleston Catholic Miscellany*, September 21, 1861.

24. *Irish News* (New York), April 27, 1861; O'Grady, *Clear*, 24–25; Gleeson, *Irish in the South*, 140; Lyons, *Brigadier-General*, 148.

25. Huntzicker, *Popular Press*, 120; Delbanco, *Portable Abraham Lincoln*, 271. For a look at Abraham Lincoln's lifelong struggle with the slavery question, see Foner, *Fiery Trial*.

26. Susannah Bruce, "Irish-Americans," 1036; *Irish-American* (New York), March 14, 1863; Kenny, *American Irish*, 125; *Pilot* (Boston), January 10, 1863; *Irish-American* (New York), July 4, 1863; January 17, 1863; Susannah Bruce, *Harp and the Eagle*, 177; Spann, "Union Green," 204.

27. Reprinted in *Irish News* (New York), May 18, 1861.

28. Welsh, *Irish Green*, 70, 62, 66; Hanchett, *Irish*, 70.

29. Rubin, *Shattered Nation*, 105; Quigley, *Shifting Grounds*, 197; Cavanagh, *Memoirs*, 470; U.S. War Department, *War of the Rebellion*, 586–92; O'Grady, *Clear*, 230, 265–66.

30. Rubin, *Shattered Nation*, 105–6. Lee is cited in Jones, "Georgia Lowcountry," 91; Gleeson, *Irish in the South*, 153; *Irish Citizen* (New York), July 9, 1870.

31. Bernstein, *New York City*, 10–11; *Irish-American* (New York), July 25, 1863; Bernstein, *New York City*, 27–31, 6; Spann, "Union Green," 204.

32. Redfield, *Comparative Physiognomy*, 254; Spann, "Union Green," 205; Susannah Bruce, *Harp and the Eagle*, 183; *New York Times*, July 25, 1863; *New York Evangelist*, July 23, 1863.

33. Curtis, *Anglo-Saxons and Celts*, 58–60; *Harper's Weekly*, August 1, 1863.

34. *Irish-American* (New York), July 25, 1863; *Daily Cleveland Herald*, July 28, 1863; Welsh, *Irish Green*, 110, 113.

35. *Daily Cleveland Herald*, July 28, 1863.

36. Huntzicker, *Popular Press*, 115–61. The "watermelons and whiskey" quote is cited on page 139. For more on the popular press during the Civil War, see Andrews, *The North Reports* and *The South Reports*; Harper, *Lincoln and the Press*; Nerone, *Violence*; Reynolds, *Editors Make War*.

37. *Irish-American* (New York), February 22, 1862; Thomas Meagher, *Letters*, 1–2. After publication in the *United Irishman and Galway American*, Meagher's letter was reprinted in the *Pilot* (Boston), November 7, 1863. Welsh, *Irish Green*, 37; McCarter, *My Life*, 213.

38. Welsh, *Irish Green*, 55; Corby, *Memoirs*, 259; Conyngham, *Irish Brigade*, 225–26.

39. Huntzicker, *Popular Press*, 140; Conyngham, *Irish Brigade*, 87; Welsh, *Irish Green*, 55.

40. *Irish Citizen* (New York), May 14, 1870; *Daily Enquirer* (Richmond), October 17, 1862; Dillon, *Life of John Mitchel*, 2:173, 205.

41. *Irish Citizen* (New York), June 4, 1870; July 2, 1870; Dillon, *Life of John Mitchel*, 2:179. Henrietta's death was reported in the *Irish-American* (New York), May 16, 1863, and the *Irishman* (Dublin), April 28, 1863.

42. Wilson, *Thomas D'Arcy McGee*, 2:116–22; Skelton, *Life of Thomas D'Arcy McGee*, 475–80.

43. *Freeman's Journal* (Sydney), December 24, 1862; November 7, 1863. For other editorials on the American Civil War and slavery, see, inter alia, July 24, 1861; September 18, 1861; October 12, 1861; January 4, 1862; June 28, 1862; December 24, 1862; March 21, 1863; May 23, 1863.

44. *Freeman's Journal* (Sydney), November 28, 1863; November 18, 1863.

45. Hernon, *Celts, Catholics*, 1; *Irish-American* (New York), December 5, 1863. For more on Hughes's and Bannon's tours of Ireland, see Gleeson, *Green and the Gray*, 168–74, Lonn, *Foreigners in the Confederacy*, 74–79, and *Foreigners in the Union*, 429, 433.

46. *Dublin Evening Mail*, January 26, 1863. See also May 28, 1863. Both gleaned from Larcom, MS 7724, NLI; *Dublin University Magazine* cited in Hernon, *Celts, Catholics*, 46–47. In November 1861, a federal ship stopped the British mail packet *Trent* on the high seas and arrested two Confederate diplomats on board. After two months of saber rattling between the United States and Britain, the *Trent* and its prisoners were released without further incident or official apology.

47. *Limerick Chronicle*, October 26, 1861, reprinted in *Nation* (Dublin), October 26, 1861, *Irish-American* (New York), November 9, 1861, and *Freeman's Journal* (Sydney), February 8, 1862; WSOB, MS 23/M/62, RIA, reprinted in *Nation* (Dublin), June 21, 1862, and *Irish-American* (New York), July 19, 1862; *Limerick Chronicle*, November 5, 1863, reprinted in *Nation* (Dublin), November 7, 1863, and *Irish-American* (New York), November 21, 1863; J. Martin to W. J. O'Neill Daunt, August 9, 1865 (O'Neill Daunt papers, MS 8047 (1), NLI); *Nation* (Dublin), September 24, 1864, reprinted in *Irish-American* (New York), October 15, 1864.

48. Hernon, *Celts, Catholics*, 106; Thomas Meagher, *Letters*, 12, 6, 14–15, reprinted in *Pilot* (Boston) and *Irish-American* (New York), November 7, 1863.

49. Hernon, *Celts, Catholics*, 55; *Nation* (Dublin), September 24, 1864, reprinted in *Irish-American* (New York), October 15, 1864; P. J. Smyth to W. S. O'Brien, n.d. (WSOB, MS 448/3307, NLI); P. J. Smyth to W. S. O'Brien, n.d. (WSOB, MS 448/3308, NLI).

50. *Nation* (Dublin), February 28, 1863.

51. *Tammany Society*, 28.

Chapter Five

1. John Bruce, *Lectures*, 94, 95, 100, 99. O'Gorman's speech was reprinted in American, Irish, and Australian newspapers including the *Irish-American* (New York), August 24, 1867, *Nation* (Dublin), August 31, 1867, and *Freeman's Journal* (Sydney), December 14, 1867. Dillon, *Life of John Mitchel*, 2:218, 238.

2. The statistics are from Miller, *Emigrants and Exiles*, 569. Calculating how many Irish migrants headed to Britain during this period is difficult. MacRaild, *Irish Diaspora in Britain*, 29 estimates that until 1880, Britain attracted "more than half the number of emigrants who went to the United States" but that its share dwindled thereafter until the 1930s. Kenny, *American Irish*, 141–49, 158–63; Diner, "The Most Irish City."

3. Higham, *Strangers in the Land*, 14, 45; Freeman, *Life and Letters*, 2:242; Gordon, *Orange Riots*, 14; Kenny, *American Irish*, 158–59.

4. Kenny, *American Irish*, 3, 158–59; Gordon, *Orange Riots*, xiv, 4, 11, 21; MacRaild, "Orange Atlantic"; Miller, "Ulster Presbyterians," 262.

5. Gleeson, *Green and the Gray*, 187–220; Blight, *Race and Reunion*, 74; Samito, *Becoming American*, 192–93; Susannah Bruce, *Harp and the Eagle*, 233–62.

6. John Bruce, *Lectures*, 57; Lyons, *Brigadier-General*, 195; John Bruce, *Lectures*, 27; Susannah Bruce, *Harp and the Eagle*, 257; Lyons, *Brigadier-General*, 202.

7. Conyngham, *Irish Brigade*, 9, 10, 5, 160, 106, 443. African Americans are notably absent from Conyngham's description of the marching army, as are Irishmen from Ulster, the predominantly Protestant province to the north. Conyngham may have been seeking to undermine both groups' participation in the war effort.

8. Samito, *Becoming American*, 2–4; McCarter, *My Life*, 221.

9. Smythe, *Gilded Age Press*, ix–x, 203–4; Joyce, *Editors and Ethnicity*, 155, 157; Frawley, *Patrick Donahoe*, 205. The four New York weeklies were the *Freeman's Journal*, *Irish World*, *Irish Citizen*, and *Irish-American*.

10. Jenkins, *Fenian Problem*, 25–27; De Nie, *Eternal Paddy*; Jenkins, *Fenians and Anglo-American Relations*, 28–31; D'Arcy, *Fenian Movement* (originally published by the Catholic University of America Press in 1947). Newspaper reports of the November 1863 convention appeared in Irish newspapers on three continents, including in the *Irish-American* (New York), November 21, 1863, *Nation* (Dublin), November 28, 1863, and *Freeman's Journal* (Sydney), March 9, 1864. J. Stephens to J. O'Mahony, December 16, 1861 (MCIH, Box 4, folder 64, NYPL); J. Stephens to J. O'Mahony, November 16, 1861 (MCIH, Box 4, folder 64, NYPL); J. Martin to George C. Mahon, November 16, 1861 (George C. Mahon papers, MS 22,194, NLI).

11. J. Stephens to J. O'Mahony, October 14, 1863 (MCIH, Box 4, folder 64, NYPL); *Irish People* (Dublin), November 28, 1863; Jenkins, *Fenian Problem*, 28–29; Garvin, *Nationalist Revolutionaries*, 34; Sullivan cited in Comerford, *Fenians in Context*, 109.

12. Comerford, *Fenians in Context*, 129; Jenkins, *Fenian Problem*, 36–37; *Irish People* (New York), January 4, 1868; "aristocratic steeples" quote cited in Joyce, *Editors and Ethnicity*, 111; *Times* (London), September 18, 1865; *New York Herald*, March 16, 1866; *Irish Times* (Dublin), June 5, 1866.

13. Casey, *Galtee Boy*, 64, 85, 126, 174, 190–92. For an interesting case of prison spies using newspapers to bait Fenian prisoners, see Jeremiah O'Donovan Rossa's letter from Chatham jail, published in the *Irish People* (Dublin), March 19, 1870, and reprinted in the *Southern Celt* (Charleston), April 2, 1870. For more on the *Universal News* during this period, see McNicholas, "Co-operation, Compromise."

14. Casey, *Mingling of Swans*, 58, 155, 124, 30, 97, 112, 118, 153, 99, 251; Cusack, *Journal of a Voyage*, n.p. For examples of Casey's letters from Australia, see the *Irishman* (Dublin), August 29, 1868; December 5, 1868; December 12, 1868; December 19, 1868; April 10, 1869; April 17, 1869; *Flag of Ireland* (Dublin), March 20, 1869. Letters of his were also published in the Australian *Fremantle Herald* and the New York *Irish People* (see Casey, *Mingling of Swans*, 24, 118).

15. *Irish Citizen* (New York), October 19, 1867; January 18, 1868; February 22, 1868.

16. Rowell, *Men Who Advertise*, 665, 701; P. O. Aherne to J. Mitchel, November 25, 1867 (Spec. MS Coll. Meloney-Mitchel, Box 1, BLCU); untitled Aherne circular, n.d. [1868] (Spec. MS Coll. Meloney-Mitchel, Box 6, BLCU); J. S. Barrett to P. O. Aherne, July 3, 1868 (Spec. MS Coll. Meloney-Mitchel, Box 1, BLCU); J. A. Duffy to P. O. Aherne, July 3, 1868 (Spec. MS Coll. Meloney-Mitchel, Box 1, BLCU); M. Sarpy to P. O. Aherne, July 19, 1868 (Spec. MS Coll. Meloney-Mitchel, Box 3 BLCU); J. Mitchel to P. J. Smyth, November 2, 1871 (Fr. W. Hickey papers, MS 3226, NLI).

17. *Irish Citizen* (New York), November 20, 1869; October 15, 1870. For an example of an Irish American newspaper poaching and reprinting an Australian correspondent's report from the Dublin *Irishman*, see *Irish Citizen* (New York), May 22, 1869.

18. Foner, *Short History*, 10. For a useful overview of the historiography of Reconstruction, see ibid., xi–xiv. Blight, *Race and Reunion*, 3, 4.

19. Gleeson, *Irish in the South*, 173–78, 186; Gleeson, *Green and the Gray*, 197–98.

20. *Irish Citizen* (New York), November 9, 1867; May 30, 1868.

21. Ibid., April 11, 1868; May 28, 1870; April 1, 1871.

22. Frawley, *Patrick Donahoe*, 80–83; *Pilot* (Boston), June 13, 1874; December 30, 1871; McManamin, *American Years*, 213.

23. Foner, *The Story*, 50–51, 77; Foner, *Give Me Liberty!*, 601–9.

24. T. F. Meagher to Thomas Meagher [father], June 15, 1867 (Thomas F. Madigan papers, NYPL); Athearn, *Thomas Francis Meagher*, 131–47; Lyons, *Brigadier-General*, 196; Axline, "With Courage," 179–80; John Bruce, *Lectures*, 51. Thomas Meagher, "Rides through Montana," also describes native Amerindians. Any study of the Irish in the American West must begin with Emmons, *Butte Irish* and *Beyond the American Pale*.

25. John Bruce, *Lectures*, 55, 42, 62, 64; Athearn, *Thomas Francis Meagher*, 158, 164. The mysterious nature of Meagher's death has been debated ever since. For a full

discussion of the various opinions, from drunken mishap to cold-blooded murder, see Emmons, "Strange Death."

26. Kwitchen, *James Alphonsus McMaster*, 202–7.

27. For Irish working-class racism on the West Coast, see Gyory, *Closing the Gate*; Saxton, *Indispensable Enemy*; Shumsky, *Evolution of Political Protest*; Lee, *At America's Gates*. *Irish Citizen* (New York), September 4, 1869; *Southern Celt* (Charleston), February 22, 1873.

28. Casey, *Galtee Boy*, 87; Casey, *Mingling of Swans*, 197; *Irish People* (Dublin), August 26, 1865 [gleaned from Larcom papers, MS 7726, NLI].

29. Grant, *Passing of the Great Race*; Spencer, *Principles of Biology*, 453; Curtis, *Anglo-Saxons and Celts*, 92–97; Solomon, *Ancestors and Immigrants*, 59–81; Saveth, *American Historians*, 9–10, 13–121; Young, *Idea of English*, 199–200, 225; *New York Times*, December 28, 1867; September 28, 1868.

30. *Irish Citizen* (New York), February 27, 1869; February 5, 1870.

31. *Declaration of Principles*, 20–21; John Bruce, *Lectures*, 35, 23.

32. *Irish Citizen* (New York), October 1, 1870; October 19, 1867, reprinted in *Freeman's Journal* (Sydney), February 15, 1868; *Declaration of Principles*, 20, 23; *Irish Citizen* (New York), February 18, 1871; J. B. O'Reilly to Edwin P. Whipple, March 20, 1878 (John Boyle O'Reilly papers, MS 219, BPL). See also Snay, *Fenians, Freedmen*.

33. Wilson, *Thomas D'Arcy McGee*, 2:404–5; Skelton, *Life of Thomas D'Arcy McGee*, 341–42, 510–11; Phelan, *Ardent Exile*, 250, 301.

34. *Declaration of Principles*, 21–23; *Irish Citizen* (New York), November 26, 1870; *ZL—472 (Thomas Sweeny papers, NYPL).

35. *Irish Citizen* (New York), January 27, 1872; May 7, 1870; August 26, 1871. Martin's appeals reached an international audience through the *Nation* (Dublin), July 1, 1871, and March 30, 1872, and the *Freeman's Journal* (Sydney), January 21, 1871.

36. Duffy, *Why Is Ireland*, 4, 18, 17. A copy of this pamphlet is held in the Leon O'Broin papers (MS 31,671, NLI). The speech was reprinted in the *Freeman's Journal* (Sydney), February 26, 1870, and advertised for sale as a pamphlet in the *Nation* (Dublin), April 30, 1870. The Sydney *Irish Citizen*'s first editorial was quoted in the *Irish Citizen* (New York), March 9, 1872, and the *Nation* (Dublin), February 3, 1872. It hoped to achieve in Australia what its predecessor "does for the national cause of Ireland in America."

37. Dilke, *Greater Britain*, 1:269, 2:155–56, 1:318; Froude cited in *Irish World* (New York), October 26, 1872; Julia Markus, *J. Anthony Froude*, 124–25; Mitchel, *Crusade of the Period*, 20. *The Crusade of the Period* was comprised of articles Mitchel had written during Froude's visit. Father Burke's attacks were published as *Ireland's Case Stated in Reply to Mr. Froude* (1873). Froude's American tour provided the basis for his three-volume *The English in Ireland in the Eighteenth Century* (1872–1874). Anti-Froude opinions were reprinted in Irish newspapers outside America, including the Dublin *Nation* (November 2, November 9, November 23, December 28, 1872) and the Sydney *Freeman's Journal* (January 4, February 8, February 15, February 22, May 3, 1873). For more on Dilke and Froude's pan-Saxonism, see Young, *Idea of English*, 196–204, 215–19.

A full examination of Froude's views on Ireland can be found in Brady, *James Anthony Froude*, 262–96.

38. O'Leary, *Ireland among the Nations*, 151–52; *Irish World* (New York), December 21, 1872.

39. Rodechko, *Patrick Ford*, 27–35, and "An Irish-American Journalist"; *New York Times*, September 24, 1913; Kenny, *American Irish*, 174–75.

40. *Irish World* (New York), December 31, 1870; May 27, 1871; September 2, 1871. The circulation statistics are from Rowell, *American Newspaper Directory*, 238, Alden, *American Newspaper Catalogue*, 224, 438, Joyce, *Editors and Ethnicity*, 157, and Rodechko, *Patrick Ford*, 48–49.

41. *Irish World* (New York), November 12, 1870; January 28, 1871; February 24, 1872. John McElheran's "The Celt and the Saxon" series originally appeared in Patrick Donahoe's Boston *Pilot* between April 5 and July 12, 1856. It was subsequently published as McElheran, *Condition of Women*.

42. *Irish World* (New York), December 31, 1870; June 24, 1871; July 5, 1873; July 26, 1873; December 27, 1873.

43. Rodechko, *Patrick Ford*, 58–64; *Irish World* (New York), December 21, 1878; January 13, 1871; September 26, 1874; February 13, 1875. Ford's national and working-class identities were not mutually exclusive. In a classic essay, Eric Foner shows that there was a "symbiotic relationship between class-conscious [trade] unionism and Irish national consciousness" in the postbellum period. See Foner, "Class, Ethnicity," 176.

44. *Irish World* (New York), April 26, 1873; April 19, 1879.

45. Ibid.; Rodechko, *Patrick Ford*, 186; *Irish World* (New York), December 31, 1870; September 1, 1877; September 13, 1873. For more on Irish American political cartoons in this period, see McMahon, "Caricaturing Race and Nation."

46. *Irish World* (New York), December 16, 1871; January 28, 1871.

47. Ibid., March 18, 1871; March 25, 1871; March 22, 1872; March 25, 1871.

48. Ibid., November 23, 1872.

Conclusion

1. Keown, "Irish Race Convention," 365; *Nation* (Dublin), April 17, 1847; *Irish World* (New York), December 27, 1873.

2. Carlyle, *Past and Present*, 7; *Nation* (Dublin), June 17, 1843.

3. *Irish Citizen* (New York), May 7, 1870.

4. *Nation* (Dublin), February 28, 1863; Gerber, "Forming a Transnational Narrative," 68; J. Martin to George C. Mahon, July 12, 1873 (MS 22,202, NLI).

5. R. R. Madden to R. O'Gorman, April 9, 1873 (R. R. Madden papers, MS 15,770, NLI); O'Connor, *Secret World*, 12; Fitzgerald and Lambkin, *Migration*, 278.

6. Giddens, *Modernity and Self-Identity*, 18.

BIBLIOGRAPHY

Manuscript Collections

Ireland
  National Library of Ireland
    Alan Queale papers
    A. M. Sullivan papers
    Charles Gavan Duffy papers
    Connell family papers
    George C. Mahon papers
    John Martin papers
    Kevin Izod O'Doherty papers
    O'Neill Daunt papers
    Richard Robert Madden papers
    Sir Thomas Aiskew Larcom papers
    Thomas Davis papers
    William Hickey papers
    William Smith O'Brien papers
  Royal Irish Academy
    Autograph Collection
    Gavan Duffy papers
    John Windele papers
    William Smith O'Brien papers
  Trinity College Dublin Archives
    John Blake Dillon papers
United States
  Boston Public Library
    Anti-Slavery Collection
    John Boyle O'Reilly papers
  Butler Library, Columbia University
    Spec. MS Coll. Meloney-Mitchel
  New York Public Library
    Jane Verner Mitchel papers
    Maloney Collection of Irish Historical Papers
    Thomas F. Madigan collection [Thomas F. Meagher letters, 1848–1867]
    Thomas Sweeny papers

Newspapers

Australia
  Freeman's Journal (Sydney)
  Irish Exile and Freedom's Advocate (Hobart Town)
Ireland
  Anglo-Celt (Cavan)
  Belfast News-Letter
  Dublin Evening Mail
  Freeman's Journal and Daily Commercial Advertiser (Dublin)
  Irishman (Dublin)
  Irish People (Dublin)
  Irish Times (Dublin)
  Nation (Dublin)
  Vindicator (Belfast)
United States
  American Celt (Boston)
  American Celt and Adopted Citizen (Buffalo)
  American Celt and Catholic Citizen (Boston)
  Boston Pilot
  Brownson's Quarterly Review (New York)
  Charleston Catholic Miscellany
  Citizen (New York)
  Daily Enquirer (Richmond)
  Freeman's Journal and Catholic Register (New York)
  Harper's New Monthly Magazine (New York)
  Harper's Weekly (New York)
  Irish-American (New York)
  Irish Citizen (New York)
  Irish News (New York)
  Irish People (New York)
  Irish World [*and American Industrial Liberator*] (New York)
  Nation (New York)
  Pittsburgh Catholic
  Southern Celt (Charleston)
  United States Catholic Miscellany (Charleston)

Electronic Newspaper Databases

America's Historical Newspapers
Proquest Historical Newspapers: The New York Times, 1851–2009

Times [*London*] *Digital Archive, 1785–1985*
TROVE Digitised Newspapers [*National Library of Australia*]

Printed Primary Sources

Alden, Edwin. *American Newspaper Catalogue*. Cincinnati: Edwin Alden, 1884.
Bruce, John P., ed. *Lectures of Gov. Thomas Francis Meagher, in Montana, together with His Messages, Speeches, &c. to Which Is Added the Eulogy of Richard O'Gorman, Esq., Delivered at Cooper Institute, New York*. Virginia City, MT: Bruce and Wright Printers, 1867.
Burke, T. N. *Ireland's Case Stated in Reply to Mr. Froude*. New York: P. M. Haverty, 1873.
Carlyle, Thomas. *Chartism*. Boston: Charles C. Little and James Brown, 1840.
———. *Past and Present*. London: Chapman and Hall, 1843.
Casey, John Sarsfield. *The Galtee Boy: A Fenian Prison Narrative*. Edited by Mairead Maume, Patrick Maume, and Mary Casey. Dublin: University College Dublin Press, 2005.
———. *A Mingling of Swans: A Cork Fenian and Friends "Visit" Australia*. Edited by Mairead Maume, Patrick Maume, and Mary Casey. Dublin: University College Dublin Press, 2010.
Cavanagh, Michael, ed. *Memoirs of Gen. Thomas Francis Meagher, Comprising the Leading Events of His Career Chronologically Arranged, with Selections from His Speeches, Lectures and Miscellaneous Writings Including Personal Reminiscences*. Worcester, Mass.: Messenger Press, 1892.
Conyngham, David Power. *The Irish Brigade and Its Campaigns*. Edited by Lawrence Frederick Kohl. New York: Fordham University Press, 1994. First published 1867.
Corby, William. *Memoirs of Chaplain Life: Three Years with the Irish Brigade in the Army of the Potomac*. Edited by Lawrence Frederick Kohl. New York: Fordham University Press, 1992.
Cusack, Martin Kevin, ed. *Journal of a Voyage from Portland to Fremantle on Board the Convict Ship 'Hougoumont' Cap Cozens Commander October 12th 1867 by John S. Casey Mitchelstown Ireland*. Bryn Mawr: Dorrance and Co., 1988.
De Beaumont, Gustave. *Ireland: Social, Political, and Religious*. Edited by W. C. Taylor. Cambridge, Mass.: Belknap Press of Harvard University Press, 2006. First published 1839.
Declaration of Principles, by the Representatives of the Fenian Brotherhood, in Congress Assembled. Cleveland: n.p., 1867.
Dilke, Charles Wentworth. *Greater Britain: A Record of Travel in English-Speaking Countries during 1866 and 1867*. 2 vols. London: Macmillan, 1869.
Dillon, William. *Life of John Mitchel*. 2 vols. London: Kegan, Paul, Trench and Co., 1888.
Doheny, Michael. *The Felon's Track; or, History of the Attempted Outbreak in Ireland: Embracing the Leading Events in the Irish Struggle from the Year 1843 to the Close of 1848*. New York: W. H. Holbrooke, 1849.

Duffy, Charles Gavan. *Four Years of Irish History, 1845–1849: A Sequel to "Young Ireland."* London: Cassell, Petter, Galpin and Co., 1883.

——. *My Life in Two Hemispheres.* 2 vols. New York: Macmillan, 1898.

——, ed. *The Voice of the Nation: A Manual of Nationality.* Dublin: James Duffy, 1844.

——. *Why Is Ireland Poor and Discontented?* Melbourne: Stillwell and Knight, 1870.

——. *Young Ireland: A Fragment of Irish History, 1840–1845.* Dublin: M. H. Gill and Son, 1884.

Ellis, George. *Irish Ethnology Socially and Politically Considered: Embracing a General Outline of the Celtic and Saxon Races; With Practical Inferences.* Dublin: Hodges and Smith, 1852.

Fitzpatrick, David, ed. *Oceans of Consolation: Personal Accounts of Irish Migration to Australia.* Ithaca, N.Y.: Cornell University Press, 1994.

Freeman, Edward A. *The Life and Letters of Edward A. Freeman.* Vol. 2. Edited by W. R. W. Stephens. London: Macmillan, 1895.

Froude, James Anthony. *The English in Ireland in the Eighteenth Century.* 3 vols. London: Longmans, Green, and Co., 1872–1874.

Grant, Madison. *The Passing of the Great Race; or, The Racial Basis of European History.* New York: Charles Scribner's Sons, 1916.

Griffith, Charles. *The Present State and Prospects of the Port Philip District of New South Wales.* Dublin: William Curry and Co., 1845.

Halpine, Charles G. *The Life and Adventures, Songs, Services, and Speeches of Private Miles O'Reilly.* New York: Carleton, 1864.

Killen, John, ed. *The Decade of the United Irishmen: Contemporary Accounts, 1791–1801.* Belfast: Blackstaff Press, 1997.

Knox, Robert. *The Races of Men: A Fragment.* Philadelphia: Lea and Blanchard, 1850.

Kohl, J. G. *Travels in Ireland.* London: Bruce and Wyld, 1844.

Lyons, W. F., ed. *Brigadier-General Thomas Francis Meagher: His Political and Military Career, with Selections from His Speeches and Writings.* New York: D. and J. Sadlier and Co., 1870.

MacPherson, James. *Fragments of Ancient Poetry, Collected in the Highlands of Scotland, and Translated from the Gaelic or Erse Language.* Edinburgh: G. Hamilton and J. Balfour, 1760.

McCarter, William. *My Life in the Irish Brigade: The Civil War Memoirs of Private William McCarter, 116th Pennsylvania Infantry.* Edited by Kevin O'Brien. Campbell, Calif.: Savas Publishing, 1996.

McElheran, John. *The Condition of Women and Children among the Celtic, Gothic, and Other Nations.* Boston: Patrick Donahoe, 1858.

Meagher, Thomas Francis. *The Last Days of the 69th in Virginia: A Narrative in Three Parts.* New York: Lynch and Cole, 1861.

——. *Letters on Our National Struggle by Brig.-Gen. Thos. Francis Meagher.* Pamphlets issued by the Loyal Publication Society from February 1, 1863, to February 1, 1864 [no. 38]. New York: Loyal Publication Society, 1864.

——. *Meagher of the Sword: Speeches of Thomas Francis Meagher in Ireland, 1846–1848*. Edited by Arthur Griffith. Dublin: M. H. Gill and Son, 1916.

——. "Rides through Montana." *Harper's New Monthly Magazine* 35, no. 209 (October 1867): 568–85.

Mitchel, John. *The Crusade of the Period*. New York: Lynch, Cole and Meehan, 1878.

——. *Jail Journal*. Edited by Thomas Flanagan. Dublin: University Press of Ireland, 1982.

——. *The Life and Times of Aodh O'Neill*. New York: P. M. Haverty, 1868. First published 1845.

Moore, Frank, ed. *The Rebellion Record: A Diary of American Events*. Part 3: *Poetry*. New York: G. P. Putnam, 1861.

O'Connell, Daniel. *A Memoir on Ireland, Native and Saxon*. New York: Greeley and McElrath, 1843.

O'Connor, Rt. Rev. Dr. [Michael], ed. *Celts and Saxons, Nativism and Naturalization: A Complete Refutation of the Nativism of Dr. Orestes Brownson; By the Catholic Press of the United States*. Boston: Thomas Sweeney, 1854.

O'Leary, J[ames]. *Ireland among the Nations; or, The Faults and Virtues of the Irish Compared with Those of Other Races*. New York: J. A. McGee, 1874.

Quetelet, L. A. J. *A Treatise on Man and the Development of His Faculties*. Edinburgh: William and Robert Chambers, 1842.

Redfield, James W. *Comparative Physiognomy; or, Resemblances between Men and Animals*. New York: Redfield, 1852.

Rigney, J. *An Account of the Life and Missionary Labours of the Late Archdeacon McEncroe*. Sydney: J. G. O'Connor, 1868.

Rowell, George P. *American Newspaper Directory*. New York: Rowell, 1879.

——. *The Men Who Advertise: An Account of Successful Advertisers, together with Hints on the Method of Advertising*. New York: Nelson Chesman, 1870.

Saunders, Frederick, and Thomas Bangs Thorpe. *A Voice to America; or, The Model Republic, Its Glory, or Its Fall*. New York: Edward Walker, 1855.

Smiles, Samuel. *History of Ireland and the Irish People under the Government of England*. London: W. Strange, 1844.

Smith O'Brien, William. *"To Solitude Consigned": The Tasmanian Journal of William Smith O'Brien, 1849–1853*. Edited by Richard Davis. Sydney: Crossing Press, 1995.

Spencer, Herbert. *The Principles of Biology*. London: Williams and Norgate, 1864.

Tammany Society; or Columbian Order Annual Celebration in Honor of the Eighty-Sixth Anniversary of American Independence, at Tammany Hall, on Friday, July 4th 1862. New York: Baptist and Taylor, 1862.

Turner, Sharon. *The History of the Anglo-Saxons, Comprising the History of England from the Earliest Period to the Norman Conquest*. London: Longman, Hurst, Rees, Orme, and Brown, 1823. First published 1799–1805.

U.S. War Department. *The War of the Rebellion: A Compilation of the Official Records of the Union and Confederate Armies*. Series 1, vol. 52, part 2. Washington, D.C.: Government Printing Office, 1888.

Welsh, Peter. *Irish Green and Union Blue: The Civil War Letters of Peter Welsh*. Edited by Lawrence Frederick Kohl and Margaret Cosse Richards. New York: Fordham University Press, 1986.

Winthrop, Robert C. *Addresses and Speeches on Various Occasions by Robert C. Winthrop*. Boston: Little, Brown, 1852.

Secondary Sources

Akenson, Donald H. *If the Irish Ran the World: Montserrat, 1630–1730*. Montreal: McGill–Queen's University Press, 1997.

———. *The Irish Diaspora: A Primer*. Belfast: Institute of Irish Studies, 1993.

———. *The Irish in Ontario: A Study in Rural History*. Montreal: McGill–Queen's University Press, 1984.

Anbinder, Tyler. *Nativism and Slavery: The Northern Know Nothings and the Politics of the 1850s*. New York: Oxford University Press, 1992.

Anderson, Benedict. *Imagined Communities: Reflections on the Origin and Spread of Nationalism*. London: Verso, 1991.

Andrews, J. Cutler. *The North Reports the Civil War*. Pittsburgh: University of Pittsburgh Press, 1983.

———. *The South Reports the Civil War*. Pittsburgh: University of Pittsburgh Press, 1985.

Arnesen, Eric. "Whiteness and the Historians' Imagination." *International Labor and Working-Class History* 60 (Fall 2001): 3–32.

Athearn, Robert G. *Thomas Francis Meagher: An Irish Revolutionary in America*. New York: Arno Press, 1976.

Atkinson, Alan. *The Europeans in Australia*. Vol. 2. Melbourne: Oxford University Press, 2004.

Axline, Jon. "With Courage and Undaunted Obstinacy: Meagher in Montana, 1865–67." In *Thomas Francis Meagher: The Making of an Irish American*, edited by John M. Hearne and Rory T. Cornish, 176–94. Dublin: Irish Academic Press, 2006.

Azuma, Eiichiro. *Between Two Empires: Race, History, and Transnationalism in Japanese America*. New York: Oxford University Press, 2005.

Barker, Hannah. *Newspapers, Politics, and English Society, 1695–1855*. London: Longman, 2000.

Barr, Colin. "Giuseppe Mazzini and Irish Nationalism, 1845–70." In *Giuseppe Mazzini and the Globalization of Democratic Nationalism*, edited by Christopher A. Bayly and Eugenio F. Biagini, 125–44. Oxford: Oxford University Press, 2008.

———. "'Imperium in Imperio': Irish Episcopal Imperialism in the Nineteenth Century." *English Historical Review* 123, no. 502 (June 2008): 611–50.

Bartlett, Thomas. *Ireland: A History*. Cambridge: Cambridge University Press, 2010.

Baum, Bruce. *The Rise and Fall of the Caucasian Race: A Political History of Racial Identity*. New York: New York University Press, 2006.

Baumgartner, Apollinaris W. *Catholic Journalism: A Study of Its Development in the United States, 1789–1830.* New York: Columbia University Press, 1931.

Bayly, Christopher A. "Ireland, India, and Empire: 1780–1914." *Transactions of the Royal Historical Series,* 6th series, 10 (2000): 377–97.

Belchem, John. "Nationalism, Republicanism, and Exile: Irish Emigrants and the Revolutions of 1848." *Past and Present* 146 (February 1995): 103–35.

Berlin, Ira. *Slaves without Masters: The Free Negro in the Antebellum South.* New York: The Free Press, 2007.

Bernstein, Iver. *The New York City Draft Riots: Their Significance for American Society and Politics in the Age of the Civil War.* Oxford: Oxford University Press, 1990.

Berthoff, Rowland. "Celtic Mist over the South." *Journal of Social History* 52, no. 4 (November 1986): 523–46.

Birchley, D. *John McEncroe: Colonial Democrat.* Melbourne: Collins Dove, 1986.

Birt, H. N. *Benedictine Pioneers in Australia.* London: Herbert and Daniel, 1911.

Blainey, Geoffrey. *The Rush That Never Ended: A History of Australian Mining.* Melbourne: Melbourne University Press, 2003.

Blight, David W. *Race and Reunion: The Civil War in American Memory.* Cambridge, Mass.: Belknap Press of Harvard University Press, 2001.

Boyce, D. G. *Nationalism in Ireland.* Baltimore: Johns Hopkins University Press, 1982.

——. *Nineteenth Century Ireland: The Search for Stability.* Dublin: Gill and Macmillan, 2005.

Boyce, D. G., and P. Wingate, eds. *Newspaper History: From the 17th Century to the Present Day.* London: Constable, 1978.

Brady, Ciaran. *James Anthony Froude: An Intellectual Biography of a Victorian Prophet.* Oxford: Oxford University Press, 2013.

Broome, Richard. *Aboriginal Australians: Black Responses to White Domination, 1788–2001.* 3rd ed. St. Leonards: Allen and Unwin, 2002.

——. "Aboriginal Victims and Voyagers, Confronting Frontier Myths." *Journal of Australian Studies* 18, no. 42 (1994): 70–77.

Brown, Malcolm. *The Politics of Irish Literature: From Thomas Davis to W. B. Yeats.* Seattle: University of Washington Press, 1972.

Brown, Thomas N. *Irish-American Nationalism, 1870–1890.* Philadelphia: Lippincott, 1966.

Bruce, Susannah Ural. *The Harp and the Eagle: Irish-American Volunteers and the Union Army, 1861–1865.* New York: New York University Press, 2006.

——. "Irish-Americans." In *Encyclopedia of the American Civil War: A Political, Social, and Military History,* edited by David S. Heidler and Jeanne T. Heidler, 1036–37. New York: W. W. Norton, 2002.

Brundage, David. "Matilda Tone in America: Exile, Gender, and Memory in the Making of Irish Republican Nationalism." *New Hibernia Review* 14, no. 1 (Spring 2010): 96–111.

Burton, William L. *Melting Pot Soldiers: The Union's Ethnic Regiments.* New York: Fordham University Press, 1998.

Campbell, Malcolm. *Ireland's New Worlds: Immigrants, Politics, and Society in the United States and Australia, 1815–1922*. Madison: University of Wisconsin Press, 2008.

Cantrell, James P. *How Celtic Culture Invented Southern Literature*. Gretna, La.: Pelican Publishing, 2006.

Carey, Hilary M. *God's Empire: Religion and Colonialism in the British World, c. 1801–1908*. Cambridge: Cambridge University Press, 2011.

Cha-Jua, Sundiata Keita. "The Changing Same: Black Racial Formation and Transformation as a Theory of the African American Experience." In *Race Struggles*, edited by Theodore Koditschek, Sundiata Keita Cha-Jua, and Helen A. Neville, 9–47. Urbana: University of Illinois Press, 2009.

Chapman, Malcolm. *The Celts: The Construction of a Myth*. New York: St. Martin's Press, 1992.

Choate, Mark. *Emigrant Nation: The Making of Italy Abroad*. Cambridge, Mass.: Harvard University Press, 2008.

Cochrane, Peter. *Colonial Ambition: Foundations of Australian Democracy*. Melbourne: Melbourne University Press, 2006.

Comerford, R. V. *The Fenians in Context: Irish Politics and Society, 1848–1882*. Dublin: Wolfhound Press, 1998.

Cornish, Dudley Taylor. *The Sable Arm: Black Troops in the Union Army, 1861–1865*. Lawrence: University Press of Kansas, 1987.

Cornish, Rory T. "An Irish Republican Abroad: Thomas Francis Meagher in the United States, 1852–65." In *Thomas Francis Meagher: The Making of an Irish American*, edited by John M. Hearne and Rory T. Cornish, 139–62. Dublin: Irish Academic Press, 2006.

Costigan, Giovanni. "Romantic Nationalism: Ireland and Europe." *Irish University Review* 3, no. 2 (Autumn 1973): 141–52.

Cullen, J. H. *Young Ireland in Exile: The Story of the Men of '48 in Tasmania*. Dublin: Talbot Press, 1928.

Curley, Thomas M. *Samuel Johnson, the Ossian Fraud, and the Celtic Revival in Great Britain and Ireland*. Cambridge: Cambridge University Press, 2009.

Curtin, Nancy J. *The United Irishmen: Popular Politics in Ulster and Dublin, 1791–1798*. Oxford: Clarendon Press, 1994.

Curtis, L. P. *Anglo-Saxons and Celts: A Study of Anti-Irish Prejudice in Victorian England*. Bridgeport, Conn.: Bridgeport University Press, 1968.

Daniels, Roger. *Coming to America: A History of Immigration and Ethnicity in American Life*. 2nd ed. New York: HarperCollins, 2002.

D'Arcy, William. *The Fenian Movement in the United States: 1858–1886*. New York: Russell and Russell, 1971. First published 1947.

Davis, Richard. *Revolutionary Imperialist: William Smith O'Brien, 1803–1864*. Sydney: Crossing Press, 1998.

———. *The Young Ireland Movement*. Dublin: Gill and Macmillan, 1987.

Delbanco, Andrew. *The Portable Abraham Lincoln*. New York: Viking Penguin, 1992.

De Nie, Michael. *The Eternal Paddy: Irish Identity and the British Press, 1798–1882*. Madison: University of Wisconsin Press, 2004.

Dickson, R. J. *Ulster Emigration to Colonial America, 1718–1785*. Belfast: Ulster Historical Foundation, 1966.

Diner, Hasia R. *Erin's Daughters in America: Irish Immigrant Women in the Nineteenth Century*. Baltimore: Johns Hopkins University Press, 1983.

———. "'The Most Irish City in the Union': The Era of the Great Migration, 1844–1877." In *The New York Irish*, edited by Ronald H. Bayor and Timothy J. Meagher, 87–106. Baltimore: Johns Hopkins University Press, 1996.

Dolan, Jay P. *The Immigrant Church: New York's German and Irish Catholics*. Baltimore: Johns Hopkins University Press, 1975.

Doorley, Michael. *Irish-American Diaspora Nationalism: The Friends of Irish Freedom, 1916–1935*. Dublin: Four Courts Press, 2005.

Dowd, Christopher. *Rome in Australia: The Papacy and Conflict in the Australian Catholic Missions, 1834–1884*. Leiden: Koninklijke Brill NV, 2008.

Doyle, David N. *Ireland, Irishmen, and Revolutionary America, 1760–1820*. Cork: Mercier Press, 1981.

———. "The Irish in North America, 1776–1845." In *Making the Irish American: History and Heritage of the Irish in the United States*, edited by J. J. Lee and Marion R. Casey, 171–212. New York: New York University Press, 2006.

Dwan, David. *The Great Community: Culture and Nationalism in Ireland*. Dublin: Field Day, 2008.

Elliott, Marianne. "The Origins and Transformation of Early Irish Republicanism." *International Review of Social History* 23, no. 2 (1978): 405–28.

Emmons, David M. *Beyond the American Pale: The Irish in the West, 1845–1910*. Norman: University of Oklahoma Press, 2010.

———. *The Butte Irish: Class and Ethnicity in an American Mining Town, 1875–1925*. Urbana: University of Illinois Press, 1989.

———. "The Strange Death of Thomas Francis Meagher: Tribal Politics in Territorial Montana." In *Thomas Francis Meagher: The Making of an Irish American*, edited by John M. Hearne and Rory T. Cornish, 223–39. Dublin: Irish Academic Press, 2006.

Feingold, Ruth. "From Empire to Nation: The Shifting Sands of Australian National Identity." In *A Companion to Australian Literature since 1990*, edited by Nicholas Birns and Rebecca McNeer, 61–71. Rochester, N.Y.: Camden House, 2007.

Fields, Barbara J. "Whiteness, Racism, and Identity." *International Labor and Working-Class History* 60 (Fall 2001): 48–56.

Fitzgerald, Patrick, and Brian Lambkin. *Migration in Irish History, 1607–2007*. Basingstoke: Palgrave Macmillan, 2008.

Fitzpatrick, David. "Ireland and the Empire." In *The Oxford History of the British Empire*, vol. 3, edited by Andrew Porter, 495–521. Oxford: Oxford University Press, 2001.

Fleche, Andre M. *The Revolution of 1861: The American Civil War in the Age of National-ist Conflict*. Chapel Hill: University of North Carolina Press, 2012.

Foik, Paul J. *Pioneer Catholic Journalism*. New York: United States Catholic Historical Society, 1930.

Foner, Eric. "Class, Ethnicity, and Radicalism in the Gilded Age: The Land League and Irish America." In *Politics and Ideology in the Age of the Civil War*, 150–200. New York: Oxford University Press, 1980.

——. *The Fiery Trial: Abraham Lincoln and American Slavery*. New York: W. W. Norton, 2010.

——. *Give Me Liberty! An American History*. Vol. 2. New York: W. W. Norton, 2011.

——. *A Short History of Reconstruction, 1863–1877*. New York: Harper and Row, 1988.

——. *The Story of American Freedom*. New York: W. W. Norton, 1998.

Frawley, Mary A. *Patrick Donahoe*. Washington, D.C.: Catholic University of America Press, 1946.

Gabaccia, Donna R. *Italy's Many Diasporas*. London: UCL Press, 2000.

Garvin, Tom. *Nationalist Revolutionaries in Ireland, 1858–1928*. Dublin: Gill and Macmillan, 1987.

Gerber, David A. "Forming a Transnational Narrative: New Perspectives on European Migrations to the United States." *History Teacher* 35, no. 1 (November 2001): 61–78.

Gibbons, Luke. *Transformations in Irish Culture*. Notre Dame, Ind.: University of Notre Dame Press, 1996.

Giddens, Anthony. *Modernity and Self-Identity: Self and Society in the Late Modern Age*. Stanford: Stanford University Press, 1991.

Gilley, Sheridan. "The Roman Catholic Church and the Nineteenth-Century Irish Diaspora." *Journal of Ecclesiastical History* 35, no. 2 (April 1984): 188–207.

Gilmore, Huston. "'The Shouts of Vanished Crowds': Literacy, Orality, and Popular Politics in the Campaign to Repeal the Act of Union in Ireland, 1840–48." *19: Interdisciplinary Studies in the Long Nineteenth Century* 18 (2014): 1–27.

Gilmore, Peter. "Rebels and Revivals: Ulster Immigrants, Western Pennsylvania Presbyterianism, and the Formation of Scotch-Irish Identity, 1780–1830." Ph.D. diss., Carnegie Mellon University, 2009.

Gleeson, David T. *The Green and the Gray: The Irish in the Confederate States of America*. Chapel Hill: University of North Carolina Press, 2013.

——, ed. *The Irish in the Atlantic World*. Columbia: University of South Carolina Press, 2010.

——. *The Irish in the South, 1815–1877*. Chapel Hill: University of North Carolina Press, 2001.

——. "Irish Rebels, Southern Rebels: The Irish Confederates." In *Civil War Citizens: Race, Ethnicity, and Identity in America's Bloodiest Conflict*, edited by Susannah J. Ural, 133–56. New York: New York University Press, 2010.

———. "Securing the 'Interests' of the South: John Mitchel, A. G. Magrath, and the Reopening of the Transatlantic Slave Trade." *American Nineteenth Century History* 11, no. 3 (September 2010): 279–97.

———. "'To Live and Die [for] Dixie': Irish Civilians and the Confederate States of America." *Irish Studies Review* 18, no. 2 (May 2010): 139–53.

Goldstein, Eric L. *The Price of Whiteness: Jews, Race, and American Identity.* Princeton: Princeton University Press, 2006.

Goodman, David. *Goldseeking: Victoria and California in the 1850s.* Sydney: Allen and Unwin, 1994.

Gordon, Michael A. *The Orange Riots: Irish Political Violence in New York City, 1870 and 1871.* Ithaca, N.Y.: Cornell University Press, 1993.

Gray, Peter. *Famine, Land, and Politics: British Government and Irish Society, 1843–50.* Dublin: Irish Academic Press, 1999.

Griffin, Patrick. *The People with No Name: Ireland's Ulster Scots, America's Scots Irish, and the Creation of a British Atlantic World, 1689–1764.* Princeton: Princeton University Press, 2001.

Guglielmo, Thomas A. *White on Arrival: Italians, Race, Color, and Power in Chicago, 1890–1945.* Oxford: Oxford University Press, 2003.

Gyory, Andrew. *Closing the Gate: Race, Politics, and the Chinese Exclusion Act.* Chapel Hill: University of North Carolina Press, 1998.

Habermas, Jürgen. *The Structural Transformation of the Public Sphere: An Inquiry into a Category of Bourgeois Society.* Cambridge, Mass.: MIT Press, 1991.

Hanchett, William. *Irish: Charles G. Halpine in Civil War America.* Syracuse: Syracuse University Press, 1970.

Handlin, Oscar. *Boston's Immigrants: A Study in Acculturation.* Cambridge, Mass.: Belknap Press of Harvard University Press, 1941.

Harper, Robert S. *Lincoln and the Press.* New York: McGraw-Hill, 1951.

Hernon, Joseph M. *Celts, Catholics, and Copperheads: Ireland Views the American Civil War.* Columbus: Ohio State University Press, 1968.

Higham, John. *Strangers in the Land: Patterns of American Nativism, 1860–1925.* 2nd ed. New Brunswick, N.J.: Rutgers University Press, 1988.

Hirst, John. *The Strange Birth of Colonial Democracy: New South Wales, 1848–1884.* Sydney: Allen and Unwin, 1988.

Hobsbawm, Eric, and Terence Ranger, eds. *The Invention of Tradition.* Cambridge: Cambridge University Press, 1983.

Hoppen, K. Theodore. *Elections, Politics, and Society in Ireland, 1832–1885.* New York: Oxford University Press, 1984.

Horowitz, Tony. *Confederates in the Attic: Dispatches from the Unfinished Civil War.* New York: Pantheon Books, 1998.

Howe, Stephen. *Ireland and Empire: Colonial Legacies in Irish History and Culture.* Oxford: Oxford University Press, 2000.

Huggins, Michael. "The *Nation* and Giuseppe Mazzini, 1842–48." *New Hibernia Review* 17, no. 3 (Autumn 2013): 15–33.

Humphrey, Carole Sue. *The Press of the Young Republic, 1783–1833*. Westport, Conn.: Greenwood Press, 1996.

Huntzicker, William E. *The Popular Press, 1833–1865*. Westport, Conn.: Greenwood Press, 1999.

Ignatiev, Noel. *How the Irish Became White*. New York: Routledge, 1995.

Inglis, K. S. *The Australian Colonists: An Exploration of Social History, 1788–1870*. Carlton: Melbourne University Press, 1974.

Jacobson, Matthew Frye. *Whiteness of a Different Color: European Immigrants and the Alchemy of Race*. Cambridge, Mass.: Harvard University Press, 1998.

James, Simon. *The Atlantic Celts: Ancient People or Modern Invention?* Madison: University of Wisconsin Press, 1999.

Janis, Ely M. "Nationalism, Gender, and Ethnicity in the Gilded Age: The Land League Movement and the United States in the 1880s." Ph.D. diss., Boston College, 2008.

——. "Petticoat Revolutionaries: Gender, Ethnic Nationalism, and the Irish Ladies' Land League in the United States." *Journal of American Ethnic History* 27, no. 2 (Winter 2008): 5–27.

Jenkins, Brian. *The Fenian Problem: Insurgency and Terrorism in a Liberal State, 1858–1874*. Montreal: McGill–Queen's University Press, 2008.

——. *Fenians and Anglo-American Relations during Reconstruction*. Ithaca, N.Y.: Cornell University Press, 1969.

Jensen, Richard. "'No Irish Need Apply': A Myth of Victimization." *Journal of Social History* 36, no. 2 (2002): 405–29.

Jones, Jacqueline. "Georgia Lowcountry Battlegrounds during the Civil War." In *Breaking the Heartland: The Civil War in Georgia*, edited by John D. Fowler and David B. Parker, 67–93. Macon, Ga.: Mercer University Press, 2011.

Joyce, William Leonard. *Editors and Ethnicity: A History of the Irish-American Press, 1848–1883*. New York: Arno Press, 1976.

Kazal, Russell A. *Becoming Old Stock: The Paradox of German-American Identity*. Princeton: Princeton University Press, 2004.

Kelly, Mary C. *The Shamrock and the Lily: The New York Irish and the Creation of a Transatlantic Identity, 1845–1921*. New York: Peter Lang, 2005.

Kenny, Kevin. *The American Irish: A History*. Harlow, UK: Longman, 2000.

——. "Diaspora and Comparison: The Global Irish as a Case Study." *Journal of American History* 90, no. 1 (June 2003): 134–62.

——. *Making Sense of the Molly Maguires*. New York: Oxford University Press, 1998.

Keown, Gerard. "The Irish Race Convention, 1922, Reconsidered." *Irish Historical Studies* 32, no. 127 (May 2001): 365–76.

Kiberd, Declan. *Inventing Ireland: The Literature of the Modern Nation*. Cambridge, Mass.: Harvard University Press, 1997.

Kibler, M. Alison. "The Stage Irishwoman." *Journal of American Ethnic History* 24, no. 3 (Spring 2005): 5–30.

Knobel, Dale T. "'Celtic Exodus': The Famine Irish, Ethnic Stereotypes, and the Cultivation of American Racial Nationalism." In *Fleeing the Famine: North America and Irish Refugees, 1845–1851*, edited by Margaret M. Mulrooney, 79–93. Westport: Praeger, 2003.

——. *Paddy and the Republic: Ethnicity and Nationality in Antebellum America.* Middletown, Conn.: Wesleyan University Press, 1986.

Knowlton, Steven R. "The Politics of John Mitchel: A Reappraisal." *Éire-Ireland* 22, no. 2 (Summer 1987): 38–55.

Koditschek, Theodore. "Capitalism, Race, and Evolution in Imperial Britain, 1850–1900." In *Race Struggles*, edited by Theodore Koditschek, Sundiata Keita Cha-Jua, and Helen A. Neville, 48–79. Urbana: University of Illinois Press, 2009.

——. *Liberalism, Imperialism, and the Historical Imagination: Nineteenth-Century Visions of a Greater Britain.* Cambridge: Cambridge University Press, 2011.

Kolchin, Peter. "Whiteness Studies: The New History of Race in America." *Journal of American History* 89, no. 1 (June 2002): 154–73.

Kwitchen, Mary A. *James Alphonsus McMaster: A Study in American Thought.* Washington, D.C.: Catholic University of America Press, 1949.

Lee, Erika. *At America's Gates: Chinese Immigration during the Exclusion Era, 1882–1943.* Chapel Hill: University of North Carolina Press, 2003.

Lee, James Melvin. *History of American Journalism.* Garden City, N.Y.: Garden City Publishing Co., 1923.

Legler, John B., Richard Sylla, and John J. Wallis. "U.S. City Finances and the Growth of Government, 1850–1902." *Journal of Economic History* 48, no. 2 (June 1988): 347–56.

Lengel, Edward G. *The Irish through British Eyes: Perceptions of Ireland in the Famine Era.* Westport, Conn.: Praeger, 2002.

Leyburn, James G. *The Scotch-Irish: A Social History.* Chapel Hill: University of North Carolina Press, 1962.

Litwack, Leon F. *North of Slavery: The Negro in the Free States, 1790–1860.* Chicago: University of Chicago Press, 1965.

Lonn, Ella. *Foreigners in the Confederacy.* Gloucester, Mass.: Peter Smith, 1965.

——. *Foreigners in the Union Army and Navy.* Westport, Conn.: Greenwood Press, 1969.

Lynch, Niamh. "Defining Irish Nationalist Anti-Imperialism: Thomas Davis and John Mitchel." *Éire-Ireland* 42, nos. 1/2 (Spring/Summer 2007): 82–107.

——. "'Live Ireland, Perish the Empire': Irish Nationalist Anti-Imperialism c. 1840–1900." Ph.D. diss., Boston College, 2006.

MacDonagh, Oliver. *The Emancipist: Daniel O'Connell, 1830–1847.* Basingstoke: Palgrave Macmillan, 1989.

MacDougall, Hugh A. *Racial Myth in English History: Trojans, Teutons, and Anglo-Saxons.* Montreal: Harvest House, 1982.

MacGrath, Kevin. "Writers in the 'Nation,' 1842–5." *Irish Historical Studies* 6, no. 23 (1949): 189–223.

MacIntyre, Angus. *The Liberator: Daniel O'Connell and the Irish Party, 1830–1847.* London: Hamish Hamilton, 1965.

MacIntyre, Stuart. *A Concise History of Australia.* 3rd ed. Melbourne: Cambridge University Press, 2009.

MacRaild, Donald M. *The Irish Diaspora in Britain, 1750–1939.* 2nd ed. Basingstoke: Palgrave Macmillan, 2011.

——. "The Orange Atlantic." In *The Irish in the Atlantic World,* edited by David T. Gleeson, 307–26. Columbia: University of South Carolina Press, 2010.

Madgwick, R. B. *Immigration to Eastern Australia, 1788–1851.* London: Longmans, Green, and Co., 1937.

Magruder, Caleb Clarke, ed. *Year-Book of American Clan Gregor Society.* Charlottesville: Michie Co., 1912.

Mandler, Peter. *The English National Character: The History of an Idea from Edmund Burke to Tony Blair.* New Haven: Yale University Press, 2006.

Markus, Andrew. *Australian Race Relations, 1788–1993.* St. Leonards: Allen and Unwin, 1994.

Markus, Julia. *J. Anthony Froude: The Last Undiscovered Great Victorian.* New York: Scribner, 2005.

Martin, Ged. "Australia's History: 'Australian' or 'British'?" *Historical Journal* 23, no. 4 (December 1980): 1009–18.

McCarthy, Angela. *Scottishness and Irishness in New Zealand since 1840.* Manchester, UK: Manchester University Press, 2011.

McGovern, Bryan P. *John Mitchel: Irish Nationalist, Southern Secessionist.* Knoxville: University of Tennessee Press, 2009.

McGrath, Ann. "Shamrock Aborigines: The Irish, the Aboriginal Australians, and Their Children." *Aboriginal History* 34 (2010): 55–84.

McGregor, Russell. "The Necessity of Britishness: Ethno-Cultural Roots of Australian Nationalism." *Nations and Nationalism* 12, no. 3 (July 2006): 493–511.

McKeown, Adam. "Global Migration, 1846–1940." *Journal of World History* 15, no. 2 (2004): 155–89.

McLean, Ian W. *Why Australia Prospered: The Shifting Sources of Economic Growth.* Princeton: Princeton University Press, 2012.

McMahon, Cian T. "Caricaturing Race and Nation in the Irish American Press, 1870–1880: A Transnational Perspective." *Journal of American Ethnic History* 33, no. 2 (Winter 2014): 33–56.

——. "International Celebrities and Irish Identity in the United States and Beyond, 1840–1860." *American Nineteenth Century History* 15, no. 2 (2014): 147–68.

——. "Ireland and the Birth of the Irish-American Press, 1842–1861." *American Periodicals: A Journal of History and Criticism* 19, no. 1 (2009): 5–20.

———. "The Pages of Whiteness: Theory, Evidence, and the American Immigration Debate." *Race & Class* 56, no. 4 (2015).

———. "Transnational Dimensions of Irish Anti-Imperialism, 1842–54." In *Irish and Scottish Encounters with Indigenous Peoples*, edited by Graeme Morton and David A. Wilson, 92–107. Montreal: McGill–Queen's University Press, 2013.

McManamin, Francis G. *The American Years of John Boyle O'Reilly*. New York: Arno Press, 1976.

McMichael, Philip. *Settlers and the Agrarian Question: Capitalism in Colonial Australia*. Cambridge: Cambridge University Press, 2004.

McNamara, Heather. "The *New Zealand Tablet* and the Irish Catholic Press Worldwide, 1898–1923." *New Zealand Journal of History* 37, no. 2 (2003): 153–70.

McNicholas, Anthony. "Co-operation, Compromise, and Confrontation: The *Universal News*, 1860–1869." *Irish Historical Studies* 35, no. 139 (May 2007): 311–26.

———. *Politics, Religion, and the Press: Irish Journalism in Mid-Victorian England*. New York: Peter Lang, 2007.

McWhiney, Grady. *Cracker Culture: Celtic Ways in the Old South*. Tuscaloosa: University of Alabama Press, 1988.

McWhiney, Grady, and Perry D. Jamieson. *Attack and Die: Civil War Military Tactics and the Southern Heritage*. Tuscaloosa: University of Alabama Press, 1982.

Meagher, Timothy J. *Inventing Irish America: Generation, Class, and Ethnic Identity in a New England City, 1880–1928*. Notre Dame, Ind.: University of Notre Dame Press, 2001.

Meaney, Neville. "Britishness and Australian Identity: The Problem of Nationalism in Australian History and Historiography." *Australian Historical Studies* 32, no. 116 (April 2001): 76–90.

Miller, Kerby A. "Class, Culture, and Immigrant Group Identity in the United States: The Case of Irish-American Ethnicity." In *Immigration Reconsidered: History, Sociology, and Politics*, edited by Virginia Yans-McLaughlin, 96–129. New York: Oxford University Press, 1990.

———. *Emigrants and Exiles: Ireland and the Irish Exodus to North America*. Oxford: Oxford University Press, 1985.

———. *Ireland and Irish America: Culture, Class, and Transatlantic Migration*. Dublin: Field Day, 2008.

———. "Ulster Presbyterians and the 'Two Traditions' in Ireland and America." In *Making the Irish American: History and Heritage of the Irish in the United States*, edited by J. J. Lee and Marion R. Casey, 255–70. New York: New York University Press, 2006.

Miller, Kerby A., Arnold Schrier, Bruce D. Boling, and David N. Doyle, eds. *Irish Immigrants in the Land of Canaan: Letters and Memoirs from Colonial and Revolutionary America, 1675–1815*. Oxford: Oxford University Press, 2003.

Mitchell, Jessie. "'The galling yoke of slavery': Race and Separation in Colonial Port Phillip." *Journal of Australian Studies* 33, no. 2 (2009): 125–37.

Moloney, Deirdre M. "Land League Activism in Transnational Perspective." *U.S. Catholic Historian* 22, no. 3 (Summer 2004): 61–74.

Morton, Graeme, and David A. Wilson, eds. *Irish and Scottish Encounters with Indigenous Peoples.* Montreal: McGill–Queen's University Press, 2013.

Mott, Frank Luther. *American Journalism: A History of Newspapers in the United States through 260 Years, 1690–1950.* Rev. ed. New York: Macmillan, 1950.

Mulligan, Adrian N. "A Forgotten 'Greater Ireland': The Transatlantic Development of Irish Nationalism." *Scottish Geographical Journal* 118, no. 3 (2002): 219–34.

Murphy, Angela F. "Abolition, Irish Freedom, and Immigrant Citizenship: American Slavery and the Rise and Fall of the American Associations for Irish Repeal." Ph.D. diss., University of Houston, 2006.

———. *American Slavery, Irish Freedom: Abolition, Immigrant Citizenship, and the Transatlantic Movement for Irish Repeal.* Baton Rouge: Louisiana State University Press, 2010.

Nally, David P. *Human Encumbrances: Political Violence and the Great Irish Famine.* Notre Dame, Ind.: University of Notre Dame Press, 2011.

Nelson, Bruce. *Irish Nationalists and the Making of the Irish Race.* Princeton: Princeton University Press, 2012.

Nerone, John. *Violence against the Press: Policing the Public Sphere in U.S. History.* New York: Oxford University Press, 1994.

Newsinger, John. "John Mitchel and Irish Nationalism." *Literature and History* 6 (1980): 182–200.

Nowlan, Kevin B. *Ireland and the Italian Risorgimento.* Dublin: Italian Institute, 1960.

———. "O'Connell and Irish Nationalism." In *Daniel O'Connell: Portrait of a Radical,* edited by Kevin B. Nowlan and Maurice R. O'Connell, 9–18. New York: Fordham University Press, 1985.

Ó Ciosáin, Niall. *Print and Popular Culture in Ireland, 1750–1850.* New York: St. Martin's Press, 1997.

O'Conner, Rebecca. *Jenny Mitchel, Young Irelander: A Biography.* Dublin: O'Conner Trust, 1985.

O'Connor, Joseph. *The Secret World of the Irish Male.* Dublin: New Island, 1994.

O'Farrell, Patrick. *The Catholic Church and Community: An Australian History.* 3rd rev. ed. Kensington: New South Wales University, 1985.

———. *The Irish in Australia.* Sydney: University of New South Wales Press, 1986.

———. *Vanished Kingdoms: Irish in Australia and New Zealand.* Sydney: University of New South Wales Press, 1990.

Öfele, Martin W. *True Sons of the Republic: European Immigrants in the Union Army.* Westport, Conn.: Praeger, 2008.

Ó Gráda, Cormac. "Across the Briny Ocean: Some Thoughts on Irish Emigration to America, 1800–1850." In *Ireland and Scotland, 1600–1850: Parallels and Contrasts in Economic and Social Development,* edited by T. M. Devine and David Dickson, 118–30. Edinburgh: John Donald, 1983.

———. *Black '47 and Beyond: The Great Irish Famine in History, Economy, and Memory.* Princeton: Princeton University Press, 1999.

O'Grady, Kelly J. *Clear the Confederate Way! The Irish in the Army of Northern Virginia.* Mason City, Iowa: Savas Publishing, 2000.

O'Malley, T., and C. Soley. *Regulating the Press.* London: Pluto Press, 2000.

Osofsky, Gilbert. "Abolitionists, Irish Immigrants, and the Dilemmas of Romantic Nationalism." *American Historical Review* 80, no. 4 (October 1975): 889–912.

Owens, Gary. "Constructing the Repeal Spectacle: Monster Meetings and People Power in Pre-Famine Ireland." In *People Power: Proceedings of the Third Annual Daniel O'Connell Workshop*, edited by Maurice R. O'Connell, 80–93. Dublin: Institute of Public Administration, 1993.

———. "Hedge Schools of Politics: O'Connell's Monster Meetings." *History Ireland* 2, no. 1 (1994): 35–40.

———. "Nationalism without Words: Symbolism and Ritual Behavior in the Repeal 'Monster Meetings' of 1843–5." In *Irish Popular Culture, 1650–1850*, edited by James S. Donnelly Jr. and Kerby A. Miller, 242–69. Dublin: Irish Academic Press, 1998.

Painter, Nell Irvin. *The History of White People.* New York: W. W. Norton, 2010.

———. "Ralph Waldo Emerson's Saxons." *Journal of American History* 95, no. 4 (March 2009): 977–85.

Pappin, Joseph L. *The Metaphysics of Edmund Burke.* New York: Fordham University Press, 1993.

Park, Robert E. *The Immigrant Press and Its Control.* New York: Harper and Brothers, 1922.

Payne, George Henry. *History of Journalism in the United States.* Reprint. Westport, Conn.: Greenwood Press, 1970.

Phelan, Josephine. *The Ardent Exile: The Life of Thomas Darcy McGee.* Toronto: Macmillan, 1951.

Phillips, P. K. "McEncroe, John (1794–1868)." *Australian Dictionary of Biography*, http://adb.anu.edu.au/biography/mcencroe-john-2398/text3167, accessed April 23, 2013.

Price, Charles A. *The Great White Walls Are Built: Restrictive Immigration to North America and Australasia, 1836–1888.* Canberra: Australian National University Press, 1974.

Quigley, Paul. *Shifting Grounds: Nationalism and the American South, 1848–1865.* New York: Oxford University Press, 2011.

Quinn, James. "John Mitchel and the Rejection of the Nineteenth Century." *Éire-Ireland* 38, nos. 3/4 (Fall/Winter 2003): 90–108.

Rafferty, Oliver P. "The Catholic Church, Ireland, and the British Empire, 1800–1921." *Historical Research* 84, no. 224 (May 2011): 288–309.

Ramold, Steven J. *Slaves, Sailors, Citizens: African Americans in the Union Navy.* DeKalb: Northern Illinois University Press, 2002.

Reece, Bob. "Irish Convicts." In *The Australian People: An Encyclopedia of the Nation, Its People, and Their Origins*, edited by James Juup, 447–51. Cambridge: Cambridge University Press, 2002.

Reynolds, Donald E. *Editors Make War: Southern Newspapers in the Secession Crisis.* Nashville: Vanderbilt University Press, 1970.

Riach, Douglas C. "Daniel O'Connell and American Anti-slavery." *Irish Historical Studies* 20, no. 77 (March 1976): 3–25.

———. "Ireland and the Campaign against American Slavery, 1830–1860." Ph.D. diss., Edinburgh University, 1975.

———. "O'Connell and Slavery." In *The World of Daniel O'Connell*, edited by Donal McCartney, 175–85. Dublin: Mercier Press, 1980.

———. "Richard Davis Webb and Antislavery in Ireland." In *Antislavery Reconsidered: New Perspectives on the Abolitionists*, edited by Lewis Perry and Michael Fellman, 149–67. Baton Rouge: Louisiana State University Press, 1979.

Roberts, Stephen H. *The Squatting Age in Australia, 1835–1847.* 2nd ed. Melbourne: Melbourne University Press, 1971.

Rodechko, James P. "An Irish-American Journalist and Catholicism: Patrick Ford of the Irish World." *Church History* 39 (December 1970): 524–40.

———. *Patrick Ford and His Search for America: A Case Study of Irish American Journalism, 1870–1913.* New York: Arno Press, 1976.

Rodgers, Nini. *Ireland, Slavery, and Antislavery, 1612–1865.* Basingstoke: Palgrave Macmillan, 2007.

Roediger, David. *The Wages of Whiteness: Race and the Making of the American Working Class.* 2nd ed. New York: Verso, 1999.

Rubin, Anne Sarah. *A Shattered Nation: The Rise and Fall of the Confederacy, 1861–1868.* Chapel Hill: University of North Carolina Press, 2005.

Ryan, Lyndall. "Settler Massacres on the Port Phillip Frontier, 1836–1851." *Journal of Australian Studies* 34, no. 3 (2010): 257–73.

Samito, Christian G. *Becoming American under Fire: Irish Americans, African Americans, and the Politics of Citizenship during the Civil War Era.* Ithaca, N.Y.: Cornell University Press, 2009.

Saveth, Edward N. *American Historians and European Immigrants, 1875–1925.* New York: Russell and Russell, 1965.

Saxton, Alexander. *The Indispensable Enemy: Labor and the Anti-Chinese Movement in California.* Berkeley: University of California Press, 1971.

Serle, Geoffrey. *The Golden Age: A History of the Colony of Victoria, 1851–1861.* Melbourne: Melbourne University Press, 1963.

Shumsky, Neil Larry. *The Evolution of Political Protest and the Workingmen's Party of California.* Columbus: Ohio State University Press, 1992.

Skelton, Isabel. *The Life of Thomas D'Arcy McGee.* Gardenvale, QC: Garden City Press, 1925.

Smith, Anthony. *The Newspaper: An International History.* London: Thames and Hudson, 1979.

Smith, John David. "Introduction." In *Black Soldiers in Blue: African American Troops in the Civil War Era*, edited by John David Smith, xiii–xxiii. Chapel Hill: University of North Carolina Press, 2002.

——. "Let Us All Be Grateful That We Have Colored Troops That Will Fight." In *Black Soldiers in Blue: African American Troops in the Civil War Era*, edited by John David Smith, 1–77. Chapel Hill: University of North Carolina Press, 2002.

Smythe, Ted Curtis. *The Gilded Age Press, 1865–1900*. Westport, Conn.: Greenwood Press, 2003.

Snay, Mitchell. *Fenians, Freedmen, and Southern Whites: Race and Nationality in the Era of Reconstruction*. Baton Rouge: Louisiana State University Press, 2007.

Snyder, Edward D. *The Celtic Revival in English Literature, 1760–1800*. Gloucester, Mass.: Peter Smith, 1965.

Solomon, Barbara Miller. *Ancestors and Immigrants: A Changing New England Tradition*. Cambridge, Mass.: Harvard University Press, 1956.

Spann, Edward K. "Union Green: The Irish Community and the Civil War." In *The New York Irish*, edited by Ronald H. Bayor and Timothy J. Meagher, 193–209. Baltimore: Johns Hopkins University Press, 1996.

Stocking, George W. *Victorian Anthropology*. New York: The Free Press, 1987.

Thorpe, Bill. "Frontiers of Discourse: Assessing Revisionist Australian Colonial Contact Historiography." *Journal of Australian Studies* 19, no. 46 (1995): 34–45.

Toomey, Michael. "'Saving the South with All My Might': John Mitchel, Champion of Southern Nationalism." In *Thomas Francis Meagher: The Making of an Irish American*, edited by John M. Hearne and Rory T. Cornish, 123–38. Dublin: Irish Academic Press, 2006.

Touhill, Blanche. "*The Times* versus William Smith O'Brien." *Victorian Periodicals Review* 15, no. 2 (Summer 1982): 52–63.

——. *William Smith O'Brien and His Irish Revolutionary Companions in Penal Exile*. Columbia: University of Missouri Press, 1981.

Townend, Paul A. "Between Two Worlds: Irish Nationalists and Imperial Crisis, 1878–1880." *Past and Present* 194, no. 1 (February 2007): 139–74.

——. *Father Mathew, Temperance, and Irish Identity*. Dublin: Irish Academic Press, 2002.

Ural, Susannah J. "Introduction." In *Civil War Citizens: Race, Ethnicity, and Identity in America's Bloodiest Conflict*, edited by Susannah J. Ural, 1–10. New York: New York University Press, 2010.

Walsh, Victor A. "'A Fanatic Heart': The Cause of Irish-American Nationalism in Pittsburgh during the Gilded Age." *Journal of Social History* 15, no. 2 (1981): 187–204.

Watson, Ritchie Devon. *Normans and Saxons: Southern Race Mythology and the Intellectual History of the American Civil War*. Baton Rouge: Louisiana State University Press, 2008.

Way, Peter. *Common Labor. Workers and the Digging of North American Canals, 1780–1860*. Baltimore: Johns Hopkins University Press, 1997.

Whelan, Kevin. *The Tree of Liberty: Radicalism, Catholicism, and the Construction of Irish Identity, 1760–1830*. Notre Dame, Ind.: University of Notre Dame Press, 1996.

Whelehan, Niall. *The Dynamiters: Irish Nationalism and Political Violence in the Wider World, 1867–1900*. Cambridge: Cambridge University Press, 2012.

———. "Skirmishing, the *Irish World*, and Empire, 1876–86." *Éire-Ireland* 42, nos. 1/2 (Spring/Summer 2007): 180–200.

———. *Transnational Perspectives in Modern Irish History*. Oxford: Routledge, 2014.

White, Richard. *Inventing Australia*. St. Leonards: Allen and Unwin, 1991.

Wiebe, Robert H. *Self-Rule: A Cultural History of American Democracy*. Chicago: University of Chicago Press, 1996.

Willging, Eugene P., and Herta Hatzfeld. *Catholic Serials of the Nineteenth Century in the United States: A Descriptive Bibliography and Union List*. Washington, D.C.: Catholic University of America Press, 1967.

Williams, John. *Ordered to the Island: Irish Convicts and Van Diemen's Land*. Sydney: Crossing Press, 1994.

Williams, Kevin. *Read All About It! A History of the British Newspaper*. London: Routledge, 2010.

Williams, Raymond. *The Long Revolution*. London: Chatto and Windus, 1961.

Wilson, David A. *Thomas D'Arcy McGee*. 2 vols. Montreal: McGill–Queen's University Press, 2008, 2011.

———. *United Irishmen, United States: Immigrant Radicals in the Early Republic*. Ithaca, N.Y.: Cornell University Press, 1998.

Wilson, David A., and Mark G. Spencer, eds. *Ulster Presbyterians in the Atlantic World*. Dublin: Four Courts Press, 2006.

Wolfe, Patrick. *Settler Colonialism and the Transformation of Anthropology: The Politics and Poetics of an Ethnographic Event*. London: Cassell, 1999.

Young, Robert J. C. *The Idea of English Ethnicity*. Malden, Mass.: Blackwell, 2008.

INDEX

Abbe and Yates, 87

Abolitionism, 3–4, 95, 109–10, 170, 181, 190
(n. 39); debate in Ireland in 1840s, 34–36,
67–68; and "Alabama Article," 101–9;
during American Civil War, 114–15,
126–27, 129, 132, 133; and Sydney
Freeman's Journal, 138. *See also*
Emancipation Proclamation; Slavery

Aboriginal Australians, 4, 45, 66–72, 75,
162–63, 181, 193 (nn. 40, 43)

Aborigines Protection Society, 67, 68

Act of Union, 12, 14, 15, 23, 32, 124

Adams, Herbert Baxter, 164

Adams, John (aka John West), 58

Adelaide, Australia, 51

Advocate (Melbourne), 178

Afghanistan, 4, 21, 36, 181

Africa, 7, 8, 33, 67, 69, 146, 179

African Americans, 1, 4, 102, 133, 172,
176–77, 203 (n. 7); during antebellum era,
80–81; armed service during American
Civil War, 113, 116, 129; during
Reconstruction, 146–48, 150, 158–59

Aherne, P. O., 155

Alden, Edwin, 171

Alfred the Great, 166

Allen, Richard, 35

American Celt (aka *Adopted Citizen* and
Catholic Citizen; Boston, Buffalo), 86, 88,
94, 102, 110, 137

American Civil War, 3, 6, 10, 78, 80, 88, 110,
111; and Irish military service, 112–19,
147–50; Irish attitudes on African
Americans, 113, 126–29, 132–33; Irish
ethnic regiments, 115–18, 120, 124–25, 128,
170, 200 (n. 16); Irish disillusionment
over, 120–21, 126–27; New York draft riots,
129–32; and Irish popular press, 133–43.
See also Abolitionism; Emancipation

Proclamation; Irish Brigade; Lincoln,
Abraham; Meagher, Thomas Francis;
Mitchel, John; Slavery

American Constitution, 1, 150, 174–76, 180;
and slavery, 4, 36, 103–4, 109, 181; and
nativism, 94, 119; and African Americans'
rights, 146–47, 156, 176

American Declaration of Independence, 107,
171, 174

American Newspaper Catalogue, 171

American Protective Association, 149

American Protestant Association, 95

American War of Independence, 9, 78, 172

American Whig Review, 94

Amerindians, 1, 3, 80, 81, 159–60, 204
(n. 24); Catlin's traveling show in Dublin,
33–34; Irish sympathy for, 34, 69, 72,
161–62, 163, 172, 173; Irish bigotry against,
146, 160–61. *See also* McMaster, James
Alphonsus; Meagher, Thomas Francis

Anderson, Benedict, 3, 5, 66, 185 (n. 3)

Andrew, John Albion, 117

Andrews, Sgt. W. M., 113

Anglicans, 7, 12, 14, 15, 16, 25, 28, 94, 147

Anglo-Celt (Cavan), 106, 189 (n. 31)

Anglo-Saxonism, 2, 104, 129, 140, 144, 145,
169; in America, 3, 78, 92–93, 100, 121–23;
in Australia, 9, 58–59; Anglo-Saxon
"myth," 13, 14, 69, 92, 98, 147–48, 163–64,
168; Irish opposition to, 60, 65, 71, 93–95,
101, 105, 109, 112, 158, 163, 164, 171–72, 176.
See also Celticism

Antietam, Battle of, 117, 126

Anti-imperialism, 4, 32–34, 36, 71, 181, 189
(n. 36). *See also* Imperialism

Antipodes. *See* Australia

Antislavery. *See* Abolitionism

Anti-Slavery Standard (New York), 36, 103

Appomattox, 145, 160

Cannibals, 68, 71, 170

Cape of Good Hope, 49. *See also* South Africa

Capitalism, 1, 12, 41, 180, 183

Carlyle, Thomas, 13, 14, 29, 179

Casey, John Sarsfield, 153–54, 156, 159, 163

Cashel, Co. Tipperary, 24, 27, 50, 165

Castlebar, Co. Mayo, 26

Catholic Church, 7, 81–82; on slavery, 9, 104; in Ireland, 23; in Australia, 51; in United States, 51, 79. *See also* Hughes, Archbishop J. J.; McEncroe, John; Polding, Archbishop John

Catholic Emancipation, 15, 16, 23

Catholic Herald (Philadelphia), 84

Catholic Telegraph (Cincinnati), 84, 126

Catholic Total Abstinence Society, 146

Catlin, George, 33–34

Cavaliers, 121

Celtic Association of Philadelphia, 164

Celticism: and Catholicism, 2, 7, 12, 31, 147; as global community, 2, 45, 75, 78, 96–97, 98, 101, 112, 116, 139, 143–44, 163, 165, 169, 177; as opposite of Anglo-Saxons, 2, 94–95, 164–65, 169, 171, 180; racial discourse of, 3, 13–14, 21, 36, 41, 60, 61, 65, 75, 96, 112, 166, 171, 180; as colonial settlers, 9, 10, 45, 60, 66, 74, 75, 180; and Irish independence, 9, 11–12, 24–32, 38, 41–42, 180; as migrants, 9, 12, 43, 63–65, 92–93, 179; as democrats/republicans, 9, 95, 109, 166, 167, 180; and American citizenship, 10, 78, 94, 99, 100, 109, 140, 143–44; and nativism, 10, 92–93, 109; as soldiers, 10, 112, 116–25 passim, 139, 143–44, 149; and people of color, 105, 130–32, 173, 181; and Confederate identity, 122–23. *See also* Anglo-Saxonism; Civic pluralism; Ethnic solidarity; Global nationalism

Celtic Revival, 13–14

Celtic Tiger economy, 182

Central America, 50, 110

Chamberlain, Brig. Gen. Joshua, 115

Charleston, S.C., 51, 111, 124, 125, 162

Charleston Catholic Miscellany, 124–25

Charleston Gazette, 170

China, 21, 33, 36, 50, 162

Chinese, 4, 71, 80, 104, 141, 146, 162–63, 173, 177

Christian Intelligencer (New York), 93

Church of Saint Francis Xavier (Manhattan), 145

Cicero, 20

Cincinnati, Ohio, 151

Cincinnati Repeal Association, 35

Citizen (New York), 83, 87, 89, 90, 97, 101, 106–8, 177

"Citizen House," 87

Citizenship, 2, 169, 180, 183; in United States, 6, 10, 94, 99–101, 146, 148, 150, 156, 172, 176–77; Irish-American status, 10, 78, 81, 109–10; as ancient principle, 20; and slavery debate, 34, 35, 109–10; in Australia, 59, 168; during American Civil War, 111, 112, 114, 119, 131, 132, 144

City Point, Va., 134

Civic nationalism. *See* Civic pluralism

Civic pluralism, 2, 10, 15, 41, 99, 124, 179, 180; in Ireland, 15, 30, 41; in Australia, 58, 73, 75; during Reconstruction, 165–67, 169, 172, 175, 177

Civic republicanism, 9; in antebellum United States, 78, 99, 100, 101, 109; during American Civil War, 112, 117, 120, 121, 144; during Reconstruction, 148

Civil War, U.S. *See* American Civil War

Claremorris, Co. Mayo, 26

Cleburne, Maj. Gen. Patrick R., 128–29

Clontarf, Co. Dublin, 28, 40

Cobh, Co. Cork, 47

Coghlan, P. G., 87

Colored Orphans Asylum (New York), burning of, 131–32

Compromise of 1877, 156–57

Conciliation Hall (Dublin), 23

Confederate armed forces, Irish service in, 111, 113–14, 121, 123–25

Confederate States of America, 133, 136, 149, 160, 202 (n. 46); firing on Fort Sumter, 111;

Young Irelanders' opinion of, 111, 122–23, 136–38, 140–41, 155; Irish military service in, 113–16, 124–25, 200 (n. 16); Confederate draft law, 114; relations with England, 118, 123; and Celticism, 121–23; African American service in, 128–29, 138; Irish public opinion of, 139–42; and "Lost Cause," 148. *See also* Davis, Jefferson; Mitchel, John

Connell Family (Tasmania), 63–64, 66

Conscription Act, 127, 130, 132

Constitution, U.S. *See* American Constitution

Convicts (Australia), 45–48, 56, 58, 63, 64, 70, 71–72

Conway, J. J., 88

Conyngham, David Power, 117, 135–36, 149–50

Coolies, 4, 71–72, 102, 107, 162–63, 177

Cooper Union (Manhattan), 145, 157

Corby, Fr. William, 120, 134

Corcoran, Brig. Gen. Michael, 116

Courier (Charleston, S.C.), 103

Cremona, Battle of, 118

Cullen, Paul, 7

Curragh of Kildare, 26

Curtin, Andrew G., 116

Daily Cleveland Herald, 132

Daily Enquirer (Richmond), 122, 136–37

Dalton, William and Eliza, 55–56

Daly, Charles Patrick, 117, 144

Daniel, John M., 137

Darwin, Charles, 164

Daunt, W. J. O'Neill, 25

Davis, Jefferson, 111, 122, 129, 136, 144

Davis, Thomas, 11, 17, 20, 22, 28, 38, 42, 70, 87, 99; background, 16; death, 21, 31; on Irish nationality, 24–26, 29–30, 32, 38, 180; on anti-imperialism, 32–34

Davitt, Michael, 174

Dawes Act, 160

Day, Benjamin Henry, 83

De Beaumont, Gustave, 33

Declaration of Independence, U.S., 107, 171, 174

Delane, John Thadeus, 28

Democracy, 159, 161, 165, 172, 173; in Ireland, 16; in Australia, 46; in United States, 51, 78, 80; and Anglo-Saxonism, 64, 147, 164; and Celticism, 78, 95–96, 109, 116, 169, 175; and Catholicism, 81, 82, 99; and slavery, 103; during American Civil War, 111, 125, 144

Democratic Party, 83; Irish support for, 9, 34, 78, 146–48, 157, 160, 181; and slavery, 34, 35, 87–88, 104, 105, 109, 177

Denmark, 40

Diamond City, Mont., 160

Diaspora, 4, 182, 185 (n. 2)

Dilke, Charles Wentworth, 168

Dillon, John Blake, 11, 16, 17, 40, 42, 77, 87, 99, 144

Disney, D. T., 35

Doheny, Michael, 26, 91, 116, 165, 190 (n. 50); on slavery, 4, 102, 105, 108, 110; death, 178

Donahoe, Patrick, 18–20, 200 (n. 12)

Doorly, Charles, 89

Dromalane House, Co. Down, 178

Dromedary (prison hulk), 49

Dublin Corporation, 21

Dublin Evening Mail, 106, 140

Dublin Quarterly Journal of Medical Science, 63

Dublin University Magazine, 140

Duff, Sir James, 26

Duffy, Charles Gavan, 17, 28, 33, 37, 76, 124, 143, 178; and Dublin *Nation*, 11, 16, 17–18, 21–23, 30–31, 53, 106, 190 (n. 43), 195 (n. 14); background, 16; on Irish identity, 20, 25, 38–40, 98, 99, 168, 179; and 1848 rebellion, 40, 42; and state prisoners in Australia, 44, 53, 54, 57, 62, 74, 85; in Australia, 75, 110, 144; and exiles in United States, 85–88; attack on John Mitchel, 90, 198 (nn. 44, 45)

Duffy, James A., 155

Dunne, Patrick, 154

Edgerton, Gov. Sidney, 160

Edinburgh Review, 60

Globe and Emerald (New York), 84

Godlonton, Robert, 68

Gold "diggings" (Australia), 46, 55, 71, 73

Graham, Fr., 176–77

Grant, Madison, 163

Grant, Ulysses S., 161

Gray, Peter, 31

Gray, Thomas, 13

Gray, Wilson, 17

Great Famine, 9, 39, 47, 55, 75, 84, 170; and
Irish migration, 6, 12, 14, 41, 42, 48, 79, 81,
140, 169; outbreak of, 21, 31; London *Times*
opinion on, 31

Greeley, Horace, 83, 126, 133

Gregory XVI (pope), 107

Griffith, Charles, 68

Habeas corpus, 40, 158

Habermas, Jürgen, 3

Halpine, Charles G., 112–13, 128, 132

Hargraves, Edward, 46

Harper's Weekly (New York), 131, 171

Haughton, James, 35–38, 101, 103–6

Helena, Ark., 128

Hengist and Horsa, 14, 93

Hermitage Hall (New York), 105

Higgins, Michael D., 182

Hindus, 141, 176

Hobart Town, Australia, 52, 62

Hobbes, Thomas, 166

Hobsbawm, Eric, 14

Hogan, Ned and Johanna, 55–56, 57

Homer, 44

Home Rule, 167, 178

Hosmer, James K., 164

Hougoumont (ship), 153

Hughes, Archbishop J. J., 79, 85, 151; and
slavery, 34, 102, 104, 113, 127, 132, 139, 202
(n. 45)

Hughes, Timothy Edward, 88

Huxley, Thomas Henry, 164–65

Hystuns, G. E., 113

Imperialism, 50, 183; and people of color, 3,
4, 32–34, 36, 67, 69, 71, 108, 181

Independent (New York), 104

India, 4, 33, 50, 97, 98, 104, 174

Ireland: socio-economic statistics, 12; and
Act of Union, 14; and literacy rates, 17–18;
outbreak of Great Famine, 31; travel
literature on, 33; rural violence during
Great Famine, 39; revolutionary
excitement in 1848, 40; convict transportation to Australia, 47; outrage over Smith
O'Brien's imprisonment, 56–57; migration
statistics to North America, 78–79, 146;
mortality during Great Famine, 79;
twentieth-century migration mindset, 182

Irish-American (New York), 83, 85, 89,
104, 115, 126–27, 130–32, 140, 155, 171,
195 (n. 14)

Irish Brigade, 145, 149, 150; and Irish
identity, 116–21; and African Americans,
126–29, 132; and newspapers, 134, 138,
141, 142. *See also* American Civil War;
Meagher, Thomas Francis; Mitchel, John

Irish Catholic Benevolent Union, 146

Irish Citizen (New York), 154–55, 158, 168

Irish Citizen (Sydney), 168, 205 (n. 36)

Irish Confederation, 37–40, 103

Irish Directory, 73

Irish Exile & Freedom's Advocate (Hobart
Town), 52–53, 63, 70–71

Irish Free State, 182

Irish language, 8, 12, 13, 26, 30, 32

Irish League, 40

Irishman (Dublin), 122, 141–42, 154, 163

Irish music, 39

Irish News (New York), xiii, 105, 110, 118, 124,
125, 143; and Irish-American press, 83,
87–92; and Irish identity, 96–98

Irish People (Dublin), 152–55, 163

Irish People (New York), 152–54

Irish Race Convention (1922), 179, 182

Irish Shield and Monthly Milesian (New
York), 84

Irish Times (Dublin), 153

Irish World (aka *American Industrial
Liberator*; New York), 1–2, 170–77; and
"Spread the Light" campaign, 174

McMahon, Thomas, 124

McManus, Terence Bellew, 54, 57, 90; and 1848 rebellion, 40, 43; voyage to Australia, 44; escape from Australia, 72; funeral, 151

McMaster, James Alphonsus, 93, 161, 163, 177

Meagher, Thomas Francis, 21, 39, 42, 44, 54, 57, 62, 72, 76, 91, 95–98, 101, 124, 125, 130, 145, 161, 196 (n. 16), 197 (n. 23), 198 (n. 38); "Meagher of the Sword" speech, 37; and 1848 rebellion, 40–41; life in Van Diemen's Land, 48–49; and Irish-American press, 83, 86–89; and people of color, 101, 160–161, 163; antebellum sectional allegiances, 111; and Irish Brigade, 116–21; and newspapers during American Civil War, 134, 138, 139; and opinion in Ireland during American Civil War, 140–42; in Montana, 144, 145, 160–61, 163, 165, 204 (n. 24); and Irish global nationalism, 148–50

Meagher Guards, 124

Meehan, Fr. C. P., 37

Melbourne, Australia, 46, 51, 168

Melbourne Morning Herald, 58

Melville, Herman, 69

Memphis, Tenn., 157

Mersey, August, 115

Methodists, 12

Mexican-American War, 81, 115, 159

Mexican immigrants, 80, 81

Mexico, 69, 123, 159

Milesians, 14, 20, 38

Mississippi River, 63, 83, 159, 161

Missouri River, 145, 161

Mitchel, Henrietta, 137, 202 (n. 41)

Mitchel, James, 154

Mitchel, Jenny [Jane Verner], 21, 62, 89, 106, 193 (n. 32)

Mitchel, John, 37, 42, 69, 71, 91, 110, 139, 140, 142, 153; background, 21–22; and newspapers, 21–22, 39, 49, 53, 83, 87, 89–90, 136–37, 154–56; on Irish identity, 38, 64, 66, 97, 164–67, 169, 177; transportation of, 40,

43, 49, 53, 61–63, 73, 76; on American citizenship, 94–95, 99–101; on slavery, 101–10, 127, 129, 132, 181, 190 (n. 48), 198 (n. 39); and Confederacy, 114, 122–24, 136–37, 144, 145; and people of color, 158, 162, 163; on Reconstruction, 158, 163; death, 178

Mitchel, Willie, 136

Mitchel Light Guards, 124

Molly Maguires, 172

Monster Meetings, 23–24, 26–28, 42, 112, 188 (n. 20)

Montana Post (Virginia City), 160

Montana Territory, 144, 145, 160–61, 165, 204 (n. 24)

Montesquieu, 14

Montieth, William, 117

Montreal, 110, 137, 176

Mooney, Thomas, 27

Moore, Thomas, 15

Morris, Lewis, 13

Moses, 101

Mount Jerome Cemetery (Dublin), 31

Mountstewart Elphinstone, 42, 44

Music Hall (Boston), 99, 119

Mutual aid societies, 146

Myall Creek Massacre, 67

Napoleonic Wars, 79

Nast, Thomas, 131

Nation (Dublin), 6, 21, 26–28, 30, 39, 40, 77, 84, 114, 123, 124, 139, 178; on Irish identity, 9, 11, 20, 24, 38, 40, 75, 98, 123, 177; founding of, 16–17, 42; circulation of, 17–20, 22–23, 27, 37, 187 (n. 11); and international popular press, 18–20, 27, 45, 52, 53–54, 62, 70, 85, 87, 90, 143, 152, 181; and people of color, 32–36, 68, 102, 106; and state prisoners, 53–54, 57, 62, 70. See also Davis, Thomas; Duffy, Charles Gavan

Nation (New York), 83–85, 87, 89, 90, 94, 96, 103, 177

Nativism, 10, 59, 82, 115, 146; Irish-American challenges to, 3, 83, 92, 94–95, 119, 125. See also Know Nothings

Naturalization, 81, 146–48, 176, 183